THE TREASURERS OF ATHENA

LONDON : HUMPHREY MILFORD

OXFORD UNIVERSITY PRESS

TAMIAS   Ἡ παράδοσις τῶν χρημάτων   ATHENA

THE TREASURERS OF ATHENA

BY

WILLIAM SCOTT FERGUSON

MᶜLEAN PROFESSOR OF ANCIENT AND MODERN HISTORY
HARVARD UNIVERSITY

CAMBRIDGE, MASSACHUSETTS

HARVARD UNIVERSITY PRESS

1932

COPYRIGHT, 1932
BY THE PRESIDENT AND FELLOWS OF HARVARD COLLEGE

PRINTED AT THE HARVARD UNIVERSITY PRESS
CAMBRIDGE, MASS., U.S.A.

TO

MY WIFE

PREFACE

THIS is a work for specialists. It is first and foremost an attempt to win from the lapidary records of the custodians of the Athenian temples more of their rich stock of historical information. In a field where August Boeckh, Adolf Kirchhoff, Eduard Meyer, Eugène Cavaignac, Henri Francotte, Wilhelm Bannier, Ulrich Köhler, Hans Lehner, Julius Beloch and Walther Kolbe have harvested, the gleanings are likely to be few. But the author has been able, he trusts, to determine more sharply than his predecessors the chronology of certain essential documents; and, in exploiting the results reached by Mr. Dinsmoor in his study of the inscriptions dealing with the Erechtheum, he has stumbled upon materials which have enabled him to extend yet farther the Tribal Cycle of the Secretary of the Treasurers of Athena, to which he devoted a few lines in his first scientific publication (*The Athenian Secretaries*, The Macmillan Co., New York, 1898). Thus aided, and advantaged yet further by the publication of new records and by the devoted labor of Hiller von Gärtringen, Johannes Kirchner, and their associates on the *Editio Minor* of the Attic inscriptions, he has interrogated anew the entire body of texts available for the study of Athenian temple finance during the epoch of the Peloponnesian War and thereafter. More questions have been raised than can be answered now; and oftentimes merely tentative solutions have been reached. But it seemed wise to include them in the belief that further finds and the insight of others will turn them eventually to profit.

Studies of this sort are limited necessarily by the state of the sources. For reasons known best to themselves the Athenians did not record on stone the inflow and outflow of their revenues, domestic or imperial. The receipts and expenditures of their many officials who handled money were booked and audited yearly; but of these accounts lapidary records were not made. The financial transactions of which Athens pre-

served publicly a permanent annual record were the advances
of money made to the state by the national deities and the
transfers of temple properties from one board of custodians
to the next. The loans were made by the Treasurers of Athena,
and the Treasurers of the Other Gods, who were also the keep-
ers of the most valuable temple properties. Their accounts tell
their story directly; their inventories elucidate financial transactions only when they note, or we note, deductions of articles
of gold and silver for assignable purposes. These records have
a grave defect in common: many of the stone tablets on which
they were inscribed are lost, or preserved in fragments alone.
The first task which confronts us is to identify these fragments,
piece them together, and restore them where possible. It is a
fascinating undertaking, and the author has done the best he
could, with the aid of friends and without the privilege of sorting stones in the Epigraphical Museum in Athens. But the
science of architectural epigraphy, perfected in the main by
American scholars, has yet to be applied to many of these
records. It augurs well for future progress that Mr. A. B. West
and Mr. A. M. Woodward have now joined hands and wits and
techniques in measuring, scrutinizing, and fitting together the
disjecta membra of the post-Eukleidean inventories. *Non cuivis
homini contingit adire Athenas.*

Messrs. B. H. Hill, W. B. Dinsmoor, and B. D. Meritt have
helped the author repeatedly when he was in difficulties. Their
contributions are acknowledged specifically in the text; but
the whole work has profited from materials, information, and
suggestions generously given by these scholars. The author is
deeply grateful to them, and he wishes particularly to thank
Mr. Meritt for his constant readiness to discuss moot points and
to furnish more reliable readings of pertinent texts. The work
on which he is now engaged, *Athenian Financial Documents in
the Fifth Century*, will furnish the evidence for which it has been
possible to cite in this book his name alone. Mr. E. T. Newell
has been consulted with profit on some numismatic questions;
and Mr. A. D. Nock has been kind enough to read the proof.
Κοινὰ μὲν τὰ φίλων, ἰδία δὲ ἡ εὔθυνα. Thanks are also due to M.
Roussel, Director of the French School in Athens, for obtain-

ing permission to reproduce from Volume II, Plate X, of the *Bulletin de correspondance Hellénique* the sculptured relief of the inventory of the Tamiae of Athena for the year 398/7 B.C. (*IG*² II 1392) which appears as the frontispiece of the book. It is finally a duty and a pleasure to acknowledge the financial aid received from the Fund for "Studies in the Humanities" of Harvard University without which publication would have been difficult, if not impossible.

The design on the cover is a reproduction of a stater struck by Lachares from the gold obtained through the melting down of the votive offerings in charge of the Treasurers of Athena. The chances are that this issue has preserved for us some of the gold of the chryselephantine statue of the Goddess that once stood in the Parthenon.

WILLIAM SCOTT FERGUSON

CAMBRIDGE, MASSACHUSETTS
    June, 1931

CONTENTS

ABBREVIATIONS

AJA	American Journal of Archaeology
AJP	American Journal of Philology
BCH	Bulletin de Correspondance hellénique
CAH	Cambridge Ancient History
GGA	Göttingische Gelehrte Anzeigen
JHS	Journal of Hellenic Studies
REA	Revue des études anciennes
REG	Revue des études grecques
SEG	Supplementum Epigraphicum Graecum

THE TREASURERS OF ATHENA

I

THE TREASURERS OF ATHENA AND
THE OTHER GODS

THE plan drafted by the Athenians in 411 B.C. for the eventual establishment of a moderately aristocratic government — that of the Five Thousand — contained a list of officials who were to be chosen by a double process of election from the membership of the Council. Among them appear in Aristotle's version of this plan ταμίαι τῶν ἱερῶν χρημάτων τῇ θεῷ καὶ τοῖς ἄλλοις θεοῖς δέκα, καὶ ἑλληνοταμίαι καὶ τῶν ἄλλων ὁσίων χρημάτων ἁπάντων εἴκοσιν οἱ διαχειριοῦσιν (*Ath. Pol.* 30 2). It has been known for some time that the project of enlarging the number and functions of the Hellenotamiae was put into effect. The evidence on which this conclusion rests is found in the records of the period immediately following the fall of the Five Thousand. In 410/09 B.C. the enlarged board of Hellenotamiae was in existence; for eleven members, and possibly more, were named in *IG*² I 304A.[1] Moreover, the *kolakretae*, whose duties they were to absorb in part, disappear after 411 B.C. Another feature of the plan was a sharp distinction of the funds of the state into such as were sacred (ἱερά) and such as were secular (ὅσια): the Tamiae were to administer the one and the Hellenotamiae the other. This portion of the plan was also put into effect. It, too, continued in operation thereafter. For it was along this line that the functions of the *kolakretae* were divided between the Hellenotamiae and the Tamiae. As is well known

[1] For a criticism of current explanations of the appearance of eleven Hellenotamiae in 410/09 B.C. see Busolt, *Griech. Staatsk.*, II, p. 1132, n. 3. Meritt has now proved, what he had earlier assumed (*Athenian Calendar*, p. 19), that the term of the Hellenotamiae ran from Panathenaia to Panathenaia (*IG*² I 304B, l. 89: new reading). He contends that the first two Hellenotamiae mentioned in *IG*² I 304A, Kallimachos and Phrasitelides, belonged to 411/0 B.C.; the rest, two from each *phyle*, to 410/09 B.C. If this contention is valid, and the partiality of the reformers of 411 B.C. for the selection of officials κατὰ φυλάς is in its favor (*below*, p. 151), we should have yet stronger evidence that the board was enlarged to twenty.

(Meyer, *Forsch.*, II, pp. 136 ff.), the contingent expenses of the
demos prior to 411 B.C. had been met by payments from the
treasury of the *kolakretae* irrespective of whether they were
religious or secular in character. For example, the *kolakretae*
had been required by decrees of the people to furnish the
salaries of priests and priestesses and the funds needed by
hieropoii, as well as to defray the costs of the *anagraphe* of
public records. After 411 B.C., on the other hand, the Hellenotamiae paid for inscribing documents on stone tablets while
the Tamiae furnished money for *hieropoii* and *athlothetae* to be
used for the Panathenaia (*IG*² I 304A, 410/09 B.C.; 305,
406/05 B.C.).[1]

It might be supposed, therefore, that the project of amalgamating the two boards of Tamiae, that of Athena, of im-
memorial antiquity, and that of the Other Gods, created only
twenty-three years since, was also realized in the government
of the Five Thousand. But the evidence is irreconcilable with
this conclusion. The title ταμίαι τῶν ἱερῶν χρημάτων τῆς Ἀθηναίας
καὶ τῶν ἄλλων θεῶν makes its first appearance in our lapidary
record in 403/02 B.C. (*IG*² II 1370, 1371); and notwithstanding that the allusion in the inventories of the Tamiae of this
year to their predecessors in office makes it fairly clear that the
Treasurers of 404/03 B.C. were also Treasurers both of Athena
and of the Other Gods (Lehner, *Ueber die athen. Schatzverzeichnisse des vierten Jahrhunderts*, p. 13; cf. Panske, *Leipz.
Stud.*, 1890, pp. 4 ff.; Ferguson, *Athenian Secretaries*, p. 73;
Kirchner, *IG*² II 1370, note); and notwithstanding that the
decree of the year 405/04 B.C. quoted by Andocides (I 77)
mentions τοὺς ταμίας τῆς θεοῦ καὶ τῶν ἄλλων θεῶν, the view still
holds its ground that the consolidation of the two boards into
a single board, contemplated in 411 B.C., was not consummated
till 404/03 B.C. (Kirchner, *IG*² II 1498, note) or the democratic
restoration in the archonship of Eukleides (Bannier, *Rh. Mus.*,
1915, p. 405, n. 1; Couch, H. N., *The Treasuries of the Greeks
and Romans*, p. 65).

---

[1] The payments made by them to the Hellenotamiae were "loans" of sacred
moneys. For the rôle of the *logistae* in 407/06 B.C., see *below*, p. 31, n. 2.

The alternative view more commonly accepted (cf. Busolt, *Griech. Staatsk.*, II, p. 1139) is that the amalgamation was effected in 406/05 B.C., at the beginning of a Panathenaic *penteteris* (Ol. 93 3); and in the following study we shall find reasons to confirm it; but for the moment we shall have to content ourselves with the demonstration that the two boards remained separate till 406 B.C.

The primary reason for holding that the consolidation was deferred thus long is that in the five years following 412/1 B.C. the Treasurers of Athena appear as a separate board (*IG*² I 298, 251, 304A, 373, l. 91;[1] 374, l. 115; II 1655, cf. *below*, p. 48). Not only is the board that made disbursements during this period entitled ταμίαι τῆς θεοῦ or ταμίαι τῶν ἱερῶν χρημάτων τῆς Ἀθηναίας, but the source of the disbursements, when specified (*IG*² I 298, 304, 301, 305), is the fund of Athena Polias or Athena Nike or Hermes [Propylaios][2] (Meyer, *Forsch.*, II, p. 120, n. 4). On the other hand, there is no evidence in contemporary records of this period establishing the existence of a separate board of Treasurers of the Other Gods; so that we are compelled to raise the question whether this board was not abolished altogether in 411 B.C. Since we have only one inventory of this board for the fifth century (*IG*² I 310, 429/8 B.C.) and only one set of accounts in which funds disbursed by it are recorded, — those of the Commissioners of the two statues of the Hephaestion (*IG*² I 370/1, 421/0–416/5 B.C.), — the argument *ex silentio* has little or no value. And as a matter of fact, Treasurers of the Other Gods continued to exist after 411 B.C. This is shown by *IG*² II 1498, which has not hitherto been utilized as it deserves on this point. I, for one, have overlooked it completely (*Class. Phil.*, 1926, p. 75). It is a catalogue, made during the administration of Lycurgus (*c.* 335 B.C.), of objects

---

[1] The *lacuna* following θεō is to be filled by the name of the Chairman, Φι[λίνο] Παι-α|νιέος. Line 91 has then 33 letters, like line 103.

[2] The accounts of the Treasurers of Athena for the years 426/5–423/2 B.C. (*IG*² I 324) show that this Hermes belonged to the competence of the Tamiae of the Goddess. A different Hermes appears in association with Artemis in the inventory of the Treasurers of the Other Gods for 429/8 B.C. (*IG*² I 310, l. 192). For Pyletes as a variant for Propylaios (*Paus.* I 22 8) see Wilhelm, *Beiträge z. griech. Inschriftenkunde*, p. 95.

on the Acropolis, apparently of bronze.[1] As we have it on the stone, which is badly mutilated at the beginning, it opens with a list of *stelae* or *stelïdia* of Tamiae of Athena and Tamiae of the Other Gods, with one from the archonship of [Pythodoros] [2] (404/03 B.C.) of the Tamiae of Athena and the Other Gods. The decisive significance of this text is that in the archonships of [Κλ]ε[όκριτος] (413/2 B.C.), [Γλαύκιπ]πος (410/09 B.C.), and Δ[ιοκλῆς] (409/08 B.C.) Tamiae of the Other Gods set up *stelae* on the Acropolis. *Stelae* of the Tamiae of the Goddess were, we learn, dedicated in the archonships of [Glaukippos], Diokles, and Antigenes (407/06 B.C.). One was dedicated in yet another archonship (l. 20). The name of the Archon is lost. Kirchner (note) suggests Alexias (405/04 B.C.); but a name with four more letters is required to fill the line out to the normal length of forty letters, or five or three more to fill it out to the occasional length of forty-one or thirty-nine letters, when we restore the word following the Archon's name as στήλη. I suggest Euktemon (408/07 B.C.).[3] Alexias seems excluded. It is not only too short for the space, but it would require us to conclude that the Tamiae of Athena continued to exist as a separate board after 407/06 B.C.

[1] The heading which contained the definition of the articles to be catalogued is lost. The inference that we have to do with a *catalogus signorum ex aere factorum* has been drawn from the descriptions of the articles listed under the subtitle [τάδ' ἀναθήματ]α [κ]αὶ κει[μήλια τῶν ταμιῶ]ν τῆς [θεοῦ]. One of the objects in the initial section is described as "a little bronze tablet set with precious stones," if the restorations are correct. Fourteen other *stelidia* of the Tamiae of the Goddess are characterized as [ἠ]λεφ[αντω-μένα], "inlaid or framed with ivory." The *stelae* cannot possibly be identified with the marble inventories which have reached us, if for no other reason because in that case most of them, and not one alone (l. 7), must have been described as "handed over by the four archae" (see *below*, p. 100, n. 1). They were all, probably, small votive or commemorative tablets of some such character as the bronze *lamella* of the sixth century of which the inscription, with the names of 8 Tamiae (2 from each *phyle* doubtless), is published in *IG*² I 393.

[2] See *below*, p. 148, n. 1.

[3] If we must have a line of forty letters at this point, for which I see no necessity (l. 30 has thirty-nine), we may restore the name Kallias and date the dedication in 412/1 B.C.; or, if 412/1 is excluded because of the dedication made by the "four archae" of the *penteteris* 414/3–411/0 B.C., the name Euphemos (417/6 B.C.) will serve. The deficiency can then be made up by restoring the next word as στηλίδιον, as suggested by Kirchner, instead of στήλη.

With the evidence thus far collected (Tamiae of the Other Gods in 409/08; Tamiae of Athena in 407/06; Tamiae of Athena and the Other Gods in 405/04 B.C.) we have narrowed down the time when the two boards were amalgamated to two points, the beginning of the year 406/05 or the beginning of the year 405/04 B.C.; and there we shall leave the problem for the present (see *below*, pp. 104 ff.).

II

THE TRIBAL CYCLE OF THE SECRETARIES
OF THE TREASURERS: I

IN MY *Athenian Secretaries* (pp. 70 ff.) I pointed out that
during two periods of five and four years respectively
(434/3–430/29 and 416/5–413/2 B.C.) the Secretary of the
Treasurers of Athena was chosen from the *phylae* in the reverse of the official order. Since, however, between and after
these epochs of regular tribal sequence the succession of the
secretaries' *phylae* was irregular, and since in the intervals of
irregularity no care was taken to give each *phyle* representa-
tion in this office in any ten-year cycle, it could be thought that
in one or both the periods defined the regularity was accidental
(Brillant, *Les secrétaires athéniens*, p. 58). In the same work
(p. 72) I observed further that during the period when the
Treasurers of Athena were amalgamated with the Treasurers
of the Other Gods to form a single board of Treasurers of Athena
and the Other Gods (406/05–386/5 B.C.) the secretaries of the
joint board also succeeded one another in the reverse of the
official order; and so far as I know this observation has been
generally accepted as valid.

It seemed curious that this cycle should have begun in 406/05
B.C. with the fifth *phyle*, Akamantis (Brillant, p. 58, n. 5); and
Brillant sought to explain *ce point de départ bizarre* by the suggestion that prior to 406/05 B.C. the secretaries of the Treasurers of the Other Gods had been chosen from the *phylae* in the
reverse of the official order, and that the Secretary of the joint
board was taken from the fifth *phyle* in 406/05 B.C. because
the cycle of these secretaries had reached that point in this year.
The suggestion was a good one and may be correct; but since
we do not know the *phylae* of any of the secretaries of the
Treasurers of the Other Gods after 418/7 B.C., it could not and
cannot be supported by evidence. The feeling that the cycle

followed between 406/05 and 386/5 B.C. should have begun with the first *phyle*, Erechtheis, was, however, justifiable; and, as the following table shows, it can now be justified:

TABLE I

Year	Chairman of Tamiae	Secretary of Tamiae	Phyle	Ol.
416/5	Dexitheos of Phyle	Lysikles of Bate	II	
415/4	Leochares (9) or (10)	Teleas of Pergase	. I	
414/3	Teisamenos of Paiania	Polymedes of Atene	X	91, 3
413/2	Polyxenides of Acharnai	Leukaios of Aphidna	IX	
412/1	Kallaischros of Eupyridai	Autokleides of Phrearrhoi	IV	
411	Asopodoros of Kydathenaion	Euandros of Euonymon	I	
411/0	Ameiniades —	— -s	10	
410/9	Kallistratos of Marathon		9	92, 3
409/8	Phi[linos]? of Paiania	. . . . es of Eleusis	VIII	
408/7	Aresaichmos of Agryle	— son of Dorotheos of [Phlya]?	7	
407/6	¹[Philippos] of Probalinthos		6	
406/5			5	93, 3
405/4	²Kalli- — (?)	— of Leukonoe	IV	
404/3		Dromokleides —	3	
403/2	Lysik- — (?)	-las of Kollytos	II	
402/1	— of Teithras (?)	Kleisophos of Euonymon	I	94, 3
401/0			10	
400/9	Meidon of Euonymon(?)	Thersilochos of Oinoe	IX	
399/8	Sokrates of Lamptrai(?)	Chairion of Eleusis	VIII	
398/7	Epichares of Euonymon (?)	Mnesiergos of Athmonon	VII	95, 3
397/6	-atos of Euonymon (?)	Morychos of Butadai	VI	
396/5	Euretos of Alopeke		5	
395/4			4	
394/3			3	96, 3
393/2			2	
392/1			1	
391/0	(10) -s of Rhamnus		10	
390/9		-res of Aphidna	IX	97, 3
389/8			8	
388/7			7	
387/6			6	
386/5			5	98, 3

It thus appears that after two false starts, prolonged the first for five years (434/3–430/29 B.C.), the second for four years

---

¹ See *below*, pp. 48 f.

² For a few years, possibly ten (406/05–397/6 B.C.), the Treasurer from the first *phyle* represented seems to have been Chairman (cf. *IG*² II 1370/1, 1377, l. 8; 1378 l. 10; 1388, 1392, l. 14, and *IG*² II 1395, l. 9). Otherwise the board had no Chairman at all, which seems improbable.

(416/5–413/2 B.C.), the tribal cycle succeeded in getting under way with Erechtheis[1] in 411 B.C., to continue in unbroken sequence until 386/5 B.C. when the two boards of Tamiae were again separated.

Two obstacles have prevented us from making this observation till now: (1) IG^2 I 254 has been assigned wrongly to the year 408/07 B.C. We owe it to Dinsmoor (*Ap.* Paton, *The Erechtheum*, p. 649, n. 1; cf. *AJA*, 1913, pp. 255 ff.; Bannier, *Rh. Mus.*, 1915, p. 406 ff.; *below*, pp. 50 ff.; 27, n. 1) that this mistake has been rectified. Perfectly certain already, the attribution of IG^2 I 254 to 409/08 B.C. has been made doubly sure by the fact that the tribal cycle demands a secretary from Hippothontis in this year. The secretary in IG^2 I 254, ... ες -οχάρος Ἐλευσίνιος, belongs to Hippothontis. (2) It seemed established that — Εὐ]θιο Λευκονοιεύς, the Secretary mentioned in IG^2 I 255a,[2] belonged to 407/06 B.C.; whereupon no cyclic relation could be made out between his *phyle* (Leontis) and the *phylae* which had the secretaryship in adjacent years. It is true that the name of the Archon is missing on the stone, but the restoration of Kirchhoff, Ἀντιγένος, seemed clinched by the appearance of the name of Antigenes' successor, Κ]αλλίο, later, in line 329; and the content of the document seemed to

---

[1] The cycle followed during the five-year period 434/3–430/29 B.C. began with Erechtheis. A new epoch in the history of the Tamiae opened in 434 B.C. (*below*, pp. 153 ff., 163, n. 1), and this may have determined the choice of Erechtheis for the ensuing year. But Professor Meritt has called my attention to the fact that when the cycle is retrojected from 434/3 B.C., it calls for a secretary from Oineis (VI) in 439/8 and one from Hippothontis (VIII) in 441/o B.C.; and that the secretaries for these two years (. . . . . Λα[κ]ιάδες, IG^2 I 347; . . . . . . ίνος Περαι[εύς], IG^2 I 293) belong to these *phylae*. Of the difficulties presented by IG^2 I 355: 293 and IG^2 I 359: 351, 365 he will, I trust, find and give us the solution. It may be noted that Professor Meritt has also made the very interesting observation that the secretaries of the Hellenotamiae follow the tribal cycle, in reverse order, for the decade between 439/8 (438/7) and 430/29 (432/1) B.C., beginning with the tenth *phyle* and ending with the first. It seems clear that the abandonment of the cycle by the secretaries of the Tamiae in 429 B.C. is connected with the completion of the cycle by the secretaries of the Hellenotamiae. I wonder if the plague had anything to do with it, as it probably had with the incompleteness of the board of Tamiae of the Other Gods in 429/8 B.C. (Kolbe, *Sitz. Ber. Akad.*, 1927, p. 324).

[2] For convenience of citing I have given the number 255a to lines 323 to 331 of IG^2, I 255.

prove the case conclusively. For this is the famous record of the *tradition* of the dedications of Athena in the Pronaos to the Hellenotamiae for use, it was thought, in the crisis of Arginusae.

Until Dinsmoor dated *IG*² I 254 in 409/08 B.C. this restoration was invulnerable; but it is so no longer. For the moving back of *IG*² I 254 necessitates the retrocession by a year of *IG*² I 255, as Dinsmoor saw. Between the end of 254 and the beginning of 255 there was left vacant on the stone a space of 0.08 for the usual prescript, which for some reason or other (see *below*, p. 73) was never filled in. *IG*² I 254 is bound fast to *IG*² I 255 in that frg. c of the stone contains at the left margin the beginnings of the last three lines of the former and the first six lines of the latter: the two inventories belong to consecutive years, i.e. 409/08 and 408/07. Between the end of 255 and 255a a vacancy of 0.10 was left. Since frg. d contains parts of 255 and 255a, the vacancy alone separates the two inventories. For this reason it was natural to think that 255 contains the record for the following year, now 407/06 B.C.; and such was the conclusion of Dinsmoor. This conclusion was all the more plausible in that 407/06 B.C. was the last year of a Panathenaic *penteteris;* so that it could be thought that this Tablet contained the inventories for 410/09–407/06 B.C.

But there are serious difficulties. Kirchhoff's restoration required for its syntax the attribution of 255 and 255a to the same year: παραδεξάμενοι (l. 303) had as its object the inventory which follows and, despite the vacancy, it qualified ταμίαι (l. 323 of 255a); while ταμίαι in turn was the subject of παρέδοσαν restored in line 328. The object of παρέδοσαν was then the same as that of παραδεξάμενοι, namely, the inventory that precedes in lines 303–322 of 255. This syntax labored all along under the disadvantage of leaving quite unmotivated the *lacuna* between 255 and 255a; for the inventory 255 is complete, as a comparison with the inventory 254 shows. In fact, Kirchhoff's syntax fell to pieces once Dinsmoor showed that in the *lacuna* between *IG*² I 254 and 255 the usual prescript was contemplated in which would have appeared, had it been incised,[1] the verb παρέδοσαν with the inventory 255 as its object.

It thus becomes necessary to reconsider Kirchhoff's restoration. We have to find an object for the verb [παρέδοσαν] of which ταμίαι (l. 323) is the subject. It was clear to Kirchhoff from the beginning (*Abh. Berl. Akad.*, 1864, p. 50) that the inscription cut after the last *lacuna* (255a) contained more letters to the line than were found in the lines of the earlier parts of the stone. It seemed, therefore, for this reason, as well as from the *lacuna*, to be a new record. None the less Kirchhoff ignored these considerations and reconstructed his text as one continuous whole. In this initial lapse into error he has been followed by all subsequent editors. We shall consider *IG*[2] I 255a as an entirely separate document.

The clue to a correct restoration is given by the fact that the Secretary of the Treasurers of Athena in this year, — Εὐ]θίο Λευκονοιεύς of the *phyle* Leontis, is assigned by the tribal cycle, not to 407/06, but to 405/04 B.C. Following this lead the completion of the text is simple (see p. 13).

The only epigraphical comment that requires to be made is to refer to Kirchner's note on *IG*[2] II 1686 for the word ἀφελόμενοι: it is vouched for by ἀφῃρέθη in lines 8 and 15 of this document (*IG*[2] I 379, l. 3 has ἐ[χσ]ελον); and to refer to *IG*[2] II 1686 for the spelling of κατελέφθε: it is vouched for by ἐλήφθη in line 23.

The interpretation of the document as thus completed gives us an important bit of new information: it was in Kallias' archonship (406/05 B.C.) that the *demos* voted to turn over the *ex-votos* to the Hellenotamiae for conversion into money to defray the expense of the war; but it was not till the following year that this vote was executed in so far as it concerned the offerings deposited in the Pronaos. We shall return to this point later (*below*, pp. 85 ff.).

In Table I, I have made 386/5 B.C. the last year of this tribal cycle. Thirty-two years ago (*Athenian Secretaries*, p. 74) the suggestion was thrown out that it ended a year earlier. The

---

[1] The case is not without parallel. In 399/8 B.C. (*IG*[2] II 1377, 1378) space was left on the stone for the names of the Tamiae of the following year; but they were never added. So too in 374/3 B.C. (*IG*[2] II 1421; cf. Kolbe, *Philologus*, 1930, p. 263).

(*IG*² I 255a (405/04 B.C.))

[hοιἐντο͂ιἐπὶʼΑλεχσιοἄρχοντοςἐνιαυτο͂ιἄ]ρχσαντεςταμίαι:Καλλι . . . .]

[. . . . :: ΦίλιπποςΦιλεσίοΠροβ[αλίσιι]

[ος . . . . εὐς::ΜενέστρατοςΜενεσ[τράτο.]

[. . . . . .ʼΕλε]υσίνιος::ʼΑντιφονʼΑντιφ . . . .]

[— — — , hοῖς — — — — Εὐ]θιοΔευκονοιεὺςἐγρα[μμάτευε],

[παρέδοσαντἀτ͂εςθεο͂χρέματαhελενοταμ]ίαιςΧαριάδειΧαριοʼΑγ[ρυλ͂εθεν]

[καισυνάρχοσι,φσεφισαμένοτο͂δέμοἐπὶΚ]αλλίοἄρχοντος,ἐπιτ͂εςβο[λ͂εςh͂ει]

[. . . . . πρ͂οτοςἐ]γραμμάτευεΞἐκτο͂Προνέ[οάφελὄ]

[μενοι.κατελέφθεστέφανοςΧρυσο͂ς,σταθμ]ὸντούτο:ΔΔΔ⊢⊢||| v.]

reason by which I was then actuated turns out to have been unfounded. So long as the cycle was thought to have started in 406/05 B.C. there was some plausibility in the view that it terminated after two revolutions were completed. Now that the beginning of the cycle has been fixed in 411 B.C. no ground exists for supposing that it ended in 387/6 B.C. 386/5 B.C. was a Great Panathenaic year (Ol. 98 3). That is undoubtedly a suitable moment for the separation of the two boards of Treasurers, by which the ending of the cycle was conditioned; but the *penteteric* period ended on Hekatombaion 28th, 386 B.C., whereas it was not till Hekatombaion 28th,[1] 385 B.C. that the Tamiae of *IG*[2] II 1407 entered office. In the fourth century, however, it was in the year following the completion of a *penteteris* rather than in its final year that changes affecting the Tamiae and their treasures were made. Thus, as noted *below* (pp. 117 ff., notes) crises of this character occurred in 378/7 (Ol. 100 3), 346/5 (Ol. 108 3), and 342/1 (Ol. 109 3). We have further to evaluate in this connection the fact observed by Köhler (*IG*[1] II 667, note) that the Tamiae of Athena for 385/4 B.C. failed to mention as usual their predecessors in office. The reason assigned by him for this omission — that they were preceded, not by Tamiae of Athena, but by a different board, namely, Tamiae of Athena and the Other Gods — has been accepted by Kirchner (*IG*[2] II 1407, note), and is probably correct. It is true, as was pointed out by Panske (*Leipz. Stud.*, 1890, pp. 18 ff.), that in another year in which the inventory of the Tamiae began with the chryselephantine statue of Pheidias (cf. *below*, p. 119, n. 1) the same omission occurred (*IG*[2] II 1410, 377/6 B.C.), the inference being that, since this was the most valuable object catalogued and was transmitted not annually but quadrennially, the Tamiae could not certify in the prescript of their inventory of either year that they had received the objects, of which a list was appended, from their immediate predecessors. It should be remarked, however, that this consideration did not prevent the Tamiae of 344/3 B.C. (*IG*[2] II 1443) from acknowledging the receipt of the *anathemata* from the Tamiae of 345/4

[1] For the time of year at which the Tamiae of the fourth century assumed office see *below*, p. 138, n. 2.

B.C.; and, as will be pointed out later (*below*, p. 118), in the year 378/7 B.C. the votives of Athena were completely overhauled with a view to segregating for melting down a lot of articles of gold. It is natural to assume that this work was entrusted to an extraordinary Commission, like the one of which Andro- tion was a member (Philoch. in *Harpocr.*, s.v. πομπεῖα = *FHG*, 124; cf. Michaelis, *Parthenon*, p. 303, XXIII; Lehner, *op. cit.*, p. 92; Kirchner, *PA*, 915), and the πομπεῖον ἐπιστάται of 420/ 19 B.C. (*IG*² I 379). This being the case, it was from the Com- missioners, and not from the Tamiae of 378/7 B.C., that the Tamiae of 377/6 B.C. received the *anathemata*. Since the failure of the Tamiae of 321/0 B.C. to mention the transmitting body (*IG*² II 1468) is also due to exceptional circumstances (*below*, p. 124), the omission of 385/4 B.C. is an isolated occurrence [1] and Köhler's explanation of it holds. That the year 386/5 B.C. was in fact the year in which the two boards were separated is confirmed by an observation discussed below (pp. 142 ff.).

[1] We do not know the practice of the Tamiae of the Other Gods on this point be- tween 386/5 and 342/1 B.C. Only one prescript has reached us (*IG*² II 1445, 376/5 B.C.), and this omits the names of the secretaries as well as a reference to the board of the preceding year (cf. *below*, p. 141, n. 1).

III

THE ACCOUNTS OF THE TREASURERS OF ATHENA FOR THE YEAR 409/08 B.C.

B ELOCH (*Griech. Gesch.*, II, 2, pp. 349 f.) attributes to the last years of the Peloponnesian War the accounts of the Treasurers of Athena [1] published in *IG*² I 301 as of the years 422/1–419/8 B.C. Beloch's opinion is connected with his contention that the decree of Kallias (*IG*² I 91/2) was enacted in

[1] Following general practice I refer to these accounts as accounts of the Treasurers, though in point of fact they were published by the state, and were whipped into shape for or by the *logistae*, through whose hands they passed after leaving the Tamiae (Meritt, *Athenian Calendar*, p. 17; cf. p. 95). The Accountants' revision might go so far as to combine in one statement the accounts of the Treasurers of Athena and the accounts of the Treasurers of the Other Gods (*IG*² I 324); ordinarily it was so slight that the Tamiae still speak in the first person (παρέδομεν, *IG*² I 296 ff., II 1686; ἐδανείσαμεν *IG*² I 302, l. 56; παρελάβομεν, ξυνελέξαμεν, *IG*² I 301). It consisted primarily of adding and subtracting items so as to translate a statement prepared for a Panathenaic year into one covering the transactions of the year for which the Council served (*IG*² I 295). Notoriously the accounts of the Tamiae of Athena are a statement of loans to the state alone. The record of receipts and expenditures, which the Treasurers, like all Athenian magistrates (*Aesch.* III 13 ff.), were required to submit to the *logistae* and the dikasts for audit at the expiry of their term, was not inscribed on stone. As is well known (Wilhelm, *Beiträge z. griech. Inschriftenkunde*, pp. 235 ff.), preservation of documents by incision on stone or bronze required specific authorization; and in Athens, for obvious reasons, this was not granted for the multitudinous accounts of the ordinary annual officials. The specific authorization given to the Tamiae of Athena is recorded in *IG*² I 92, ll. 57 ff. and that given to the Tamiae of the Other Gods in *IG*² I 91, ll. 22 ff., cf. *below*, p. 97; that given to the *epistatae* of Eleusis for one class of records is contained in *IG*² I 76, ll. 26 ff. The chances are that the case of *IG*² I 313/4 was covered by a special vote of the *demos*. Publication of accounts was obviously required of Commissions specially created to superintend the construction of public works like the Parthenon, the Propylaea, the chryselephantine statue of Athena, the temple and statue and Nikae of Athena Nike, the Erechtheum, and the various edifices built in the fourth century. It was also required for the *acta* of the Athenian Amphictyons at Delos (*IG*² I 377; *BCH*, 1884, pp. 283 ff.). The latter probably indicate approximately what the accounts of the Tamiae of Athena prepared for their *euthyna* looked like.

After the abandonment of the conciliar year, in 407/06 B.C. at the latest (Meritt, *Class. Phil.*, 1930, p. 239; cf. Dinsmoor, *The Archons of Athens in the Hellenistic Age*, pp. 347 f.), the accounts of the Tamiae which were prepared for publication ran, as did the accounts submitted at their *euthyna* at all times, from Panathenaia to Panathenaia.

418/7 B.C. Now that this document is placed finally in 434
B.C. (Kolbe, *Sitz. Ber. Akad.*, 1927, pp. 319 ff.)[1] his dating of
IG[2] I 301 falls to the ground.[2] Its attribution to *c.* 419/8 B.C.
rests on Bannier's investigation of the development of the
formulas used by the Athenians in the dating of expenditures
in public documents. *IG*[2] I 301 is, he affirms (*Rh. Mus.*, 1906,
pp. 211 ff.), earlier than *IG*[2] I 302, that is to say, than 418/7–
415/4 B.C., because it shares with *IG*[2] I 324 (426/5–423/2 B.C.),
296 (432/1 B.C.), and 295 (433/2 B.C.) the practice of adding
invariably the word πρυτανείας after the name of the prytanizing *phyle*, while *IG*[2] I 302 does so only in its first section and
the later accounts omit it altogether. We have to do, he contends, with the breaking down in 418/7 B.C. of a set form. This
may be right in a general way, though the later accounts, with
the exception of two peculiar records (*IG*[2] I 304A and B),[3] are so
badly mutilated that we have an inadequate basis of observation. But this change in form is purely a stylistic matter, disconnected with any change of institutions. It was in no sense
prescribed by public authority. And indeed the practice of
adding the word πρυτανείας continued for a long time after

---

[1] It now appears that *IG*[2] I 92 was passed on the same day as *IG*[2] I 91 (new reading
by Wade-Gery, knowledge of which I owe to Meritt). For this and other reasons I regard the article of Bannier in *Rh. Mus.*, 1926, pp. 184 ff., as completely antiquated.
Wade-Gery's recent proposal (*Class. Rev.*, 1930, p. 165) to date *IG*[2] I 91 in 422 B.C.
is as yet unsustained by argument. It will need a lot of proving. [Cf. Addendum.]

[2] For withdrawals from the reserve of Athena in the keeping of the Tamiae a preliminary vote of *adeia*, passed by the *demos* under special conditions as to attendance
and voting, was required in 434 B.C. (*IG*[2] I 91/2, ll. 44 ff.). The only accounts which
mention the passing of the vote of *adeia* are those of the years 418/7–415/4 B.C. (*IG*[2]
I 302). This is probably a peculiarity of emphasis, not of practice (*below*, p. 162).
That the disbursement of Athena's money always presupposes specific authorization
on the part of the *demos* or, during the oligarchy, of the Council (*IG*[2] I 298), is shown,
if by nothing else (*IG*[2] I 296, 304A), by the opening phrase of all the accounts: Ἀθεναῖοι
ἀνέλοσαν. Cf. *below*, p. 81, n. 1. The vote of the *demos* incorporated in *IG*[2] I 302, ll.
5 ff. is something special. It altered the destination of funds previously disbursed by
the Tamiae; Meritt, *AJA*, 1930, p. 150, Plate II.

[3] They record expenditures of Athena's income (*epeteia*), made on general authorization of the *demos* but without a special vote in each case. See *below*, pp. 27 ff., 81,
n. 1. They contained such a multitude of petty entries (*below*, p. 31) that abridgements
and omissions of formulae of dating were natural. See *below*, p. 24, n. 2. In *IG*[2] II
1686A, l. 21, and also in *IG*[2] I 304B, l. 71, the most compendious formula possible,
Ἐπὶ τῆς - - ίδος, was employed.

418/7 B.C. It was still followed in 405/04 B.C. for example (*IG²* II 1686, l. 32). Since the Treasurers might insert it when they had a mind to, there is not the slightest reason why a particular board should not have inserted it invariably. Besides, *IG²* I 301 is so badly mutilated that this word may have been omitted occasionally without our knowing it. Its omission or retention after 418/7 B.C. was purely a matter of taste or economy.

Moreover, *IG²* I 301 has several points of style and arrangement which approximate it with the accounts of the period between 411 and 404 B.C. It is badly mutilated; but, none the less, we can see that it used, at least occasionally (ll. 23 f.; cf. 10 f. and 49 ff.),[1] the practice employed at times in the later accounts of dating expenditures by simply naming the prytany and then entering the items, with or without specifying the days on which payments were made (*IG²* I 304A, 410/09 B.C.; 304B, ll. 71 ff.,[2] 407/06 B.C.; II 1686, l. 21, 405/04 B.C.; cf. *above*, p. 17, n. 3). As in the case of *IG²* I 304A, subsequent disbursements made during the prytany were introduced by the word ἕτερον without repetition of the name of the prytany.[3] More fundamental, as reflecting a change of financial system, is the feature it has in common with the later accounts: it specifies that the funds from which the money was taken belonged to Athena Polias, Athena Nike, or Hermes — a method of accounting which meets us for the first time in the annual accounts in *IG²* I 298 (411 B.C.),[4] and is adhered to thereafter (*IG²* I 304A, 304B, 305). The need of particularising in this way arose from the change of situation through which after 412 B.C. the Tamiae were under the necessity of meeting drafts by using current revenues (*below*, pp. 21 f.). It is to be noted further in this same connection that none of the payments made by the Tamiae after 412 B.C. were to the Generals directly[5] — a feature emphasized in *IG²* I 301 (ll. 64 f.) by the

---

[1] See *below*, p. 24, n. 2.   [2] New reading by Meritt.

[3] In one item headed by ἕτερον (l. 20) in *IG²* I 301 the specification τει αὐτει ἐμέραι was used. This seems to call for earlier mention of a definite day. One dating by days is found in the remnants, πέμπτε[ι] in line 36 (new reading by Meritt).

[4] See *below*, p. 21, n. 1.

[5] The sole exception (probably not really an exception) is found in *IG²* I 304A, ll. 34 f. An order was here given by the Tamiae to "the allies" (Meritt) to disburse

explicit statement that all the disbursements were to the Hellenotamiae. Between 418/7 and 414/3 B.C. (*IG*² I 302, cf. *AJA*, 1930, pp. 150, 297), as theretofore, the Generals appear regularly among the recipients. This alteration cannot be explained by the assumption that after 412 B.C. the Generals were never in Athens at the time moneys were "loaned" by the Tamiae. We must infer that part of the financial reorganization effected in 411 B.C. (*above*, p. 3) covered the point. *IG*² I 301 has the further similarity with *IG*² I 304A that they indicate, *IG*² I 304A in the case of certain moneys that originated in Samos, *IG*² I 301 in the case of moneys contributed by the allies, the source from which the sums expended came. There are, therefore, much stronger stylistic grounds for dating *IG*² I 301 in the neighborhood of 410/09 B.C. than in the neighborhood of 420 B.C.; and, indeed, the general scale of the account (without the summarization on the right margin of the stone it alone occupies sixty-four lines as against *c.* eighty-one for the entire four years of *IG*² I 302) classifies it with the later and not with the earlier records of the Tamiae.

These considerations weigh quite as strongly against dating *IG*² I 301 before 422/1 B.C. as in 422/1–419/8. Should it be thought, none the less, to belong before 422/1 B.C.,[1] the choice of year is limited to the epoch 431/0–427/6 B.C. by the preoccupation by other accounts of 433/2 and 432/1 B.C. on the one hand and 426/5–423/2 B.C. on the other. The intervening

to the Generals and other officers at Samos moneys on deposit at Samos which had been "given" to Athena but not transferred to Athens. Naturally the Hellenotamiae did not figure in this transaction. See Hiller, note and Boeckh cited *below*, p. 36, n. 2. It does not constitute an exception that in Munychion 406 B.C. Conon, the General in Samos, was probably joint recipient of money along with the Hellenotamiae and their *paredroi* (*IG*² I 304B, ll. 69 f.; Meritt). The significant thing is that the Hellenotamiae were included.

[1] Wade-Gery (*Num. Chron.*, 1930, p. 17), on grounds "historical and epigraphic," which he "reserves for another occasion" — which, I think, has not yet arrived — dates it "in one of the earliest years of the war, probably 431 B.C." There is one epigraphic factor which I have not tried to evaluate in this study — the style of writing. I distrust my competence in so delicate a matter; but, apart from this, I am indisposed to attach decisive importance to the criterion of writing, for the good and sufficient reason that the outside dates for *IG*² I 301 fall within the active lifetime of a single stone cutter, who (no startling change of general fashion having occurred in the meantime) can have used the same style in inscribing *stelae* in 430 and 408 B.C.

years (with the exceptions of one which must be reserved for
IG^2 I 299/294/308 and of another to which IG^2 I 300 belongs)
are theoretically open. But there seems to be no year free at
this point for an annual, as distinct from a *penteteric*, account
(see *below*, p. 99, n. 2). Moreover, the ratio established between
silver and gold in IG^2 I 301 seems to me to be decisive against
so early a date. In *c*. 440 B.C. (IG^2 I 355; Dinsmoor, *AJA*,
1913, p. 76) this was 14 to 1 as also in 434/3 B.C. (IG^2 I 352):[1]
in IG^2 I 301 it was 10 to 1 (Wade-Gery, *Num. Chron.*, 1930,
pp. 21 ff.), as in 408/07 B.C. (*below*, p. 87, n. 1). That gold
fell thus in value by 430 B.C. is incredible. On the other hand,
its depreciation thus far by 409/07 B.C. is easily intelligible
in view of the "copious influx of Persian gold" after 413/2
B.C. (Tod, *CAH*, V, p. 22; cf. Reinach, *L'Histoire par les monnaies*, p. 50; Gardner, *History of Ancient Coinage*, p. 278).
Of the 5000 talents given by the King to the Spartans between
412 and 405 B.C. (*Andoc.* III 29; *Isocr.* VII 97) the greatest
part was doubtless in gold, and its effect in lowering the value
of this metal was enhanced by the simultaneous disposal of the
gold reserve of Athens itself (*below*, p. 75, n. 3.). Moreover, in
431/0–427/6 B.C. items in the Treasurers' accounts were invariably dated by the days of the prytany, and the formulae
used for the purpose (τρês καὶ δέκα ἐμέραι ἐσελελθυῖαι ἐσαν; - -
ἐμέραι λοιπαὶ ἐσαν; ἐσελελθυίας πέντε ἐμέρας, κτλ. —) occupy more
space than is available in IG^2 I 301, if the lines of this inscription had, as was usual and probable, *c*. eighty-four letters
(Wade-Gery, *loc. cit.*, pp. 25, 30, n. 13) or *c*. eighty-one letters
(Meritt); nor do the remnants of the dates in IG^2 I 301 permit
the use of such periphrases (l. 36). Finally, if IG^2 I 301 belonged thus early, we should expect to find in it the formula
by which additional payments were then introduced (δευτέρα
δόσις, etc.), whereas we find ἕτερον.[2]

And for that matter, as Mr. Meritt very kindly informs me, the writing of IG^2 I 301
is so like that of IG^2 I 297 (414/3 B.C.) and 298 (411 B.C.) that "one might say that it
is identical."

[1] Restoring ⊓ΔΔΔ[ΔⲦ⊦⊦⊦] in line 22 (Meritt).

[2] A further note by Wade-Gery on this document has just appeared (*JHS*, 1930,
pp. 292 f.). A word can, therefore, be added to meet his additional reasons for the
earlier date. In line 35 the dative plural περιπόλεσι, instead of περιπόλοις, is an oddity

The contents of the document seem to me to make a decision in favor of the later date imperative. In it payments were made by the Treasurers from current revenues (*epeteia*). That is a characteristic of Athenian temple finance of the epoch following 412/1 B.C. Before this date payments from income are never mentioned in the Treasurers' accounts. Unless there is conclusive evidence to the contrary, we are bound to believe that payments from current revenues disclose the imminent or complete exhaustion of reserves. So long as there was a large accumulation of funds in the Opisthodomos deposits were naturally added to it when made, and withdrawals, even when debited to special accounts,[1] were taken from the aggregate. Thucydides informs us (VIII 76 6) that in 411 B.C. the Athenians had no more money. It is generally agreed that at the time of the Peace of Nicias there was still a balance of Athena's money in the hands of the Tamiae. Meyer (*Forsch. z. alt. Gesch.*, II, p. 130) estimates it at 700 talents over and above the 1000 talents set apart for a naval crisis; Beloch (*Griech. Gesch.*, II, 2, pp. 342, 351) reduces it to "einige hundert Talenten - - wenig mehr als der eiserne Reservefonds"; nobody denies its existence.[2] We shall give reasons later (*below*, pp. 154 ff.) for thinking that in 434 B.C. the system was inaugurated of creating a public war-fund from the surpluses of the tribute, and that when in 421–415 B.C. this system bore fruit, it led not to the augment-

on any construction. It may imply a nom. plural περιπόλεις, on the false analogy of πόλις, and, if so, it has no significance for dating; -σι παρέδομεν can be restored [φύλαχ]σι π.; on the Thasian Quota see *below*, p. 42, n. 3; the proposed restoration of lines 38 and 62 ([φύλαχσι κατὰ γὲν καὶ κατὰ] θ[άλ]ατταν) has no chronological bearing: the guards could have been described as "on the seaward and landward side" with as much appropriateness in 409/08 as in 431/0 B.C. Agis' attack on the city in 410/09 B.C. (Xen., *Hell.* I 1 35; Beloch, *Griech. Gesch.*, II 2, p. 248) and the departure of Thrasyllos for Ionia must have made necessary special precautions for the defense of the fortifications. See *below*, p. 40, n. 1.

  [1] It is clear from *IG*[2] I 324 that the funds in the custody of the Tamiae of Athena belonged to Athena Polias, Athena Nike, and Hermes; and that they were kept in three separate compartments. It could, accordingly, be specified, when it was thought desirable, from the fund of which of these three deities particular payments were made. Prior to 412 B.C. this was done only in the comprehensive accounts emanating expressly from the *logistae*. For the peculiarities of *IG*[2] I 324, see *below*, p. 99, n. 1.

  [2] Francotte (*Finances des Cités Grecques*, p. 186) estimates it at 736 talents; Cavaignac (*Études sur l'histoire financière d'Athènes*, p. 158, *Tableau*) at twice that amount.

ing of Athena's reserve, but to the accumulation of a new reserve which could be utilized without borrowing. After 421 B.C. Athena's reserve grew by the addition to it of the net yield of Athena's own revenues alone. There may have been withdrawals of which we have no knowledge between 421 and 419/8 B.C. There certainly were such in the following years; but they did not exhaust this reserve; for as late as March, 414 B.C., it was drawn on for a loan of 300 talents (*IG*² I 302, l. 64). Prior to this date there cannot have been any point at which Athena did not have an accumulated fund of at least several hundred talents over and above the 1000 talents specially segregated for a naval crisis. And if we are wrong in holding that the profits of the Empire were accumulated separately, her fund must have run rapidly up into the thousands of talents after the Peace of Nicias. Yet we are asked to believe that in 419/8 B.C. the Tamiae had inadequate reserves and were obliged to have recourse to their current revenues for the loans they made! If, on the other hand, it is contended that payments from income do not imply the absence of a reserve, but signify rather the adoption by the Athenians of a policy of keeping the revenues of the Tamiae distinct from the reserve till the end of the year and of drawing on them for military necessities instead of on the fund accumulated, why did they abandon this policy in 418/7–414/3 B.C. (*IG*² I 302, 297)?

There is yet another reason for dating *IG*² I 301 after 414/3 B.C. As is well known, Athens had a silver currency. The only gold (electron) that circulated was of foreign minting. The possibilities for the use of electron pieces were limited. This is well illustrated by the fact that the Commissioners in charge of the building of the Parthenon had in their possession at the end of construction prolonged for fifteen years the 70 Lampsacene staters and the 27 staters 1 hekte of Cyzicus which they had received in 447/6 B.C. None the less electron and gold formed part of the reserve in the Opisthodomos, in the form of foreign coins which had come in, we may suppose, as tribute or gifts, and also in the form of bullion. The state had the same experience as the Commissioners of the Parthenon, doubtless: its gold-electron was not wanted while silver existed; and the reckonings of the logistae-Tamiae for the eleven years between 434/3 and 423/2 B.C. (*IG²* I 324) deal with items of expenditure in silver alone. In 429/8 B.C. the expenditures of the Treasurers of the Other Gods were exclusively of silver notwithstanding that their funds and receipts were largely of gold and electron. But the state had a resource which the building Commissioners lacked; it could use electron for payments abroad. The first payment of electron made in the extant "accounts" of the Treasurers of Athena went to the Trierarchs who accompanied Demosthenes to Argos in 418 B.C. (*IG²* I 302, ll. 12 ff.); the next was made at the time of the Sicilian expedition.[1] It cannot be denied that the reserve of coined electron could have been drawn on in 422/1–419/8 B.C.; but this is not all. The Tamiae of *IG²* I 301 were reduced to making payments in gold bullion (ll. 103 ff.). Moreover, the silver which they paid out was partly of foreign minting or unminted (ll. 74 ff.). Its value was ascertained by weighing. Consequently, the native silver had to be designated carefully as such (ἐμεδαπόν).[2] It is incredible that in 422/1–419/8 B.C. Athens had reached the point of financial exhaustion such ex-

---

[1] Antimachos of Hermos was not one of the Generals sent to Sicily (Beloch, *Griech. Gesch.*, II, 2, p. 265). Yet he is mentioned three times in conjunction with Alcibiades, Nicias, and Lamachos in the accounts of the Tamiae concerned with the dispatch of the Sicilian expedition (*IG²* I 302). West (*AJA*, 1925, p. 4; 1929, p. 39) suggests that he was a detached *paredros* of the Hellenotamiae, and in fact in 410/09 B.C. (*IG²* I 304A, l. 20) an Hellenotamias and his *paredros* were abroad at Samos, as is shown by the fact that the money they received from the Tamiae was obviously on the island, and not in Athens. But a *paredros* does not appear anywhere isolated from his principal. Meritt (*AJA*, 1930, p. 128; cf. Plates I and II) seems to imply that exceptionally in 415 B.C. the three Generals had each a *paredros* of whom Antimachos was one. There is much to be said for this last suggestion, seeing that *paredro[i]* were in fact mentioned along with the Generals in line 40. But it seems to me possible that he was the *tamias* who, according to *IG²* I 99, l. 10, was "to sail along" with the expedition. The *lacunae* of 41 spaces each (Meritt, *loc. cit.*) in lines 43, 45, and 47 of *IG²* I 302 can be restored, on this interpretation, as follows: στρατεγοῖς ἐς Σικελίαν Ἀλκιβιάδει Λαμάχοι [Νικίαι καὶ τôι ταμίαι τôι χσυμπλέοντι μετὰ τês στρατιᾶς] Ἀντιμάχοι hΕρμείοι.

[2] The use of ἐμεδαπόν as a determinative of ἀργύριον occurs in the later accounts (*IG²* I 305, l. 16, 406/05 B.C. and 307, which Woodward, *JHS*, 1914, p. 280, n. 22, proposes, erroneously as it seems to me, to join with 301; cf. *below*, p. 75, n. 3), not in the earlier. Its appearance in the decree of Kallias (*IG²* I 91, l. 4, 434 B.C.), in the inventory of the Treasurers of the Other Gods (*IG²* I 310, l. 165, 429/8 B.C.), and in the decree substituting Attic silver for local currencies throughout the Empire (*Zeit. f. Numis.*, 1925, pp. 217 ff.) calls for no comment.

pedients imply. That the Tamiae of *IG²* I 301 were drawing off the dregs of their treasury is also evident from their utilization of "silver from the Parthenon" (ἐκ τô Παρθενôνος ἀρ[γυρίο], l. 13).[1] Once the Tamiae had come to the necessity of meeting drafts by paying out current receipts, the sole step left to be taken prior to the issuance of a gold currency was to lay their hands on the stock of ἀργυρώματα placed on display in the Pronaos, Hekatompedon, and Parthenon; and this the Tamiae of 409/08 B.C. also did.

The judgment of Boeckh (*Staatshaushaltung³*, II, pp. 64 ff.), Kirchhoff (*IG¹* I 184/5), and Meyer (*Forsch.*, II, p. 123; *Gesch. d. Alt.*, IV, p. 574) was sound when they dated *IG²* I 301 in the neighborhood of 411 B.C., though the reasons assigned by the first two editors of the *Corpus* for dividing it between two years and determining these definitely as 413/2 and 412/1 B.C. are no longer tenable. As Bannier has pointed out (*Rh. Mus.*, 1906, p. 212), it is impossible to identify the moneys drawn on in line 6 with the special naval reserve, seeing that the former was gold and the latter silver (*Thucy.* II 13 3). It is clear from Hiller's edition that *IG²* I 301 records the expenditures of a single year. Hence the view of Meyer (*loc. cit.*) and Francotte (*Finances*, pp. 191 ff.), that it included the disbursements of the last two months of 412/1, of the archonship of Mnasilochos (Meyer leaves these out), and of the archonship of Theopompos, is not tenable. Had separate boards of Tamiae been involved, they must have been mentioned at the head of the several captions of the account, as in *IG²* I 302 and all the other documents in which the accounts of different boards are inscribed on a single tablet.[2]

---

[1] This, as is well known (Meyer, *Forsch.*, II, p. 141), is a unique occurrence. The only possible explanation has been given by Meyer: "Wie es scheint, lässt sich der verstümmelte Text nur so erklären, dass Zahlungen aus den in Form von Weihgeschenken, Barren u. a. im Parthenon befindlichen Mitteln gemacht sind." We do not know what this "silver" was. The inventory of that chamber of the Temple for 412/1 B.C. (*IG²* I 288) contains several references to uncoined gold, but the silver was all in plate. Silver, coined or in specie, can have come there in 410/09 B.C. (*below*, pp. 34 ff., 53). It seems, therefore, that the *ex-votos* were broached twice during the epoch of the Decelean War, first in 409/08 B.C., during the financial crisis of that year, and secondly, and much more completely, in 406 B.C.

[2] This account grouped items of expenditure which had some reason for being combined and followed each such group by a summary (κεφάλαιον). A dating by days of

To what year then *does IG²* I 301 belong? In 412/1 B.C. the Treasurers were under no necessity of making payments of the miscellaneous character disclosed by this document, certainly not till the end of the year when the naval reserve was exhausted (*Thucy.* VIII 76 6); for it was in this year, the archonship of Kallias (Philoch., *Schol. Aristoph. Lysis.* 173 = *FHG*, 116), that they were authorized to dispose of the 1000 talents of coined silver set aside by Pericles in 431 B.C. (*Thucy.* VIII 15 1). 412/1 B.C. is thus excluded definitely. The preceding year is also excluded for a variety of reasons. If *IG²* I 301 belonged to 413/2 B.C. we should have to date the inception of the practice of making payments from current revenues before the exhaustion of the reserves; the record should have appeared on the same tablet with *IG²* I 297 (414/3 B.C.; *below*, p. 70 n. 1); and we should have to invent an expedition to the Peloponnese before or about September–October, 413 B.C. A count of the prytanies of the year of *IG²* I 301 backward from the end of the account shows (Hiller, note) that the prytany Erechtheis, during which the expenditure ἐς Πελοπόννεσον was made, cannot have been later than the third. In view of the particularity with which Thucydides (VIII 1 ff.) describes the situation that existed at the time of the Athenian disaster in Sicily, we can be certain that Athens did not dispatch an expedition to the Peloponnese at that epoch. She was expecting an attack on the

the prytany may have been entered at the head of each group, but not, I think, for each one of the items. The section entered under the prytany Oineis, with the heading ʰΕρμδ· ἀπὸ πρυ[ταυείας], is a self-contained whole containing items debited to specially designated funds. The date of the payments made from the income of Hermes may have been defined as falling between a named initial and final prytany. Wade-Gery's restoration (ἀπὸ πρυ[ταυείου], *Num. Chron.*, 1930, p. 36, n. 20) seems to me intrinsically improbable. What can Hermes Propylaios have had to do with πρυταυεῖα? Πρυταυεῖα were court-fees, and court-fees were ὅσια χρήματα, which, after 411 B.C., the Hellenotamiae, not the Tamiae, handled (*above*, p. 3). This section was preceded by a similar self-contained whole with payments earmarked as "for the Peloponnese" and dated in the prytany Erechtheis. And it is probable that other sections were marked off by summaries in lines 38 and 63. It is in the last section especially (cf. lines 41 ff.) that considerations of space forbid us to think that a specific day of the prytany was assigned to each item. Similar sections with separate additions of the items contained in them appear in the accounts for 405/04 B.C. (*IG²* II 1686, frg. b). In this respect also *IG²* I 301 is classifiable with the later rather than the earlier accounts. In the accounts dating from the first years of the Peloponnesian War (*IG²* I 296; 299/294/308) the expenditures were grouped, not, as here, by prytanies, but "according to their destination" (Wade-Gery, *JHS*, 1930, p. 292).

city itself from all quarters. The fleet with which Hippokles endeavored to intercept the Corinthian ships returning from Syracuse (*Thucy.* VIII 13) came into action off Leucas only in the season of 412 B.C. It had probably wintered in Corcyra. Its objective could not have been described as ἐs Πελοπόννεσον. If, moreover, *IG*² I 303 is a fragment of the Treasurers' accounts for 413/2 B.C., this year is already occupied; for *IG*² I 301 and 303 do not form parts of the same stone. But I doubt the dating of *IG*² I 303.[1] It seems to me probable that *IG*² I 307 belongs to that year. We cannot date *IG*² I 301 in 411/0 B.C. We already possess the accounts of the Tamiae for Mnesilochos' archonship of two months (*IG*² I 298). Consequently, we are not allowed to treat the part of *IG*² I 301 which precedes ἀπὸ πρυ[τανείας] in line 12 as a record of expenditures made under the Four Hundred even if we should assume it to have been permissible not to note the entry of a different board of Tamiae at this point. Why should the accounts of the Tamiae of the Four Hundred have been published twice or in two parts? Nor does the balance of the year, the ten months of Theopompos' archonship, come in question. There was certainly no expedition to the Peloponnese in this period. Moreover, the prytanies under the Five Thousand were not so constituted as to be given the names of *phylae* (*Class. Phil.*, 1926, p. 75; *CAH*, V, p. 339;[2] cf. *below*, p. 75, n. 2), whereas the prytanies of *IG*² I 301 are named as usual.

*IG*² I 301 cannot belong to 410/09 B.C., for that year is preoccupied by *IG*² I 304A; and if this does not suffice, the se-

---

[1] *IG*² I 303 is written in Ionic script. This being so it is out of place in 413/2 B.C. See *below*, Appendix I. It may belong in 411/0 B.C., in the archonship of Theopompos, since the accounts of the Tamiae of the Four Hundred used the new method of writing (*IG*² I 298). If the Hippokles mentioned in it is correctly identified (Hiller, note) with the Hippokles, son of Menippos, who was General in 413/2 B.C. (*Thucy.* VIII 13), he can have been Hellenotamias under the Five Thousand. It is as Hellenotamias, rather than as *strategos*, that he appears in *IG*² I 303. But the identification is not certain. A Hippokles was one of the Ten (*Lysias* XII 55). They may of course be the same person. In any event, *IG*² I 303 may belong to the 406/04 epoch, when the Ionic script was constantly used by the Tamiae in their accounts. Query: May it have formed part of *IG*² I 305? A confrontation of the two stones is desirable.

[2] The contrary inference of De Sanctis (*R. Accad. dei Lincei, Classe di Scienza morali*, 1930, p. 334) falls with the transfer of *IG*² I 105 from 410 to 407/06 B.C.

quence of the prytanies leaves no possibility of doubt. In 410/09 B.C. Erechtheis was ninth and Oineis third (*IG²* I 304A); in *IG²* I 301 Erechtheis preceded Oineis (ll. 2, 10). And this same criterion excludes 408/07; for in this year, too, Oineis preceded Erechtheis,[1] and, what is more, Athens sent no expedition to the Peloponnese in the late summer or autumn of 408 B.C. 407/06 B.C. was barren of Athenian enterprises in the Peloponnese; 406/05 B.C. is preoccupied by *IG²* I 305; 405/04 B.C. by *IG²* II 1686 (*below*, pp. 77 ff.). The only year remaining for *IG²* I 301 is 409/08 B.C.

With this issue we have three of the four accounts for the seventh *penteteris*[2] (410/09–407/06 B.C.), namely, *IG²* I 304A,

---

[1] This conclusion rests upon the observation made by me (*Athenian Secretaries*, p. 26, n.; cf. Paton, *The Erechtheum*, pp. 371, n. 1, 398) that in 408/07 B.C. the *phylae* held the prytany in the reverse of their official order. If Hiller's restoration of *IG²* I 313, ll. 173 ff. were correct, the regularity of prytany-sequence in the latter half of this year (Oineis V, Akamantis 6, Leontis VII, Pandionis VIII, Aigeis IX, Erechtheis X) would have to be held to be accidental; for, if the secretary of the first prytany were Dorotheos, Antiochis, of which the secretary was Eukleides (*IG²* I 118), could not have held the prytany first, as demanded by the tribal cycle. But Hiller's restorations are almost certainly wrong. They require more spaces to the line than are available — thirty-five as against a maximum elsewhere (l. 129) of thirty-three; and this maximum is reached only by the crowding in of three *iotas* out of alignment (cf. Sardemann, *Eleusinische Uebergabeurkunden*, Beilage I). Meritt very kindly informs me that "the lines here contain a maximum of thirty letters though some crowding is permissible." He suggests reading

$$\tau\alpha\mu\iota\alpha[\varsigma \ h\iota\epsilon\rho\hat{o}\nu \ \chi\rho\epsilon\mu\acute{\alpha}\tau o\nu \ \tau\hat{\epsilon}\varsigma \ 'A\theta\epsilon\nu\alpha\acute{\iota}\alpha\varsigma \ (\theta\epsilon\hat{o}?)]$$
$$\grave{\epsilon}\pi\grave{\iota} \ E\grave{\upsilon}\kappa[\tau\acute{\epsilon}\mu o\nu o\varsigma \ \check{\alpha}\rho\chi o\nu\tau o\varsigma \ \kappa\alpha\grave{\iota} \ \grave{\epsilon}\pi\grave{\iota}]$$
$$\Delta o\rho o\theta\acute{\epsilon}o \ [\gamma\rho\alpha\mu\mu\alpha\tau\epsilon\acute{\upsilon}o\nu\tau o\varsigma \ \pi\alpha\rho\acute{\epsilon}\delta o\mu\epsilon\nu], \ \kappa\tau\lambda.$$

If it were permissible to assume sufficient crowding toward the ends of the lines to accommodate thirty-three letters we might read

$$\tau\alpha\mu\iota\alpha[\varsigma \ h\iota\epsilon\rho\hat{o}\nu \ \chi\rho\epsilon\mu\acute{\alpha}\tau o\nu \ \tau\hat{\epsilon}\varsigma \ 'A\theta\epsilon\nu\alpha\acute{\iota}\alpha\varsigma]$$
$$\grave{\epsilon}\pi\grave{\iota} \ E\grave{\upsilon}\kappa[\tau\acute{\epsilon}\mu o\nu o\varsigma \ \check{\alpha}\rho\chi o\nu\tau o\varsigma \ h o\hat{\iota}\varsigma \ \Delta o\rho\acute{o}\theta\epsilon o\varsigma \ ?]$$
$$\Delta o\rho o\theta\acute{\epsilon}o \ [\Phi\lambda\upsilon\epsilon\grave{\upsilon}\varsigma \ ? \ \grave{\epsilon}\gamma\rho\alpha\mu\mu\acute{\alpha}\tau\epsilon\upsilon\epsilon \ \pi\alpha\rho\acute{\epsilon}\delta o\mu\epsilon\nu], \ \kappa\tau\lambda.$$

But even if Hiller's restorations were possible, the alternative, which makes Dorotheos the secretary of the Tamiae, and not of the prytany, is preferable. In the accounts of the Commissioners of the Erechtheum for 408/07 B.C. (*IG²* I 374), as well as in those of the Tamiae for Mnasilochos' archonship, the phrase desiderated by Hiller, $\grave{\epsilon}\pi\grave{\iota} \ \tau\hat{\epsilon}\varsigma$ $\beta o\lambda\hat{\epsilon}\varsigma \ h\hat{\epsilon}\iota \ \grave{o} \ \delta\epsilon\hat{\iota}\nu\alpha \ \pi\rho\hat{o}\tau o\varsigma \ \grave{\epsilon}\gamma\rho\alpha\mu\mu\acute{\alpha}\tau\epsilon\upsilon\epsilon$, is omitted after the name of the Archon. On the other hand, it would be singular in a record of this character to find neither the Chairman nor the Secretary of the Tamiae mentioned by name.

Be that as it may, I see no reason to doubt that Oineis furnished the fifth and Erechtheis the tenth prytany in 408/07 B.C.

[2] Counting 434/3–431/0 B.C. as the first.

301, and 304B. *IG*² I 304B occupies the reverse of the *stele* which has *IG*² I 304A on its obverse. It was assigned to 407/06 B.C. by Kirchhoff (*IG*¹ I 188/9, p. 88), and though his arguments have lost much of their validity,[1] his dating is still generally accepted. We can replace Kirchhoff's arguments by others which are more cogent. Since *IG*² I 304A belongs in 410/09 B.C., and 406/05 and 405/04, besides being outside the *penteteris*, belong to *IG*² I 305 and *IG*² II 1686, the only possible alternatives for *IG*² I 304B are 408/07 and 409/08. But both of these years are excluded by the prytany-sequences. In the year of *IG*² I 304B Erechtheis had the second prytany and in the year that followed (line 92) Erechtheis had the first prytany. Since Erechtheis had the tenth prytany in 408/07 (p. 27, n. 1), *IG*² I 304B can belong to neither 408/07 nor 409/08.

The problem of relating the *stele* which gives us *IG*² I 301 with the *stele* on which, front and back, *IG*² I 304A and 304B are inscribed seems at first sight insurmountable; but with the aid of suggestions furnished by Professor Meritt, who has special knowledge of the stones (*Class. Phil.*, 1930, pp. 236 ff), the difficulty (so it appears to me) vanishes. The *stele* of the year 409/08 B.C. was of unusual thickness (23 or 24 cm. as against 18 cm. for 304). On its obverse *IG*² I 301A was inscribed and on its right side 301B, a summary of the items included in 301A. The rear face of the stone has been split off. The left part of the front and the entire left side are lost. It is, therefore, quite possible for another account — that of the year 408/07 B.C. — to have been inscribed on the reverse and the left margin; and, since this need not have been as lengthy as *IG*² I 301, there can have been space remaining for the beginning of the account for the year 407/06 B.C. Assuming that the two *stelae* were set side by side (not joined by dowels,[2] etc.),

---

[1] This much remains: *IG*² I 304B cannot belong to 408/07 B.C., seeing that in this year the eighth prytany had thirty-six days (*IG*² I 374, ll. 256 ff.; Paton, *The Erechtheum*, p. 394, ll. 8 ff., cf. p. 371, n. 1), whereas in the year of *IG*² I 304B the eighth prytany had only thirty-five days (Meritt, *Class. Phil.*, 1930, p. 238). The lengths of the sixth prytany also differed: thirty-seven days in the one instance, thirty-four in the other. It is certain that *IG*² I 374 and 304B cannot belong to the same year.

[2] The *stele* from which, front and back, *IG*² I 304A and B come has an *anaglyph* at the top, the base of which (*cymation*) is 6 cm. deep and projects slightly on each side,

the back of *stele* I was then available for the rest of the account for 407/06 B.C. (*IG²* I 304B). This begins, as is well
known, some distance (30 cm.) from the bottom of the back of
the *anaglyph* by which the *stele* is adorned, with the expenditures for the second prytany. The lower half of the *stele* is lost.
Apparently the stone was sawn horizontally in the middle at
some time or other and the lower section carried away.¹ On
the back of this section the expenditures of prytanies III–VII
of 407/06 B.C. were entered. Owing to a miscalculation of
space (accompanied by the desire to leave an ample margin
between the account and the *anaglyph*) there was no room for
those of prytanies VIII–X, which were, accordingly, posted on
the space left vacant on the top of the stone. The difficulty
that seemed insurmountable was to explain what was written
on the front of the lower section. Two solutions are suggested:
(*a*) that the accounts of the year 410/09 B.C. consisted of two
parts. Part I contained expenditures from *epeteia* alone. This
is in our possession practically intact. Part 2 consisted of expenditures from the balance in the Opisthodomos. This has
perished with the loss of the lower section of the stone. In
other words, the accounts for 410/09 B.C. were drafted in the
same fashion as those for 406/05 and 405/04 B.C., with a separation of outlays from income and outlays from the treasury.
In the account for 406/05 B.C. (*IG²* I 305) the second part is
headed by the rubric τάδε ἐκ τοῦ 'Οπ[ισ]θοδόμο[υ παρ]έδομεν.² It
can be thought that this same rubric prefaced the outlays from
the treasury recorded in the lost second half of the account for
410/09 B.C.; and that it or something similar also prefaced the
initial outlays recorded in *IG²* II 1686A frg. b (405/04 B.C.).

thus preventing a close join with any other stone. Moreover, the *stele* which gives
us *IG²* I 301 may have contained writing on its left margin.

¹ The shape of the stone indicates that only about half of it has reached us (Meritt):
the *stele* proper, as it stands, is 53 cm. in length and 77 cm. in width; the height of
the *anaglyph* is 57 cm., its width 62 cm.

² The right interpretation of this rubric has been given already (Meyer, *Forsch.*,
II, p. 140; Francotte, *Finances*, p. 200). One notation [ἐχς 'Οπισθ]οδόμο occurs elsewhere, in *IG²* I 324, l. 20. It is attached to a loan of 30 talents made in 425/4 B.C. by
the Tamiae of Athena. There it seems superfluous (cf. Meyer, *Forsch.*, II, pp. 138 f.;
Michaelis, *Arch. Jahrb.*, 1902, p. 25; Francotte, *Finances*, p. 199; Bannier, *Rh. Mus.*,
1906, pp. 205, 214; Paton, *The Erechtheum*, p. 472, n. 1).

For this fragment belongs, as Kirchner places it, at the bottom of the *stele* which gives us *IG²* II 1686 frg. a, in the first place because its broken lines cannot be fitted into the body of this text, and in the second place because it is not opisthographous, as it must have been had it belonged at the top. Yet it exhibits expenditures made during a second series of prytanies. In the first series approximately seven prytanies were involved. That the second ran parallel is shown by entries made during the fifth prytany and at least one earlier prytany. So too in *IG²* I 305 the expenditures made from the Opisthodomos are dated on the 27th of Munychion whereas the account of outlays from the *epeteia* ran down to the 27th of Hekatombaion (line 10, as restored by West, *Class. Weekly*, 1929, p. 62).

In further development of this solution we can imagine that once the *epeteia* were intercepted for current needs before they were banked in the Opisthodomos the Tamiae found it advisable to keep their accounts in two sections. In 410/09 B.C. the items entered in each were published in a group separately. In 409/08, on the other hand, the Tamiae included both in a single statement, distinguishing in each case expenditures of revenues which they themselves had collected from expenditures of moneys which they had received from their predecessors. To this chronological exposition of items they appended a summary in which the totals for the year from each source were given, the items being arranged for addition according to whether the disbursements were of silver or gold. Native silver was distinguished from foreign silver and silver that was uncoined, coined gold (electron rather) of various currencies from gold bullion, the equivalent in Attic money being entered in the case of specie and alien mintages. This kind of statement had obvious disadvantages. The main body of the account was swollen by the repetition with each entry of either one of the two phrases of specification, "from the revenue which we ourselves collected," "which we took over from the former Tamiae"; and, whether necessarily or not, it entailed a lengthy and intricate recapitulation of items prior to the final addition. It would be intelligible, therefore, that in 406/05 and 405/04 B.C. the Tamiae should follow the model of the account for 410/09. We do not know what the Tamiae of 408/07 did. What about the account for 407/06 (*IG*² I 304B)?

Despite the fact that the beginning of this account is lost it is clear from the dribs and drabs paid out in the second prytany (the amounts range from 6 drachmas, 3½ obols to 946 drachmas, 1 obol; there are twelve items in all, one on the average for every two days between Metageitnion 20th and Boedromion 14th — all for the *diobelia*; the total for twenty-four days is only *c.* 2150 drachmas) that we have to do with the paying out of sums as they were received (Wilamowitz, *Arist. u. Athen*, II, p. 212, n. 2). In other words, the account began, like *IG*² I 304A, with outlays from the *epeteia*. We cannot be sure how long this form of statement was followed; but one of two things is certain, either it was abandoned before the end of the seventh prytany was reached, or the expenditures ceased to be made with equal frequency. Otherwise, we should have to assume that 175 lines were contained in the lost lower part of the *stele*.[1] In any event, when the record was resumed on the top of the stone, notwithstanding that the script, length of line, and arrangement of letters (*stoichedon*) were maintained, there is a marked difference in the character of the entries.[2] Now we have to do with single expenditures four and five times as large as the entire aggregate for the second prytany, and one such large payment at least (TT. in line 74; cf. Meritt, *Class. Phil.*, 1930, p. 237) is credited to the *diobelia*. It was made on the fourth day of the ninth prytany (Munychion [1]9th). We might attribute its comparative largeness to the time of the year, seeing that it was in the ninth prytany that most of the public revenues were payable, if it were not that on the 23d of the eighth prytany a similarly large disbursement was

---

[1] If half the stone is lost, there was room for only about sixty-one lines.

[2] A peculiarity of this part of the account, and indeed of all the accounts which have reached us, is the appearance in it of the *logistae* (Meritt, *Class. Phil.*, 1930, p. 237). They figure on six occasions, three times as recipients (ll. 74, 76, 85), elsewhere possibly as donors. Once (l. 74) they were joint recipients with the Hellenotamiae (cf. *above*, p. 18, n. 5). The rôle played here by the Accountants remains as yet unintelligible. That they should receive sacred moneys is surprising; that they should give them, bewildering. The only explanation I can think of is that they acted as intermediaries between the Tamiae and the payees. They appear in our record for the first time on or about Munychion 3d (April), 406 B.C.

made (1 talent, 2009 drachmas, and 4 obols). A further change was made in line 77, beginning with an item dated on the 15th of the ninth prytany (Munychion 30th). Not only are the letters from this point on crowded much more closely together and the *stoichedon* arrangement abandoned, but the script becomes strongly Ionic, with the peculiarities commented on elsewhere (*below*, p. 47). The document ended in line 93 with an incomplete entry (Meritt) — not for lack of space.[1] It broke off abruptly on or shortly after Hekatombaion 20th, at just about the time when the decree of the people was passed amalgamating the two boards of Tamiae into a single *collegium* and expropriating the votives for the war (*below*, pp. 88 ff.). If the expenditures throughout were made from *epeteia*, as the continuous progression of payments in a single series of prytanies suggests, we have to conclude either that there were no expenditures from the Opisthodomos in 407/06 B.C. or that the disbursements from this source were left unrecorded.

An alternate explanation (*b*) of the failure of the Tamiae of 409/08 B.C. to post their record on the lower half of the face of *IG*[2] I 304A is adducible. For reasons which he will discuss in his forthcoming work on *Athenian Financial Documents in the Fifth Century* Meritt concludes that the Tamiae of 410/09 B.C. made outlays from *epeteia* alone, and that what we possess (*IG*[2] I 304A) is their whole account. Consequently the Tamiae of 409/08 could have begun their record on the lower half of their predecessors' *stele*. But they could not have finished it there. Owing to the form in which it was drafted, it was of unusual length. They must, therefore, have contemplated concluding it on the reverse had they used the *stele* of their predecessors at all. Since this particular *stele* was surmounted by a sculptured relief by which its front was clearly indicated, its reverse may have seemed an invidious position for their account. It seems probable, moreover, that the subject of the relief contained a

---

[1] A *lacuna* of 3½ cm. separates line 93 from line 41 (Meritt). The account may have been continued on another stone. It was obviously inscribed piecemeal. Conceivably it was enlarged suddenly by the decision to expropriate the *ex-votos*. Judging from *IG*[2] II 1686A (see *below*, p. 79), we should expect it to contain a memorandum of the articles of gold and silver surrendered for minting. This would involve a lengthy addition.

specific reference to events of the year 410 B.C. Consequently the Tamiae of 409/08 preferred to set up a *stele* of their own.[1] Perhaps we should rather say, they and their successors — the Tamiae of 408/07 — decided on a *stele*, ample (front, sides, and back) for two accounts.[2] This left the lower face of the preceding *stele* blank. That was no novelty. In the series of tablets devoted to accounts and inventories the entire face of slabs often remained uninscribed (*below*, p. 71). In July, 406 B.C., the situation of the outgoing Tamiae was altogether different. At that time Athens was resorting to the most desperate expedients to raise money. The need to economize was imperative. It was the end of a *penteteris* and at the same time the end of the existence, as a separate board, of Tamiae of Athena. Accordingly the Tamiae had no choice but to utilize tablet space left blank on the *stelae* of their fellow *archae*.[3] They posted the beginning of their account — that for the first prytany — on the unoccupied lower face of *IG* I[2] 304A and the balance on the reverse. They seem to have taken little pride in their work.

Quite apart from the epigraphical reasons to be urged by Meritt there is much to be said in favor of this second solution of our difficulty. It seems certain that the Tamiae of 410/09 B.C. inherited an empty treasury. At the time the revolution broke in 411 B.C. the reserves were exhausted: the report of Thucydides (VIII 76 6) is explicit that the Athenians had at that time no money except what the fleet at Samos could itself collect. We cannot imagine Athena being able to accumulate a new reserve during either the four months of the Four Hun-

---

[1] The total expense involved may be estimated at from 100 to 150 drachmas if the costs of making, transporting, and engraving the *stele*, and of the lead, wood, and labor used in setting it up were comparable with those prevailing in Delos in the third century (*IG* XI 2, 161A, ll. 117 ff.; Wilhelm, *Wien. Anzeiger*, XIV–XVII, 1930, pp. 98 ff.).

[2] From the fact that the Tamiae of 409/08 B.C. placed their summarization on the right margin of the stone we should naturally infer that they were not free to use the reverse. Cf. however, *IG*[2] I 216/217/231 = *SEG* V 25.

[3] From like motives of economy the Tamiae of 406/05 and 405/04 B.C. used for their inventories of the Parthenon space left blank on the *stele* of their predecessors for the *penteteris* 418/7–415/4 B.C. In both instances the penalty was incurred that the records appeared out of their chronological place in the series of tablets.

dred,[1] or the exacting months which followed, preceding the victory at Cyzicus (Xen. *Hell.* I 1 14). How then could the Tamiae of 410/09 B.C. have made payments from any source but *epeteia*? In the third prytany of the year 410/09 B.C. *syngrapheis* presented to the *demos*, and the *demos* accepted, a plan for paying back to the Goddess some of the money borrowed from her. The details of the plan are lost. All that has reached us of this important document is the prescript,[2] a mutilated line stating the object of the proposals (ἐς τὲν [ἀπόδοσιν τô χρυσô κ]αὶ τôν ὀφ[ε]ιλομένον χρεμ[άτον], and portions of the three following lines (-ται ὸς πλεῖστα χρέμ[α]τ[α - - , ἐν] ἀκροπό[λε]ι κ - - , πα]ραλ[α - -). *Subjectum*, explains Hiller (*IG*² I 109, note), *fuerit hoc ταμίαι.* What it was that the Tamiae were to do in order to have on the Acropolis as much money as possible we cannot guess; but the circumstances were favorable for success (*below*, pp. 38 ff.), and the accounts for the year 409/08 B.C. show that a considerable amount was in fact accumulated. Conceivably, the proceeds of this campaign were banked in the Opisthodomos as the nucleus of a new reserve; but they were none the less *epeteia*, and if expended by the Tamiae of 410/09 B.C. they would be debited most naturally to income. On this hypothesis the Tamiae of 409/08 B.C. were the first treasurers to cope with the problem of drawing up an account which should distinguish disbursements from balance from disbursements from income; and notwithstanding that their production was marred by long repetitions, astonishing even in these formal records, the Tamiae of 408/07 B.C. may have followed their model, if indeed they made expenditures from balances at all. How those of 407/06 B.C. proceeded we have already seen. In 406/05 and 405/04 B.C. the more simple method of preparing two separate statements

---

[1] The sum borrowed from Athena Polias on Hekatombaion 21st was 27+ and not 77+ talents (Meritt, new reading of line 19 of *IG*² I 298).

[2] Hiller's restoration of the Secretary's *demotikon* (Οἰ[έθεν) is certainly wrong: the Secretary could not belong to the prytanizing *phyle.* I have suggested 'Οτ[ρυνεύς] (*Class. Phil.*, 1926, p. 74). Οἰ[ναῖος] is preferable because the second letter seems not to have had a cross bar at the top. On the other hand, since the *epistates* was one of the officiating *prytaneis*, Αἰγηίς should be restored in line 4 of *IG*² I 125 (405/04 B.C.). The *stele* containing *IG*² I 109, like that on which the accounts of the Tamiae of Athena for the same year (410/09 B.C.) were inscribed, was surmounted by an *anaglyph.*

was employed by the joint board of Tamiae. We may doubt whether there was any reserve of sacred money to speak of after Hekatombaion 28th, 408 B.C., until the coining of the votives rehabilitated the finances of Athens in 406/04 B.C.

It appears that the *epeteia* of the Goddess amounted to over 173½ talents in 410/09 B.C. The most considerable item is a sum in excess of 90½ talents originating in Samos, the expenditure of which was subject to conditions arranged — with the fleet doubtless. This seems too large an amount to be derived by Athena from properties allocated to her on the island. Her share of the land taken from the Mytilenaeans in 427 B.C. yielded an income of only 10 talents (*Thucy.* III 50 2). But it is to be observed that after their subjugation in 439 B.C. the Samians did not pay *phoros*: no *aparche* to Athena is credited to them in the tribute-lists (Meritt). It is thinkable that the Goddess received as *epeteia*, not as in the case of Lesbos a tithe alone, but the entire amount paid by the Samians each year as tribute and indemnity combined. This would be equitable since the cost of the Samian War was borne by the Goddess (*IG²* I 293). The reduction of Samos preceded the policy inaugurated in 434 B.C. of "giving" no longer to Athena the surpluses of the Empire (*below*, p. 155). At the time of the confiscation of the lands of the Mytilenaeans, on the other hand, the natural procedure was to give Athena a tithe and to let the rest go into the public fund. But even if we hold it probable that Athena got a sum in excess of 200 talents annually from Samos in the epoch following 439 B.C., it is incredible that a tribute-indemnity of this magnitude was being still paid in 410 B.C. The costs of the Samian War were covered by 433 B.C.;[1] and during the Decelean period of the Peloponnesian War the Samians had just claims for preferential treatment.[2] It seems to me that the 90½ talents expended in this year "of the money

[1] Kolbe (*Sitz. Ber. Akad.*, 1930, p. 340, n. 1) cites *IG²* I 65, ll. 20 ff., as proof that in 425/4 B.C. Samos was required to pay tribute. We can assume that by that time the account of the Samians with Athena was squared; and, indeed, it is clear (*below*, p. 155) that it was already squared in 433 B.C. Subsequently the "tribute" in its entirety may have been paid in full to Athena; cf. West, *Trans. Amer. Phil. Assoc.*, 1930, p. 219, n. 8.

[2] In 412 B.C. Samos was given autonomy by Athens (*Thucy.* VIII 21).

from Samos" represents a contribution made to Athena's treasury from the funds which the Athenian fleet stationed at the island had collected.[1] It was "given" to Athena in such a way that it was expendable by the Tamiae, not in cash, but by a special authorization.[2] Presumably this was one of the means recommended by the *syngrapheis* for paying back some of the money borrowed from the Goddess.

The *epeteia* of money in silver belonging to Athena Polias which were expended in 409/08 B.C. amounted to more than 50 talents and less than 100 talents if lines 83 ff. of IG^2 I 301 are restored correctly. The total expenditures of silver money of Athena Polias, Athena Nike, and Hermes made in the year aggregated at least 360 + talents; [3] and in addition there were expenditures of gold and electron from the balance left by the Tamiae of the previous year (staters and bullion) to an amount which, on Wade-Gery's restoration of the figures (*Num. Chron.*, 1930, pp. 37 f.), came to 71 (70) talents, 1240 drachmas, 1 obol; [4] and of gold from the *epeteia*, of which one item (bullion) amounted to 3000 drachmas and another (staters) to 8 talents, 3600 drachmas, according again to Wade-Gery's reconstruction of the text. The total expended from the balance received from the Tamiae of 410/09 B.C. was, therefore (if we estimate arbitrarily at *c.* 75 talents the *epeteia* of silver money received by Athena Polias and at *c.* 5 talents the silver money received

---

[1] That this was *epeteia* of the Goddess, i.e., receipts for the year, has been maintained rightly by Beloch (*Griech. Gesch.*, II, 2, p. 343; *Rh. Mus.*, 1884, pp. 36 ff.). Its designation as *epeteia* is, however, reconcilable with the view that the fleet held back the income of the Goddess from the island for 412/1 and 411/0 B.C. and that the 90½ talents represent the income for three years. However, even 30 talents would be an incredibly large annual return to Athena from her private property and rights on Samos. Apart from the receipts from Samos, Beloch (*Griech. Gesch.*, II, 2, p. 327) estimates the *epeteia* of the Goddess at this epoch as 50 talents, Meyer (*Forsch.*, II, pp. 130, 123) at about 78 talents. In any event, we cannot gauge the normal revenues of the Goddess by the total expended from *epeteia* in 410/09 B.C.

[2] Ἀνομολόγεμα. Böckh (*Staatshaushaltung*[3], II, pp. 14, 20 f.) is doubtless right in insisting that the money remained at Samos notwithstanding that it was recognized as Athena's and consequently required the authorization of the Tamiae for its expenditure.

[3] Restoring the minimal figure in line 92 of IG^2 I 301 (Wade-Gery, *Num. Chron.*, 1930, p. 37): [ⲎⲎⲎ]ⲎⲔⲢ△ · ·

[4] There is an arithmetical error in Wade-Gery's calculations: ten times TⲬⲬⲬ-ⲎⲎⲎⲔⲢ△△ · is △ⲔⲢⲬⲬⲬⲔⲢⲎⲎ ·, not △ⲔⲢTⲬⲬⲬⲔⲢⲎⲎ · [Corrected, *ibid.*, p. 333.]

by Athena Nike and Hermes), about 350 + talents, and the total *income* expended by the Tamiae during the year was about 89 talents. These totals, it should be observed, are totals of expenditures: they are totals of funds only if all the balance and income was disbursed; [1] and in view of the many uncertainties inherent in the figures, they are simply hypothetical totals. All that I wish to show by these statistics is that, on the latest figures available, the expenditures attributed to the Tamiae of 409/08 B.C. are reconcilable with the hypothesis that under the plan launched in October 410 B.C. for repaying borrowings from the Goddess a reserve of something like 350 talents remained in the Opisthodomos at the end of the year — a conclusion well within the probabilities.

[1] If *epeteia* from Samos aggregating 90½ talents were received in silver in 409/08 B.C., which is highly improbable (*above*, p. 36, n. 1), they were not disbursed at all or only in small part. There cannot be much doubt, I think, that the Tamiae of 409/08 B.C. disbursed practically all the money in their possession. They would not have disposed of gold and silver bullion and silver votives from the Parthenon if they had had liquid funds in their hands.

IV

THE EXPEDITIONS OF ANYTOS AND
THRASYLLOS

IN view of the fact that the ordinary reserves must have been pretty well exhausted in 412 B.C. when the special reserve of 1000 talents was broached; in view of the further fact that the great naval effort made by Athens between the revolt of Chios and the outbreak of revolution consumed the special reserve (*Thucy.* VIII 76 6); and inferring the gravity of the financial situation during the year 411/0 B.C. from the abolition of indemnities for all non-military services, we shall do well to recognize that the Tamiae of 410/09 B.C. inherited a practically empty treasury. We have now seen that they handed over to their successors a balance of several hundred talents. The solvency of Athena at the opening of 409/08 B.C. is affirmed by further evidence: the Athenians resumed work at this moment on the Erechtheum after a suspension for a considerable period (*IG*² I 372; Paton, *The Erechtheum*, pp. 298 ff.), and, as was natural, they called upon the Goddess to finance the building operations. The sums involved were not large, the men employed few; but the significant thing is that work could have been resumed at all.

It is not difficult to understand how the finances both of Athens and of Athena came to be rehabilitated in 410/09 B.C. Early in 410 B.C., after three years of uphill struggle, the Athenians became once again undisputed masters of the sea. For the first time since its inauguration they were in a position to collect the Twentieth into which the *phoros* had been commuted in 414/3 B.C. After Cyzicus we may be sure that the subject allies made haste to square their accounts by paying arrears as well as current obligations. There came to be added the Tenth imposed and collected on all cargoes passing through the Bosporus from the Black Sea. Last but not least there was the booty. So far as naval operations were concerned the year 410/09 B.C. was singularly uneventful. Notoriously the record of Alcibiades for this year is a blank. We can explain the inactivity of the victorious Athenian fleet during these critical months only on the assumption that it was again, as before Cyzicus, broken up into squadrons and dispatched hither and yon to collect money. After all, the restoration of the imperial revenues was the *sine qua non* for the campaign, projected for 409 B.C., for the recovery of the "allies" which had revolted in 412 and 411 B.C.

The chief military enterprise of Athens during 410/09 B.C. was the expedition of Thrasyllos to Ionia. This was launched on the opening of navigation in the spring of 409 B.C. It was not paid for by moneys borrowed from the income of Athena for the year. Otherwise the payments would have been entered in *IG*² I 304A. But Athens was not dependent on Athena. The Hellenotamiae disbursed the imperial revenues and had recourse to the funds of the Goddess only in case of a shortage. They cannot have been without money in the spring of 409 B.C. The sums paid to them by the Tamiae must be regarded as supplements designed to free them from expenditures incumbent upon them which would have reduced the amounts available for military operations. The destination of the sums thus disbursed by the Tamiae from income was diverse: the *diobelia*,[1] *sitos* for the knights, the commandant at Pylos, the General ἐξ Ἐρετρίας, the commanders of the fleet at Samos. The only large amount paid to the Hellenotamiae without indication of

---

[1] The first payment for the *diobelia* of which we have knowledge was made toward the end of the prytany of Oineis in the year 410/09 B.C. (*IG*² I 304A, l. 10). Theretofore the Tamiae had made no expenditures for this donation to the people. Since it was during this same prytany that the plan of the *syngrapheis* for recreating Athena's reserve was adopted, it is reasonable to infer that one of its objects was to provide the Goddess with the money required to meet this new drain on her funds. We may suspect that Cleophon was the real author of the plan. Money for the *diobelia* went through the hands of the Hellenotamiae, but it reached for ultimate distribution an official whom Xenophon (*Hell.* I 7 2) describes as τῆς διωβελίας ἐπιμελόμενος.

destination was one of 57 talents paid out on the thirtieth day of the sixth prytany (January, 409 B.C.). This may have gone to help outfit Thrasyllos; but it went more probably to Samos, like the other moneys paid from "the fund from Samos," seeing that the expenditure of this fund was subject to conditions imposed doubtless in their own interest by the Athenian "*demos*" on the island when the money was given to Athena. No expenditures were labeled for Alcibiades or his fellow admirals.

It is intelligible that the improvement in Athens' financial position effected in 410 B.C. benefited Athena. Naturally she profited by the increased yield of the public revenues (Twentieth, Tenth, arrears, booty) on which she was entitled to levy a tithe (Meyer, *Forsch.*, II, pp. 122 ff.); but the Athenians were not content to leave it at that. As we have seen, they took measures to repay to the Goddess money previously borrowed and thus shared their newly won revenues with their patron deity. Accordingly, they came to possess by the opening of the season of 409 B.C. a reserve of money for an enlarged and, it was hoped, decisive military effort.

The specific destination of the moneys expended by the Tamiae in 409/08 B.C. is known in one case only. Many of the outlays made to the Hellenotamiae with or without specification of destination were doubtless for the *diobelia*. At two points the expenditures were described as for operations [1] καὶ κατὰ γὲν καὶ κατὰ θάλατταν. The few items preserved are not large. The largest was one of 33 talents, 2000 drachmas. The

---

[1] Restoring ἐς τὰς στρατίας in lines 38 and 62. Wade-Gery (*JHS*, 1930, p. 293) suggests φυλάχσι; but it does not seem in place in an account to specify thus topographically the stations of the guards: they were designated adequately by name alone. On the other hand, the campaigns of the spring and summer of 408 B.C., since they involved the whole region of the Hellespont, Propontis, and Bosporus and operations by land and sea with the combined forces of Thrasyllos and Alcibiades, are designated appropriately by the phrase used. That this phrase was current officially in this epoch is shown by the decree relating to Alcibiades quoted by Diodorus (XIII 69). In Athenian decrees the phrase κατὰ γῆν καὶ κατὰ θάλατταν is the regular description of wars and campaigns. Cf., e. g., *IG²* I 63 (West, *Trans. Amer. Phil. Assoc.*, 1930, p. 218), *IG²* II 649 (Dinsmoor, *Archons of Athens*, p. 7, l. 17), and Ditt., *Syll.³*, Index, s. v., γῆ.

final totals, which are summarized in *IG*² I 301B, were very considerable (see *above*, pp. 36 f.). There cannot be any doubt that the great enterprises of 409/08 B.C. strained the financial resources of Athens to the breaking point.

Two entries call for special comment. From one we learn that the Treasurers of Athena handed over to the Hellenotamiae — the statement of final totals shows that all payments were made to the Hellenotamiae — gold ingots which reached them directly or through their predecessors from Skaptesyle. The precise situation of the gold fields of Skaptesyle is disputed (Perdrizet, *Klio*, 1910, pp. 25 ff.; Casson, *Macedonia Thrace and Illyria*, pp. 68 ff.), but the location given them by Stephanos — πόλις Θρᾴκης μικρά, ἀντικρὺ Θάσου — suffices for our purpose. Skaptesyle belonged to the gold-producing *peraia* of Thasos. Thasos revolted from Athens in 411 B.C. (*Thucy.* VIII 64 2 ff. *Hell. Oxyrhy.* 2 4), drove out its democrats (who formed an ἀποικία on the adjacent mainland), and laid siege to Neopolis (near Kavala, to the west; Casson, pp. 34, 67).[1] In the spring of 410 B.C., just before the battle of Cyzicus, two Athenian fleets were operating in the North Aegean, one of which under Theramenes was summoned by Alcibiades from Macedon and the other under Thrasybulos from Thasos, both to take part in the concentration which enabled the commander-in-chief to gain his great naval victory (Xen. *Hell.* I 1 12). Xenophon says that the mission of Theramenes and Thrasybulos was to collect money (ἀμφότεροι ἠργυρολογηκότες); and of this there is epigraphic proof (*IG*² I 108). After the Athenian fleet had constituted itself at Samos as the *demos* of Athens it had taken into its own hands the collection of the contributions due (on the score of the Twentieth) or demanded (on the score of the war-necessities) from the "allies." The practice once begun was obviously not discontinued. And we cannot doubt that much of the money thus secured was spent on the spot for the payment of the crews. The Hellenotamiae can have handled during these years only a fraction of the Athenian revenues.

---

[1] See *IG*² I 108 and XII 5 109, 8 262 f.

However that may be, Theramenes had a military reason for being off Macedon (IG^2 I 105;[1] cf. Wilhelm, *Oester. Jahresh.*, 1923, pp. 123 ff.) and Thrasybulos another for being off Thasos. He was there to check the Thasians; and when he departed for the Hellespont, he doubtless left troops behind as Theramenes did simultaneously at Pydna. In 410/09 these troops were under the command of Oinobios of Decelea (IG^2 I 108, l. 38). In conjunction with the Neopolitans, who supplied them with money and materials, they waged war successfully against the Thasians. Neopolis was saved (some time before the sixth prytany of 410/09 B.C.); and during this same summer (Xen. *Hell.* I 1 32) things in Thasos took a turn against the enemies of Athens. The Spartan harmost, Eteonikos, and his partisans were expelled and the island became neutral.[2] In this way the position of Athens was reëstablished in the gold-bearing regions of Thrace. Hence the inflow into the treasury of Athena in 410/09 and 409/08 B.C. of gold ingots from Skaptesyle. In their accounts the Tamiae took pains to let it be known whence they came.[3]

The other item reserved for special comment is peculiarly significant. It is the one recording payments made ἐs Πελοπόν-νεσον. The amounts are lost, but they were obviously not inconsiderable. Bannier (*Rh. Mus.*, 1906, p. 213), to whom we

---

[1] The date of this decree is doubtless 407/06 B.C. (Meritt), not 411/0; but it cites as additional grounds for the honors then bestowed upon Archelaos the services rendered by him in 410 B.C.

[2] During the *nauarchy* of Pasippidas in 410/09 B.C. (Beloch, *Griech. Gesch.*, II, 2, pp. 273, 288). Subsequently, in the summer of 407 B.C., Thrasybulos intervened in the course of an internal struggle and regained Thasos for Athens (Xen. *Hell.* I 4 9). He also reëstablished completely Athens' position in Thrace.

[3] They did not come as *aparche* to the Goddess from Neopolis; for that was remitted as a special concession by the Athenian *demos* (IG^2 I 108, ll. 47 ff.). Other cities of the gold-producing region, less deserving of preferential treatment, may have paid their *aparche* in gold bullion. Whether the *aparche* was a relic computed on the basis of the old *phoros* (for a revival of the *phoros* in the case of Chalcedon see Xen. *Hell.* I 3 9; cf. Busolt, *Griech. Gesch.*, III, p. 1407, n. 3) or a sixtieth of the new Twentieth, it is impossible to say. It is interesting to note (Wade-Gery, *Num. Chron.*, 1930, p. 24) that the bullion from Skaptesyle (3000 drachmas) is precisely the *aparche* on the *phoros* paid by Thasos after *c.* 444 B.C. This suggests that the arrangement effected with Chalcedon was made with other places also.

owe the ill-advised transfer of IG^2 I 301 back to 422/1–419/8
B.C., connects these outlays with the dispatch in 419/8 B.C. of
1000 hoplites across the Saronic Gulf to take a hand, should
Sparta intervene, in the Argive operations against Epidauros.
But Sparta did not intervene; so the Athenians returned home
(*Thucy.* V 55 4). The occasion seems inadequate. But let
that pass. It was quite impossible for the Treasurers of 419/8
B.C. to allude with special emphasis to their contributions to
[operations] conducted by Athens "on land and sea." Apart
from the unauthorised adventure of Alcibiades "with a few
hoplites and bowmen" in the Peloponnese (*Thucy.* V 52 2),
the crossing of the Saronic Gulf without fighting is the only
military enterprise undertaken by Athens in that year. The
real campaigns in the Peloponnese and Thrace came in the
following year and are covered by the Treasurers' accounts for
418/7 B.C. (IG^2 I 302; *AJA*, 1928, pp. 346 ff., 1930, pp. 128,
150: Plates I and II). Nothing that occurred in 419/8 B.C. can
explain the heavy levies on Athena recorded in IG^2 I 301.

In 409/08 B.C. came the expedition of Anytos for the relief
of Pylos (Xen. *Hell.* I 2 18; *Diod.* XIII 64 5–7; Arist. *Ath. Pol.*
27 5). With this unsuccessful enterprise, on which Athens had
to embark while its main forces were absent in the Hellespont,[1]
we may connect with confidence the expenditures "for the
Peloponnese." They were made at precisely the right time of
the year — in or about October, 409 B.C. (see *above*, p. 25, and
Beloch, *Griech. Gesch.*, II, 2, p. 250). 409/08 B.C. was the year
during which the field army of Athens under Thrasyllos, after
joining the fleet under Alcibiades at Lampsacus, proceeded in
the spring of 408 B.C. to the major objective of this phase of the
war — the winning of the Bosporus (*CAH*, V, pp. 345 ff.). An
enterprise of great moment conducted "on land and sea"!

A new datum of decisive character for the long dispute as to
the chronology of the period from 410 to 406 B.C. is now in our

---

[1] Line 22 of IG^2 I 301 may be restored τοῦτο ἔδοθε Περι[κλεῖ Χολαργεῖ]. Since Pericles was Hellenotamias in 410/09 and *strategos* in 406/05 B.C. he may have been General
in 409/08 B.C. also. His *phyle*, Akamantis, makes no difficulty (Beloch, *Griech. Gesch.*,
II, 2, p. 268).

possession. The expedition of Anytos falls in the year 409/08
B.C. This expedition, however, synchronizes with the activity
of Alcibiades in and about Lampsacus before and during the
winter immediately following the expedition of Thrasyllos to
Ionia (Xen. *Hell.* I 1 14–18). We have therefore proved what
hitherto, for purpose of presentation, we have assumed, namely,
that it was in the spring of 409 B.C. (as maintained by Dodwell,
Annales Thucydidii et Xenophontei, Oxford, 1702, and after him
by a long list of scholars, including Clinton, Grote, Beloch,
Bury, Valeton), and not in the spring of 410 B.C. (as maintained
by Haacke, *Chron. de postremis belli Pelop. annis*, Diss. Stendal,
1822, and after him by an equally long list including Boerner,
Meyer, Busolt, Kirchhoff, Kirchner), that Thrasyllos set out
from Athens. As pointed out by me (*CAH*, V, pp. 483 ff.),
Xenophon himself distinguishes the military seasons of this
entire period with sufficient accuracy though with some vague-
ness at times. His divisions are as follows: I 1 2, winter of
411/0; I 1 37–2 1, winter of 410/09; I 3 1, winter of 409/08;
I 4 1, winter of 408/07; I 5 10, winter of 407/06; II 1 1, winter
of 406/05; II 2 16, winter of 405/04. The suspension of field
operations in the winter of 407/06 is indicated only by the
period of inactivity given to Lysander; the three months' absence of Theramenes in Sparta marks the winter of 405/04;
elsewhere Xenophon notes the seasons. The interpolator, to
whom we owe the insertion of the dates, failed to notice the
"approach of spring" of the year 408/07 (I 4 2); and, since, as
Busolt showed (*Hermes*, 1898, pp. 661 ff.), he worked backward
from the year of the Anarchy, which Xenophon himself had
designated with unmistakable clearness (II 3 2), he thus set the
campaigns of the two preceding years (in reality 409/08 and
410/09 B.C.) each a year too late. He also failed to enter dates
for the year 410/09 — the one following the winter season
noted by Xenophon in I 1 2. Had he put in an Archon here, it
would have had to be the predecessor of Euktemon (408/07:
Hell. I 2 1), that is to say, Diokles (409/08), and he would have
carried his error back to the beginning of the *Hellenica*. Perhaps the fact that Thucydides breaks off in the course of the

year 411/0 B.C. scared him off; for he had no place for Glaukippos (410/09 B.C.). He was an uncommonly poor artificer.[1]

[1] Incidentally, we may note that the decrees regarding the Selymbrians and the Clazomenians at Daphnus (*IG*² I 116, 117) belong to the summer of 407 B.C. This follows from the fact that Alcibiades, on whose motion the one was amended and the other passed, was in Athens for the four months from May to September of this year, not of 408 B.C. Busolt (*Griech. Gesch.*, III, 2, p. 1532, n.) uses *IG*² I 304B, ll. 41–65 to sustain the contention that it was not in the summer of 407 B.C. that Alcibiades was in Athens: had Athens just received the 100 talents brought back by Alcibiades (Xen. *Hell.* I 4 8 ff.) the Tamiae would not be dispensing such trifling sums as are posted in this record (*above*, p. 31), But there is not the slightest suggestion or probability that this money was given to Athena. At this time the Hellenotamiae had the handling of the χρήματα ὅσια (*above*, p. 3).

*IG*² I 122 is also dated a year too early. Hiller gives the correct dates in the *Fasti Attici* (*IG*² I, pp. 299 f.).

V

THE INVENTORY OF THE HEKATOMPEDON
FOR THE YEAR 409/08 B.C.

THE only years possible for the inventory of the Hekatompedon published by Hiller as *IG*² I 274 are 426/5, 409/08
(where Hiller, following Lehner, *op. cit.*, pp. 16 f., and Michaelis, *Parthenon*, p. 299, puts it), and 407/06 B.C., which has become available by the transfer to 408/07 of *IG*² I 255 and 275
(see *above*, p. 11). It cannot belong to 408/07. *IG*² I 275 belongs to that year and the two cannot be joined to form one
inventory. Though the two stones are badly broken, the word
[συ]νάρχουσιν: χσυνάρχο[σι] occurs in both. All other years prior
to 406/04 are similarly excluded, that is to say, by a clash
with another Hekatompedon inventory or with a board of
Treasurers whose Chairman belonged to a different *deme*. Indeed, 426/5 B.C. is also excluded. 426/5 was the initial year of
a *penteteris*, whereas *IG*² I 274 has the prescript of a non-
initial year. Moreover, in *IG*² I 274 appear objects the weights
of which identify them with objects dedicated after 426/5; for
example, the gold crown dedicated in 419/8 (*IG*² I 267, l. 99).
Accordingly, *IG*² I 274 belongs after 419/8; and, indeed, its
contents (see *below*, p. 52) show that it cannot be placed earlier
than 410/09, that is to say, since 410/09 B.C. was also the
initial year of a *penteteris*, than 409/08 B.C.

The problem is to decide whether it belongs in 409/08 or
407/06 B.C. The script used in *IG*² I 274 is strongly Ionic. In
this respect it is unique among all the inventories which we
possess. All the post-Eukleidean inventories are pure Ionic.
All the other pre-Eukleidean inventories are Attic. The inventory for the Pronaos for 409/08 B.C. (*IG*² I 254) is Attic
throughout; so is the inventory of the Parthenon which we have
assigned tentatively to that year (*below*, p. 68); and on dating *IG*² I 274 in 409/08 B.C. we shall have to assume that the

inventory of the Hekatompedon for that year differed in script from its two companions. It is to the accounts, and not to the inventories, of the Tamiae of Athena that we have to go for a parallel to IG^2 I 274; and among these there is one and one only that resembles it, viz., IG^2 I 304B, ll. 77–93, which is commonly, and, I believe, correctly,[1] assigned to 407/06 B.C. Not only do they agree in being strongly Ionic, but they agree notably in certain of their Ionicisms. Both have συν- not ξυν-, for χσυν-; neither uses *omega* at all, a striking congruity. Both have *eta* for ε̄, IG^2 I 304B, ll. 77–93 always, 274 occasionally; neither uses it for *h*. The former uses Λ for both *lambda* and *gamma* and Γ for *gamma* and Ⱶ for *lambda* besides; 274 lacks occasion to use *gamma* and uses Ⱶ for the only *lambda* in the preserved fragment. There is one notable point of dissimilarity. IG^2 I 274 uses frequently, though not always, ου for the false diphthong, whereas IG^2 I 304B follows the practice which prevailed in the Attic inscriptions till *c.* 360 B.C. in using ο (Meisterhans, *Grammatik der attischen Inschriften*[3], p. 26). It is hard to say what significance, if any, is to be attached to their agreement in the use of ο for ω and σ for χσ and in discarding η for *h*. These congruities were a common compromise in this transition epoch (*below*, Appendix I). But even though we trace them to an identical stonecutter, we do not need on this account to assign the two documents to the same year. The same stonecutter can have been at work in two years as close together as 409/08 and 407/06 B.C.; and in fact when we go outside the records of the Tamiae and bring the decrees of the People into consideration, we find one which is completely identical with IG^2 I 274 in its Ionicisms. IG^2 I 108 II (inscribed shortly after Jan., 409 B.C.), agrees with it in other particulars and uses ου for the spurious diphthong. But on general grounds it is probable that the inventory for 409/08 B.C. was not inscribed on stone till the end of the *penteteris* two years later.

Let us consider the consequences which would ensue if we were to date IG^2 I 274 in 407/06 B.C. On the same stone with this inventory, separated by a small *lacuna* from its initial line, appear some letters of the last three lines of another in-

[1] See *above*, p. 28.

ventory, which for the sake of convenience of citing we shall call 274a. They are as follows:

$$a$$
$$\sigma\tau\alpha\theta\mu\grave{o}\nu \;\; \tau o\acute{v}\tau]o : \mathsf{T} \;\; \mathsf{T} : \chi[\rho\upsilon\sigma o?$$
$$\lambda \; o \;.\; \sigma \;.\; \sigma \; \tau \; \epsilon[\phi\alpha\nu$$

Since no object weighing 2 talents appears in the inventories of the Hekatompedon prior to 411/0 B.C. (*JHS*, 1928, pp. 176 f.), we have to assume that this object was dedicated later; and in view of the position at which it is entered near the end of the inventory it may have been dedicated in the year immediately preceding that of *IG*² I 274. If *IG*² I 274 belongs to 407/06, *IG*² I 274a must be the termination of the inventory of which the badly mutilated beginning is in our possession in *IG*² I 275. This is possible. Neither 275 nor 274a was written *stoichedon*, if Kirchhoff's reproduction of the latter (*IG*¹ I 145, p. 55) can be depended upon; and both had approximately the same number of letters to the line (94–100), if the length of *IG*² I 274 and 274a was about the same, as is usually the case with two consecutive inventories on the same stone when written with letters of the same general size and spacing. It might be urged against regarding *IG*² I 275 and 274a as the beginning and ending of the same inventory that the former used punctuation after the figures (l. 190), the latter both before and after. But it is unsafe to draw conclusions from this difference. We have only one instance to judge from in each fragment; and on the same grounds we should have to divide *IG*² I 243 and 282 (cf. l. 120) into portions. Yet it must be admitted that a difference in punctuation of this sort within the body of a single inventory is rare.

There is, however, an obstacle which seems to me decisive against dating *IG*² I 274 in 407/06 B.C. When this is done, it becomes impossible to date *IG*² II 1655 in that year, as is demanded by Dinsmoor (*The Erechtheum*, pp. 648 ff.); for the Chairman of the Tamiae in the former document belonged to Paiania, in the latter to Probalinthos. Dinsmoor (*loc. cit.*) has identified the Chairman of *IG*² II 1655 with Philippos, son of Philesios, of Probalinthos, who was one of the Tamiae in 405/04

B.C. (*IG*² I 255a; see *above*, pp. 12 f.); but, on the supposition
that, if the two were identified, *IG*² II 1655 would have to fall
in 405/04 B.C., he later (letter) objects to so late a date and lets
the identification fall. The identification is, however, too good
to be discarded; and it can be maintained without carrying
*IG*² II 1655 down to 405/04 B.C. The Tamiae of *IG*² II 1655
are Tamiae of Athena, those of *IG*² I 255a Tamiae of Athena
and the Other Gods, and there was nothing in the Athenian
law against iteration of offices to prevent the Chairman of the
earlier board in 407/06 B.C. from being a member of the later
board in 405/04. Since the choice was limited to *pentakosiomedimni* (Arist. *Ath. Pol.* 8 1) there is nothing improbable in
the lot falling upon the same individual in the two years. And
there are in fact definite reasons for not dating *IG*² II 1655
in 405/04 B.C. We can get around the obstacle that the prytany
preceding the fifth in 405/04 (*IG*² II 1686, l. 33; cf. *below*, pp.
77 ff.) was not Pandionis, the *phyle* prytanizing fourth in the
year of *IG*² II 1655. All we have to do is to assume that in this
section of their accounts the Tamiae for 405/04 B.C. made no
entries of expenditures in the fourth prytany. It is much more
serious that we should have to assume that work proceeded on
the Erechtheum after the battle of Aegospotami; for it by no
means follows that such must have been the case if *IG*² II 1654,
ll. 23 ff. is dated correctly by Dinsmoor (*AJA*, 1913, pp. 264 f.)
and the authors of *The Erechtheum* (pp. 278, 416 ff., 460, n. 5)
in 405/04 B.C. The work covered by this account can have
been completed during the first prytany or two of the year, i.e.,
before Aegospotami, which came about September 1, 405 B.C.;
that involved in *IG*² II 1655 fell in the fourth prytany. The in-
superable difficulty, however, is the mention of ταμίαι τῆς [θεõ]
in *IG*² II 1655. This requires a date earlier than 406/05 (see *below*, pp. 104 ff.) or later than 386/5 B.C. (see *above*, pp. 12 ff.).
The latter epoch seems clearly excluded by the letter forms
(Dinsmoor, *The Erechtheum*, p. 649); unless we are willing to
assume that at some time after 386/5 B.C. the stonecutter made
"a conscious attempt to imitate the letters of 408/07 B.C.," and
succeeded. On the other hand, the Ionic script was not used
in the accounts of the Commissioners of the Erechtheum for

409/08 and 408/07 B.C. Hence the only year left for *IG*² II 1655 is 407/06, from which *IG*² I 274 is thereby excluded. 409/08 B.C. alone remains.

The issue thus reached is confirmed by the restorations which must then be made. We already possess the inventory of the Pronaos for 409/08, *IG*² I 254. Its prescript, with the requisite restorations, runs as given on p. 51. With the same prescript we can restore *IG*² I 274 (see p. 52).[1] To facilitate comparisons I have added the lines of the inventory of the Hekatompedon for the following year (408/07 B.C.), of which portions are preserved on the stone (*IG*² I 275).

As has been pointed out (see *above*, p. 10), a *lacuna* was left at the beginning of the inventory of the Pronaos for 408/07 (*IG*² I 255) where the names of the officials ought to have been

[1] Line 169: For Philinos of Paiania see Kirchner, *PA*, 14335 and *below*, p. 51, n. 1; line 170: I have assumed that the τοῖς was omitted before ταμίαις as in line 3 of *JHS*, 1928, p. 176 (412/1 B.C.). It might also be thought that the letters were crowded, since the inscription is *non-stoichedon* (Hiller). The Secretary of the receiving board is omitted, as in the other inventory preserved for the year 409/08 B.C. (*IG*² I 254). The omission of the phrase beginning with παραδεξάμενοι is paralleled in *IG*² I 253 (411/0 B.C.), where an error may be suspected, and in *IG*² I 273 (413/2 B.C.); line 173: the space after ἔχει will be two spaces shorter, as in line 190 of *IG*² I 275, if aspirates were used. If the identification of this Nike with the Nike of the fourth-century inventories were certain (*IG*² II 1382, 1384, 1386, *etc.*; cf. Lehner, *op. cit.*, pp. 23 f.), we might restore some phrase like τὸ ἀγάλματος χρυσὸ or ἐπὶ τῆς κεφαλῆς; line 174: the insertion of ἱερεύς is probably right, cf. *IG*² II 1534, l. 98; but ἀνδριάς is also possible, cf. *IG*² II 1424, l. 11; line 178: the gold crown which the cleruchs dedicated is identified by its position, and its weight marks it as something exceptional. It could readily have seemed appropriate to the Tamiae to record the dedicators in its case, and the same is true of the crown in line 182 which I have attributed to the cleruchs from Lesbos; cf. *IG*² II 1383. The first of these was dedicated in 418/7 B.C. (*IG*² I 268), the second in 415/4 (*IG*² I 270, cf. 272); line 180: I have been unable to fill the *lacuna* after the second τοῦτο. It reappears in the inventories for 414/3 (*IG*² I 272), 412/1 and 411 (*JHS*, 1928, pp. 176 f.). The appearance of the second τοῦτο shows that we have to do at this point with a στέφανος, and not with a στεφάνη, as surmised by Woodward; lines 180–183: the space entered for the various items agree with those given by Woodward; but I am unable to bring item 26 into the same spatial relation with item 24 as it holds in *IG*² I 272, except by assuming a dittography of στέφανος in *IG*² I 272, l. 164. A dittography of χρυσὸς has been noted by Hiller in line 162. Perhaps the stonecutter had become careless; line 185: for Dorotheos (?) of Phlya see *above*, p. 27, n. 1; line 186: for the name of the Chairman for 407/06 B.C. see *IG*² II 1655; *The Erechtheum*, p. 648; *above*, pp. 48 f.; line 187: the name of the Chairman of the board from whom the votives were received is not recorded elsewhere except as it may be restored in *IG*² I 292b (*below*, p. 68), which is also datable in 408/07 B.C.

IG² I 254 (409/08 B.C.)

[τ ά δ ε ho ι τ α μ ί α ι τ ō ν h ι ε ρ ō ν χ ρ ε μ ά τ ο ν τ] ē̂ ς Ἀ θ ε ν α ί α ς Φ ι[λ ῖ ν ος?Π α ι α ν]-¹

[ι ε ῦ ς κ α ὶ χ σ υ ν ά ρ χ ο ν τ ε ς, ho ῖ ς . . . . .]ε ς Ἐ λ ε υ σ ί ν ι ο ς ἐ[γ ρ α μ μ ά τ ε υ]-

[ε, π α ρ έ δ ο σ α ν τ ο ῖ ς τ α μ ί α ι ς, Ἀ]ρ ε[σ α ί χ μ ο ι]Ἀ γ ρ υ λ ē̂ θ ε ν κ α ὶ σ[υ ν ά ρ χ ο σ ι ν],

[π α ρ α]δ ε χ σ[ά μ ε ν ο ι π α ρ ὰ τ ō ν π ρ ο τ έ ρ ο ν τ α]μ ι ō ν h ε ν τ ō ι π ρ ό ν[ε ο ι

¹ One of the comparatively rare names Philaios, Philitos, Philotas is also possible; but none of them is found in Paiania.

IG² I 274 (409/08 B.C.)

[τάδε οἱ ταμίαι τὸν ἱερὸν χρεμάτον τἐ̑ς 'Αθεναίας, Φιλῖνος? Πα[α]αν[ι]εὺς καὶ συνάρχο[ντες, οἶ̑ς .... ἐς 'Ελευσῖνος ἐγ]-

[ραμμάτευε, παρέδοσαν ταμίαις 'Αρεταίχμοι 'Αγρυλἐ̑θεν καὶ συ]νάρχουσιν· ἐν τὀ̑ι ν[ἐὀ̑ι τὀ̑ι 'Εκατονπέδοι :¹φιάλαι χρυσαἶ̑]

170 [τρἐ̑ς, σταθμὸν τούτον ΧΧ⊢ΔΔΔΔ⊢⊦⊦⊦ :²κόρε χρυσἐ̑ ἐπὶ στέλες, ἄσ[τ]αθμος· ³ἀπορραυ[τέριον ἀργυρὸν, ἄσταθμον : τ ....]

[........ :⁴στέφανο χρυσᾶ δύο, σταθμὸν τούτον Ρ̄ΔΔΔ : ⁵[σ]τέφανο[ς χρυσὸς, ὃν ἡ Νίκη ἔχει ....,σ]-

[ταθμὸν τούτοΡ̄ΔΔ : ⁶φιάλαι ἀργυραἶ̑ ὀκτό, σταθμὸν τούτον Ρ̄ΗΗΗ :⁷κ[α]ρ[χ]ήσιον ἀρ[γυρὸν, σταθμὸν τούτο ΗΗ :⁸καρχήσιον ἀργυ]-

[ρὸν (weight as in IG² II 1382)

τοῦτο ... ⊢⊢⊦⊦ · ¹⁰ στέφανε χρυσἐ̑, σταθμὸν ταύτες Ρ̄ΔⱵ⊢ : ¹¹στέφ[ανο χρυσοῖ τέτταρ[ες, σταθμὸν τούτον ΗΔΔΔΓ⊦⊦ : ¹²στέφανος

175 χρυσὸς, σταθμὸν τούτο ΔΓ⊦⊦⊦⊦⊦⊢⊢⊦⊦⊦ : ¹³χρυσίδε δύο, σταθμὸ]ν τούτον ΗΗΡ̄ΔΔΔΔ⊢[⊢⊢⊦⊦⊦ : ¹⁴χρυσίς, σταθμὸν ταύτης ΗΔΔΔΓ⊦⊦⊦⊦⊦]·

[χρυσίς, σταθμὸν ταύτης ΗΔΓ⊦⊦⊦⊦ :¹⁶στέφανος χρυσὸς, σταθμὸν τούτο ΔΔΓ⊦⊦⊦⊦ ¹⁷ἀ[ργυρίς, σταθμὸν ταύτης ΗΓΔΔΔΔΓ⊦⊦ ·¹⁸θυμιατ]-

[έριον ἀργυρὸν, σταθμὸν τούτο Χ :¹⁹στέφανος χρυσός, ὃν? ὁ]ι κλεροῦχοι ἀνέθεσ[αν ....,σταθμὸν τούτο ΧΗΗΡ̄]·

20 [στέφανος χρυσός, σταθμὸν τούτο ... ⊦ : ²¹στέφανος χρυσός, σ]τα[θμὸν τούτο ΔΔ[ΔΓ⊦ : ²²στέφανο χρυσᾶ δύο, σταθμὸν τούτου Ρ̄⊢⊦⊦ ·

[σταθμὸν ταύτες .... ²⁴στέφανος χρυσὸς, στ]αθμὸν τούτο Δ[ΔΔ⊢⊦ · ²⁷στέφαν[ος χρυσὸς, σταθμὸν τούτο ²⁵στέφανε χρυσἐ̑,

[σταθμὸν ταύτες .... ²⁶στέφανος χρυσὸς, σταθμὸν τούτο ΔΔ⊢⊦ · ὃν οἱ κλεροῦχοι ἐγλέσ[θεσαν, σταθμὸν τούτο Ρ̄ΗΗΔΔ⊦⊦⊦·

[σταθμὸν ταύτες ... ²⁹στέφανος χρυσός, ὃν οἱ κλεροῦχοι ἀνέθ[εσαν, σταθμὸν τούτου²⁸στέφανε χρυσἐ̑],

σταθμὸν χρυσοῖ̑ τρἐ̑ς, σ[ταθμὸν τούτου

τούτ]ουν[

IG² I 275 (408/07 B.C.)

185 [τάδε hοι ταμίαι τὸν hιερὸν χρεμάτον τἐ̑ς 'Αθεναίας, 'Αρέταιχμος 'Αγρυλἐ̑θεν καὶ χσυνάρχοντες, hοἶ̑ς Δορόθεος Φλυεὺς? ἐγραμμά]-

[τευε,π]αρέδοσ[αν τοῖς ταμίαις, hοῖς .... ἐγραμμάτευεν, Φιλίππου Φιλεσίο Προβαλισίοι

καὶ χσυνάρχο[σιν, παραδεχσάμενοι παρὰ τὸν προτέρον ταμίον, Φιλίνο Παιανίεος καὶ χσυναρχόντον, hοῖς .... ἐς ....?]

οχάρος 'Ελευ[σῖνος ἐγραμμάτευε· ἐν τὀ̑ι νεὀ̑ι τὀ̑ι hεκατονπέδοι :φιάλαι χρυσαἶ̑ τρἐ̑ς, σταθμὸν τούτον ΧΧ⊢ΔΔΔΔ⊦⊦⊦ :κόρε χρυ]-

σἐ̑ ἐπὶ στέλες, [ἄσταθμος· ἀπορραντέριον ἀργυρὸν, ἄσταθμον· τ ....στέφανο χρυσοἶ̑ ΙΙ, σταθμὸν τούτουν

190 Ρ̄ΔΔΔ : στέφ[ανος χρυσός, hὸν hε Νίκε ἔχει ....,σταθμὸν τούτου Ρ̄ΔΔ· φιάλαι ἀργυραἶ̑ Γ⊦ΙΙΙ, σταθμὸν τούτον Ρ̄ΗΗΗ· καρχέσι]-

ον ἀργυρ[ὸν, σταθμὸν τούτο

entered (cf. *below*, p. 73); hence we get no help from that stone; but the Chairman of the board of Tamiae is known from the account of the Commissioners of the Erechtheum (*IG*² I 374) and the Secretary from the account of the Commissioners of Eleusis (*IG*² I 313, l. 175; cf. *above*, p. 27, n. 1). After a barren period of several years, 414/3, 413/2, 412/1, 411 B.C., during which no additions were made to the dedications in the Hekatompedon, this shrine was notably enriched in 411/10 or (and) 410/09 B.C. As already pointed out, among the additions was a single article weighing two talents (*IG*² I 274a). We shall not err, probably, in connecting this harvest with the special effort made to reëndow Athena in 410 B.C. (*above*, p. 34).

As a comparison of *IG*² I 274 with *IG*² I 275 shows, the inventory of 409/08 B.C. was not unique in the more lengthy descriptions given to a number of the articles it contained. The conclusion is obvious that the new type dates from 410/09 B.C. — the inaugural year of the seventh *penteteris*. The inscribing of the whole group was probably done in 407/06 B.C. (*below*, p. 55, n. 2); but the drafts then followed were of course prepared at the expiry of their terms by the successive boards of Tamiae. Hence we are warranted in attributing the new type to the officials of the first year of the *penteteris*. As will be shown later, the Tamiae of the seventh *penteteris* also adopted a new arrangement of the items in their inventories of the Parthenon (see *below*, pp. 59 ff.). It is intelligible that after the regimes of the Four Hundred and the Five Thousand had ended, and democratic officials were again in charge, the Tamiae of 410/09 B.C. drew up new inventories of the Hekatompedon and the Parthenon, in the one case identifying particular articles more sharply, and in the other entering the items in an order which corresponded perhaps more closely with the position of the articles in the shrine. Since no further dedications were to be accepted for display in the Pronaos, and since the articles in this part of the Temple were doubtless fastened in definite positions like those in the Hekatompedon, — the miscellaneous articles deposited in the Parthenon were much more liable to be displaced, — the old type of inventory sufficed in this case. In any event, no new one was prepared.

The inventories of the Hekatompedon may be assigned to Tablets as follows (cf. Woodward, *JHS*, 48, 1928, p. 159):

	Year of Obverse	IG²	Year of Reverse	IG²
TABLET 1	434/3–431/0	256–259	none	vacant
	430/29–427/6	260–263	none	vacant
TABLET 2	426/5–423/3	lost	none	vacant
TABLET 3	422/1–419/8	264–267	418/7–415/4	268–271
TABLET 4	414/3	272		
	413/2	273 and *JHS*, 48, p. 176		
	412/1	*JHS*, 48, p. 176	none	vacant
	411	*JHS*, 48, p. 176		
	411/0	*JHS*, 48, p. 177		
TABLET 5	410/09	274a		
	409/08	274	none	vacant
	408/07	275		
	407/06	lost		
TABLET 6	406/05 *	lost	none	vacant
	405/04	lost		

* New Style: all the remaining dedications of the Parthenon were now assembled in the Hekatompedon; but inventoried on a separate *stele*.

VI

THE LATE FIFTH CENTURY INVENTORIES OF THE PARTHENON

I. *IG²* I 284, 285, 290, 289

A MARKED feature of the inventory of the Hekatompedon for 409/08 B.C. which we have just discussed (*IG²* I 274) is the spelling out of the numerals when they express the count, not the weight, of the articles (l. 175, τέτταρες; l. 183, τρês; restorations in lines 171, 172, 173, 176). Except for δύο, which appears quite frequently, but only with the dual in certain set combinations, numbers written out appear only sporadically, and then only when very little loss in space was incurred by not using figures: μία and τρês in *IG²* I 253 (411/0 B.C.), and τρês and ὀκτό in *IG²* I 266 (420/19 B.C.), and τρês in *IG²* I 267 (419/8 B.C.) — that is the total for all the inventories,[1] if we except *IG²* I 274,[2] *IG²* I 292b, and the last two of the four inventories of the Parthenon listed at the head of this section.

These Parthenon inventories resemble one another further in that they all had lines containing only about half the number of letters of the other inventories. They were all written in pure Attic script. Hence they belong before 403/02 B.C. Hiller, following Kirchhoff, dates *IG²* I 284/5 in the fifth *penteteris* (418/7–415/4 B.C.), 289 and 290 in the seventh (410/09–407/06 B.C.).

IG² I 284 and 289 cannot belong to the same year; for the item ὁρμίσκο δύο, θαλλὸς χρυσός appears in both (*IG²* I 284, l. 146; 289, l. 1). That *IG²* I 289 belongs to a later and different year is further borne out by the fact that it is written

---

[1] The spelling out of τεττάρον in θαλλὸς χρυσὸς πετάλον τεττάρον (*IG²* I 286, l. 174; 287, l. 200; and 288, l. 227) results from the use of the descriptive genitive. Figures were substituted later — when the entry was rephrased; cf. *IG²* I 289 (*below*, p. 61) and *IG²* II 1376.

[2] This practice confirms the view that *IG²* I 274 was cut on stone in 407/06 B.C. (*above*, pp. 47, 53; *below*, pp. 101 f.).

on the reverse of the stone that gives us 284/5. It also had lines of different length — thirty-seven letters as against forty-three. The two inventories cannot belong to consecutive years; for at the bottom of 284 appears the heading of a new inventory (*IG*² I 285), which must intervene between the two. "*IG*² I 284/5, 289, and 290 are of equal thickness (.077), both finished front and back, and there is nothing in the grain or appearance of the marble to exclude their being parts of the same *stele*. Judging, however, from the letter-forms and sizes, I should doubt 290 being from the same year's account as 284/5 or 289."[1] For some reason not given Hiller infers that the tablet had three columns. The title of *IG*² I 285 is inset; and we cannot say whether the space before it in line 148 did or did not contain writing. Since a title inset in this fashion is rare (it occurs only in *IG*² I 257 and 277, both of the same year, 433/2 B.C.) and the wording τάδε παρέδ[οσαν hοι ταμίαι] is unique, the title may also have differed from the norm in other respects. Hence we are unable to calculate how much space it required. The unprecedented shortness of the lines is our warrant for thinking that there was more than one column on the *stele*. There could have been three columns of forty-three letters to the line if the letters were crowded together like those in *IG*² I 283, or if the stone had the breadth assumed for *IG*² I 292b (*below*, p. 68); but the normal length of line in these inventories is seventy-three to seventy-nine letters. We should, therefore, expect two columns only. The existence, however, of a second column impairs the evidence on the basis of which Hiller dates *IG*² I 284/5 in the fifth *penteteris*. If the inventory *IG*² I 284 ended in line 147 it must have preceded *IG*² I 286 (414/3 B.C.), since the years 413/1 B.C. are already occupied by *IG*² I 287 and 288 and the latter of these contained articles which *IG*² I 284 lacks. But since there was a second column, this may have contained the articles dedicated in 412/1 B.C. and later.

Hiller observed rightly that *IG*² I 290 contained lines of the same length as 284. Since in this case the right margin of the

---

[1] Letter from Mr. B. H. Hill, who very kindly examined the stones in the Epigraphical Museum at Athens for me.

stone is preserved, it is natural to think of placing it in Col. II
somewhere; for the length is too abnormal and the agreement
in number of letters and in the thickness of the stone too complete for it not to belong to the same *stele*. *IG*² I 290 is, however, an inventory, not of all the *ex-votos* in the Parthenon, but
of those alone which survived the cataclysm of 406 B.C. Upon
it are patterned the inventories ἐκ τô Παρθενῶνος of the fourth
century (cf. *IG*² II 1376, 1377, 1395); and since the script is
Attic, it must belong to either 406/05 or 405/04 B.C.[1] We must,
consequently, consider whether *IG*² I 284 cannot belong to
407/06.

If it belongs in 417/6–415/4 B.C. it must have had *c.* forty-
two lines, seeing that *IG*² I 283 had 1727 letter spaces and
sixty-four more have to be added for the *epeteia* of 418/7. On
the other hand, if it belongs in 407/06 B.C., the total number
of lines will have to be greater by *c.* twenty-five since the same
space was probably demanded on the average by *epeteia* in 411–
06 as in 412/1 (*IG*² I 288). Assuming that *IG*² I 290 belongs
in 406/05 and *IG*² I 289 in 405/04, the inventories may be disposed on the *stele* as follows,[2] on the hypotheses (A) that *IG*² I
284 belongs to 417/6, (B) that it belongs to 407/06 (see p. 58).
This seems to exclude the earlier date: the account for 405/04
(*IG*² I 289) would hardly have been posted thus low down on
the stone. But if we date *IG*² I 284 in 416/5 (the only alternative if it belongs to the fifth *penteteris*), 289 can have occupied the upper left-hand corner of the reverse (X in A).[3] We

---

[1] If inventories for 404/03 B.C. were publicly recorded, which is highly improbable,
they would have been written in Ionic script, doubtless, like all the other records posted
in Eukleides' archonship. Moreover, if the restoration of *IG*² II 1370 proposed *below*
(p. 150) is correct, the inventories for 404/03 B.C. were not even compiled. The *acta*
of the Thirty were annulled (*Dem.* XXIV, 56; cf. Cloché, *La restauration démocratique
à Athènes*, pp. 353 ff.). Hence we cannot connect any of these fragments with 404/03
B.C. No records of any kind of the year of the Anarchy have reached us, if we except
the bronze tablet of the Tamiae of Athena and the Other Gods mentioned in *IG*² II
1498, l. 21; and this was not a record but a dedication (see *above*, p. 6, n. 1).

[2] Since we lack the divisions of the lines in 289, we assume the division most favorable to the hypothesis in each case.

[3] Since space has to be provided for *IG*² I 290 at the bottom of Col. II the inventory for 416/5 B.C. must have appeared partly at the bottom of Col. I and partly
at the top of Col. II.

have then to assume that the Tamiae of 406/05 B.C. found room for their attenuated record in space left vacant at the close of the inventories of the fifth *penteteris* and that the Tamiae of 405/04 B.C. used the reverse so far as they needed it.

If we date *IG²* I 284 in 407/06 B.C. — the last year before the epoch of the attenuated records — we encounter several difficulties: the resultant *stele* has an unnatural shape (B); the second half of 284 was carried over to the top of Col. II instead of being inscribed on the remainder of Col. I as is to be

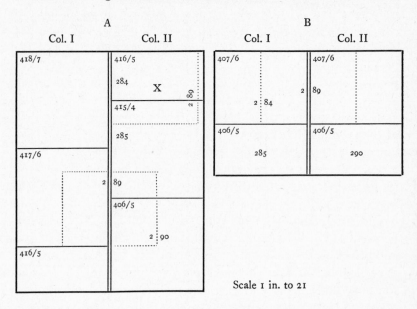

Scale 1 in. to 21

expected; and there must have been a second half. The first and third of these difficulties are not insurmountable. The shape of the *stele* can have been made to conform to the width of the others in the series. Its depth can have been lessened in view of the vote already taken at the time the *stele* was ordered to expropriate the gold and silver articles in the Parthenon. Its obverse and reverse were probably ample for the inventories of the rest of the *penteteris*. That there can have been a second half is proved by *IG²* I 292b. It is easy to imagine that this inventory is the second half of *IG²* I 284/5, line 148 of the one being continued by line 7 of the other; but this cannot be. "There is, I think, no chance that 284/5 and 292b are from the same *stele*, since 284/5, preserved front and back (289), is only .077 thick, while 292b, from which the back has been split off, is now .082 thick. There are also differences in letter forms and spacing."[1] But while this relation is excluded, we learn from *IG*² I 292b that there was a time prior to 403 B.C. when the miscellany of articles in the Parthenon catalogued by number and not by weight (nos. 8–37, 40–42) was placed at the end of the inventory — as after 403 B.C.[2] The question is, what time is this? As we have already seen, *IG*² I 292b cannot belong to the *stele* which gives us 284/5, 290, and 289. Two years are involved. Theoretically, these can be any two years between 412/1 B.C. and 406/05 B.C. (*IG*² I 288). The point is that we can reckon in 407/06 B.C. with an inventory in which, contrary to practice, the catalogue did not close with articles of silver and gold, but with the miscellaneous *kosmos* of the Goddess. It is to be observed further that these miscellaneous articles were not arranged in 292b in their earlier order. There is no possibility whatsoever to insert the usual items in the space following [Γορ]γόν[ειον], or [ἀσπίδες ἐπίχρυσοι hυπόχ]συλοι Δ[Γ], or [χσίφε] πέντε and preceding ἐπέτεια. We are bound to conclude that at some time after 412/1 B.C. the inventory of the Parthenon was rearranged, the articles of gold and silver were placed all together at the beginning, and the miscellaneous articles of the *kosmos* were listed in a new order. Since we have already seen that a new type of Hekatompedon inventory was drawn up in 410/09 B.C., it is natural to conclude that it was in this year also that the new type of Parthenon inventory was constructed. Consequently, we can place *IG*² I 292b in 410/09–409/08, 409/08–408/07, or 407/06–406/05 B.C. We shall come back to this problem later. Did 284 precede or follow the rearrangement?

[1] Mr. B. H. Hill (letter).

[2] The miscellaneous articles (nos. 8–37, 40–42) of the inventories of the Parthenon before 411 B.C. appear in the fourth-century catalogues (*IG*² II 1377, 1380, 1394, 1395) toward the end of the record; but once they were listed, if at all, near the beginning (*IG*² II 1376). The order of the items is different from that followed prior to 410/09 B.C.; and also from that followed after 375/4 B.C. ('Αρχ. Δελτίον, 1927/8, p. 128, col. III, ll. 41 ff.; *IG*² II 1425, ll. 250 ff.; 'Αρχ. Δελτίον, 1927/8, p. 126, ll. 197 ff.).

It is to be noted that in general the order of the items in 284 is the one that existed prior to 410/09 B.C. But there is one exception. No. 54, χρυσίον ἄσεμον, σταθμὸν τοῦτο ΓΗΗ, is missing. It should have appeared between 51 and 52, as it does in *IG*² I 288 (412/1 B.C.), 287 (413/2 B.C.), and 286 (414/3 B.C.). But it can be thought to have been dedicated in 415/4, if *IG*² I 284 is dated in 416/5, and to have been inserted before items 52 and 53 when taken next year out of the *epeteia*. Its weight was 7 drachmas throughout (West). It is to be noted further that a new entry of uncoined gold appears in the inventory for the last-mentioned year (*IG*² I 288, l. 228).

The real objection to dating *IG*² I 284 in 407/06 B.C. is the second in our enumeration (*above*, p. 58). It is, I think, unparalleled for a record to be carried thus forward to a second column before the first column was completed. The tribute lists (for example *IG*² I 202–204) are not analogous. There was no set order of tributaries. The entries in the two columns under the titles of each sub-section were doubtless made concurrently. The nearest approach to a parallel is found in the inventories of the Tamiae of the fourth century (*IG*² II 1421 ff., and especially ’Αρχ. Δελτίον, 1927/8, p. 128) where the gold was entered first, in Col. I, the silver afterwards, and the articles of copper, iron, ivory, etc., later. But to make this analogy apply to *IG*² I 284/5 we should have to assume that in Col. I the end of the inventory of articles of gold and silver was reached.[1] But this was not the case — if the document belongs in 407/06 B.C. — unless all the new articles of gold and silver dedicated both between 418/7 and 410/09 and between 410/09 and 408/07 were lifted further up into the body of the inventory without disturbing the sequence of items numbered 48–53.

It seems best, therefore, to conclude that *IG*² I 284 belongs to 416/5, *IG*² I 285 to 415/4, and that the Tamiae for 406/05 and 405/04 used blank space, front and back, of an earlier *stele* for their attenuated inventories. The texts are as follows:

---

[1] None the less the analogy is fairly close, especially in the case of ’Αρχ. Δελτίον, 1927/8, p. 128 (369/8 B.C.) where the columns proceeded only part way down the *stele*; but in this case the entire lower portion of the stone was reserved for the inventory of the Chalkotheke.

TABLET 5, COL. II (OBVERSE)

σ]-

IG² I 284

[τέφανος χρυσõς, σταθμὸν τοῦτο Δ]ΔΔΗΗ·στέ[φανος χρυ
σõς Ἀθεναίας Νίκες, σταθμὸν τούτ]ο ΔΔΔΗΗ·τετ[ραδρά]-
χμον χρυσõν, σταθμὸν τοῦτο ΓΗΗΙΙϹ·ὀ ν υ χ χ ρ υ σ õ σ τ ὸ[ν δ α]-
κτύλιον ℎέχον, ἄ σ τ α θ μ ο σ·ℎ ο ρ μ ι[σ κ ο δ ύ ο, θ α λ λ ὸ σ χ ρ υ[σ õ σ],
σταθμὸν τοῦτον ΔΔΔΓΙΙΙ·χρυσ ι[ο δ ύ ο, σ τ α θ μ ὸ ν τ ο ύ[τ ο ι ν]
ι τ ά δ ε π α ρ έ δ[ο σ α ν ℎ]-

[ο ι τ α μ ί α ι τ ἐ ν ℎ ι ε ρ õ ν χ ρ ε μ ά τ ο ν τ ê σ Ἀ θ ε ν α ί α ς, Λ]ε[ο χ ά ρ ε ς
[. . . . . . κ α ὶ χ σ υ ν ά ρ χ ο ν τ ε ς, ℎ ο î σ Τ ε λ έ α σ Τ ε λ ε ν ί κ ο Π]-
ε ρ γ α σ έ θ ε ν ἐ γ ρ α μ μ ά τ ε υ ε

IG² I 285

σ τ α θ μ]ὸ ν τ ο ῦ τ ο ν ΓΔ
[. . . . . ℎ ὸ ρ μ ο ι π λ α τ ê σ δ ι ἀ λ ι θ ο ι κ α ὶ σ ℎ κ ύ τ ο]σ τ ρ ο σ ὸ ν, ἀ ρ ι-
[θ μ ὸ σ π έ ν τ ε, σ τ α θ μ ὸ ν τ ο ύ τ ο ν ΓΓ·ἐ ν ο ι δ ι ο δ]ι α λ ί θ ο χ ρ υ[σ]-
[δ, ἀ ρ ι θ μ ὸ σ δ ύ ο, σ τ α θ μ ο ν τ ο ύ τ ο ι ν ΔΔΓ·σ φ ρ α γ]î δ ε σ δ κ τ ὸ τ[ε]-
[ρ ι χ ρ υ σ ο ι κ α ὶ γ ρ ῦ π ε δ ι α λ ι θ ο χ ρ υ σ ό, ἀ ρ ι θ μ ὸ σ δ ύ ο, σ τ α θ μ]-
[ὸ ν τ ο ύ τ ο ν ΔΔΔ . . .

TABLET 5, COL. II (REVERSE)

ℎ ό]-

IG² I 289

[ℎ ο ρ μ ι σ κ]ο δ ύ ο χ ρ υ σ ό, θ α[λ λ ὸ σ χ ρ υ σ õ σ, ἀ ρ ι θ μ ὸ σ π έ]-
[τ ά λ ο ν]ΙΙΙ·ζ ὀ ν ε χ ρ υ σ έ ι [
[ρ μ ο σ]ρ ὸ δ ο ν δ ι ἀ λ ι θ ο σ χ[ρ υ σ õ σ ℎ ο μ έ ζ ο ν, ἀ ρ ι θ μ ὸ σ ρ]-
[ὸ δ ο ν]ε ἴ κ ο σ ι, κ α ὶ κ ρ ι õ κ ε φ α λ έ, σ τ α θ μ ὸ ν τ ο ύ τ ο ι ν]
[ΔΔΔ·χ ρ]υ σ [ι δ ι α δ ι ά λ ι θ α σ ύ μ μ ι κ τ α π λ ι ν θ ί ο ν κ α ì]
[τ ε τ τ ί γ ο ν, σ τ α θ μ ὸ ν τ ο ύ τ ο ν ΓΓΗΗ·

---

[1] The letters of τάδε παρέδ[οσαν] are not aligned with those of *IG² I 284*: they are placed midway between those of the preceding line. Hence there is room for eta (*spiritus asper*) after παρέδ[οσαν]. The upper horizontal bar of the first *epsilon* of [Λ]ε[οχάρες] is distinctly legible on the squeeze, directly under the *epsilon* of παρέδ[οσαν].

[61]

II. IG^2 I 292b

The problem of dating IG^2 I 292b cannot be separated from the problem of finding a place for the documents which Hiller has published as IG^2 I 291, 292, and 292a. According to the report of Wilhelm, with which Hiller agrees (IG^2 I 292a, note), these fragments belong to the same *stele*. The question must be raised whether they belong to an inventory of the Parthenon at all. IG^2 I 291 contains a reference to an article or articles "from the Parthenon." Why state that certain articles were from the Parthenon if all belonged to that chamber? "From the Parthenon" clearly means "formerly in the Parthenon" (Meisterhans, *op. cit.*, p. 214, n. 1719a). If the Tamiae took certain articles away from the Parthenon, how could they have handed them over to their successors in a Parthenon inventory? The inference has been drawn (Kirchhoff, IG^1 I 169, p. 77; Kirchner, IG^2 II 1407, note) that the reference is to the removal of votives from that chamber into the Hekatompedon presupposed by the inventories of the post-Eukleidean epoch (see *below*, p. 110). The date of this transaction has been fixed erroneously as the archonship of Antigenes (407/06 B.C.). We now see that it was really the archonship of Kallias (406/05 B.C.); but, if the inventory represented by these fragments belongs to the Parthenon, we cannot ascribe it to the Tamiae of 406/05, since IG^2 I 290 belongs to them and IG^2 I 289 to their successors.[1] It is, however, unnecessary to ascribe it to them. As we shall see presently, it was in the period of Kallias' archonship which overlaps with the term of office of the Tamiae of 407/06 B.C. that the vote of the people authorizing the ἀφαίρεσις of the property of the Goddess was passed. Hence these fragments can belong to the inventory of the Tamiae of 407/06 B.C.

But it cannot well be an inventory of the Parthenon: it must be, rather, an inventory of the place to which the articles "from the Parthenon" were removed, i.e., the Hekatompedon; and, arguing thus, we are bound to conclude that the fragments are all that remain of the tablet on which was recorded

[1] See *above*, pp. 57, 60.

a combined inventory of the Hekatompedon and Parthenon made at the time of assembling in one place the *ex-votos* with a view to segregating for minting such as were mintable. For the making of this tablet the Tamiae of 407/06 B.C. can have been responsible. This result — that we have to do with a combined inventory of the Parthenon and Hekatompedon — seems, at first sight, to be confirmed by the appearance in our fragments of articles which were not found theretofore in the Parthenon inventories. It is not possible to find in the pre-Eukleidean inventories of this chamber the items recorded in lines 5, 6, 7, 10, and 11 of *IG*² I 291. Line 8 of *IG*² I 292 should probably be restored [σφρα]γίς, another novelty. Lines 2 and 5 of *IG*² I 292a are likewise alien to this set of inventories. And this list of extraneous articles must be increased. The stone which contains on its reverse *IG*² I 292a has a fragmentary inscription on its obverse (EM 57) which will be published shortly by Mr. A. M. Woodward.¹ It contains two other alien items, στλι[γγίς] and [διό]πα χρυ[σά]. Of these foreign elements all but three (λευκα, -α ἔχοσα:Δ, and -οις:) are found in the post-Eukleidean inventories of the Hekatompedon: for διόπα χρυσά cf. *IG*² II 1388, l. 76; for -ιδε πε[ριχρύσο] cf. *id.* ll. 89 f.; for σφραγίς cf. *id. passim*; for στλιγγίς cf. *IG*² II 1400, l. 50.² Other articles in the fragments can be identified similarly; e.g., -τρο- in *IG*² I 292a, l. 3, may be πλῆκτρον (*IG*² II 1388, l. 80) or ἐλύτρῳ (*IG*² II 1425, l. 267);³ -βε- (*IG*² I 292a, l. 10) may be restored as [σε]βέ[νε] and found in *IG*² II 1388, l. 75 or *IG*² I 288, l. 220. It may also be restored as [χερνι]βê[ιον] or [ἔ]βε[νος] (*IG*² II 1517, l. 73). On the other hand, θρό[νοι]⁴ (*IG*² I 292a, l. 6) appears in the fifth-century inventories of the Parthenon (*IG*²

---

¹ I owe information concerning this fragment to the kindness of Mr. B. H. Hill, who furnished me with a squeeze.

² A στλ[εγ]γίς appears in *IG*² II 1409 listed in line 14 among the *epeteia*. A golden strigil is also found in the inventories of the *epistatae* of Artemis Brauronia (*IG*² II 1517, l. 47; 1526, l. 24); but it was possibly a recent dedication at the time these records were made.

³ It can also be [κά]τρο[πτον]; cf., e.g., *IG*² II 1517, ll. 192 ff.

⁴ Or should we stress the reported absence of punctuation before θρο and resist the temptation to restore θρό[νοι]? The tip alone of a possible *iota* is visible on the squeeze before the *theta*. It might be ἐπ]ὶ θρό[νο.

I 288, l. 215; cf. IG^2 II 1394) and in the inventories of the Hekatompedon after 385/4 B.C. (IG^2 II 1415 ff.).

We are struck by the number of articles in these fragments which can be identified with things in the inventories of the Hekatompedon after 403/02 B.C. either as being then ἐν τῷ 'Οπισθοδόμῳ and belonging to Artemis Brauronia or as "from the Parthenon," i.e., transferred thence to the Hekatompedon in 406 B.C. And to this last category belongs ἐγχ[ειρίδιον] in IG^2 I 291a, l. 16;[1] cf. 'Αρχ. Δελτίον, 1927/8, p. 128, col. III, l. 45; IG^2 II 1425, l. 256. It is possible that all these articles belonged to Artemis Brauronia, but no confirmation of this can be found in the case of θρό[νοι]; and the στλεγγίς is designated expressly as a παρακαταθήκη 'Αθεναίας (IG^2 II 1400, l. 50).

This becomes important in view of the fact that these fragments are almost certainly to be joined to form one *stele* with certain fragments first published by Hondius (*Nov. Inscr. Attic.*, pp. 62 ff.; *SEG*, III, 44) and republished with fewer restorations by Hiller in IG^2 I 386/7. Mr. B. H. Hill, who has examined both sets of fragments for me in the Epigraphical Museum in Athens, reports: "The marble is practically the same, the direction of the grain identical, and the lettering very similar; 292a (EM 57) and 386/7 are of the same thickness (110 mm.) and their preserved edges are alike in tooling. . . . In fact, I should say that 291a, 292, and 292a are nearer 386/7 I than 386/7 I is to 386/7 II."[2] No actual contacts of the fragments are discernible, and I have been unable to establish textual connections; but the spacing of the letters is identical and so is the spacing of the lines. Moreover, the two groups are alike, and unique among the inventories, in style.

---

[1] If this is not the name of an article, it may be restored ἐγ χύτραι (cf. [ἐν τῶι ἀ]ρχαίω νεὼι τὸ χρυσὸ ἐγ χύτρ[αι], IG^2 II 1445, l. 43) or ἐγ χαλκῆι (cf. IG^2 II 1394, l. 12).

[2] On this point Mr. Hill writes: "The left edge of EM 5204 (386 II) is finished very roughly, that of EM 400 (386 I) is dressed very evenly with a toothchisel; the back of EM 5204 has a toothchiseled or hammered surface with a narrow smooth border, while the back of EM 400 is smooth throughout, including the 0.14 of uninscribed surface below the bottom line (387 I). If the two fragments are from the same *stele*, the differences of finish would have to be accounted for by the fact that EM 5204 is from the very bottom of the *stele*, I suppose." The thickness of EM 5204 is 111 mm. [I have subsequently learned from Mr. Hill that Mr. Woodward has also observed that IG^2 I 292a is to be associated with IG^2 I 386/7.]

The phrases ἐκ τô ἀρχαίο νεό, ἐκ τô Παρθενôνος of *IG*² I 386/7 are
matched by ἐκ τô Παρθενôνος of *IG*² I 291 and 292a (obverse);
and the phrases ἀπὸ τô λιθίνο ἕδος, ἀπὸ τês φλιᾶς, ἀπὸ τô χιτονίο'
of the former group, by χρυσίο ἀπό, ἀπὸ τês of the latter.

Now Hondius (*loc. cit.*) has, I think, proved that *IG*² I 386/7
contains articles belonging to Artemis Brauronia. The reference in ἀπὸ τô λιθίν[ο ἕδος] and [ἀπὸ τô] ἀρχαίο ἕδος can hardly
be to anything but the ἀρχαῖον ἕδος and λίθινον ἕδος which were
in the shrine of that goddess (*IG*² II 1516, ll. 7, 14; cf. Hondius,
p. 69). Moreover, the objects listed are of the same character
as those recorded in the fourth-century inventories of Artemis
Brauronia (cf. Hondius, *op. cit.*, and Hiller, *IG*² I 386/7, note),
and to the correspondences already noted may be added another, that between the μέν of line 32 of 386/7 and the μη[ν]ί[σ]κον
of *IG*² II 1524, l. 73, the chief significance of which lies in the
close association of the crescent with Artemis (*Pauly-Wissowa*,
II, 1, p. 1438). The articles listed in *IG*² I 386/7 are difficult
to identify elsewhere, so many of them belong to the *kosmos*
of any goddess. Compare, for example, the inventory of the
κόσμος τῆς θεοῦ (Hera) contained in the Samian inscription
published by C. Curtius (*Inschriften und Studien zur Geschichte
von Samos*, pp. 10 ff.) But the ὄχθοιβοι χρυσία ἔχο[ντες] of line 35
can hardly be other than the ὄχθοιβοι χρυσία ἔχοντες listed in
*IG*² II 1388, ll. 83 ff.; and the collocation of ἐλεφαντίνη, σφεν-
δόνη, ὑπάργυρος ἐπίχρυσος, μίτρα, λιθίνη, δίοπαι·χρυσαῖ, χερνιβεῖον,
and σφραγίς in *IG*² II 1448/9 recalls strikingly articles which
appear or may appear in one or other of our two sets of
fragments.

Accordingly, these fragments contained (1) items which were
in the Opisthodomos in the fourth century, listed in the inventory of the Hekatompedon until 385/4 B.C., when the
Tamiae of the Other Gods took charge of them; (2) items of
clothing, etc., belonging to the personal *kosmos* of Artemis
which are not found subsequently in the inventories of the
Opisthodomos (the λευκά in line 5 of *IG*² I 292a may qualify
ἱμάτια or something of the sort; cf. *IG*² II 1514 ff., *passim*).
Some of them are noted as detached from the statues which they
adorned; but this does not mean necessarily that they were

removed from the shrine in which the statues were situated
(cf. Hondius, *op. cit.*, p. 67); and (3) items noted above,
θρό[νοι], and στλι[γγίς], which we should connect *prima facie*
with the Parthenon and Athena.

Now that we have seen that this inventory cannot belong
in its totality to the Parthenon or to the Hekatompedon or
to Athena, there is no sound reason for dating it in 406 B.C.
But while this is true, there is also no reason for not dating it
in or about that year.[1] The letter forms accord perfectly with
this date. Without being identical, they are very like those of
*IG*² I 118 (408/07 B.C.); cf. Kern, *Inscr. Attic.*, 18; and again
without being identical, they are like those of *IG*² I 57 (424/3
B.C.); cf. Kern, *id.*, 15, and Kolbe, *Ber. Phil. Woch.*, 1926, p.
1161. Clearly they do not lead us to a definite date. Articles can
have been removed from the Erechtheum (Ancient Temple)
in 406 B.C.[2]; but they can have been removed from the Ancient
Temple equally well when the Erechtheum was begun. To
hold (Kolbe, *Ber. Phil. Woch.*, 1926, p. 1161) that the Erechtheum was not called the Ancient Temple in 409–404 B.C., but
the "Temple on the Acropolis in which is the Ancient Image,"
is to infer too much from a single instance (*IG*² I 372). If the
Erechtheum is in fact the Ancient Temple, it can hardly have
been known generally by a different name during the first

---

[1] 406 B.C. was notoriously a time when things were moved out of the Parthenon
and into the Hekatompedon to replace votives consigned to the melting pot. It may
also be mentioned for what it is worth that the insertion of the word ἀριθμός after the
name of the object (*IG*² I 291, l. 7; 292, l. 6; 386/7, ll. 4, 9) and before the figure is
a feature of the inventories of the epoch 406/05 B.C. and following (*IG*² I 290, 289;
II² 1373; cf. *above*, p. 61). It is also found in the accounts of the *epistatae* of the Erechtheum (*IG*² I 372, l. 97; 373, l. 112, 409/08 B.C.). [Cf. also [ἐκ τ̂ο νεὼ τ̂ο] ἀρχαίο ἀπενεγ[κ-
in *IG*² II 1383, which West (*below*, p. 95, n. 2) now dates tentatively in 407/5 B.C.:
a transfer from the Erechtheum to the Hekatompedon at this very time!]

[2] If the ἀρχαῖον ἄγαλμα was there in 408 B.C. (*IG*² I 372, ll. 1, 75; 373, ll. 263 ff.;
cf. Paton, *The Erechtheum*, pp. 457, 463, n. 2), other things can have been there in 406
B.C. So far as we know, the Ancient Temple may have contained only the cult image
and its *kosmos* between 406 and 394/3 B.C. (see *below*, p. 112, n. 3); but we have to reckon
with the possibility that crowns, etc., in this temple were melted down in 378/7 B.C.
(see *below*, p. 118). There is no reason for supposing that the fire reported to have occurred in the no-longer-used (παλαιός) temple of Athena in 406/05 B.C. should have
caused the removal of votives "from the Parthenon" (Paton, *The Erechtheum*, p. 473).

period of its existence;[1] if it is not, as Judeich (*Hermes*, 1929, pp. 391 ff.) still maintains — incorrectly, as I think — *ex-votos* can have been taken from the Ancient Temple at any time. The question really turns on the correctness of the identifications suggested for the items in (3) above. The thrones of Athena were not removed from the Parthenon before 411/0 B.C. (*IG*² I 288). If they really appear in our fragments, we must conclude, I think, that in *IG*² I 386/7, 291, 292, 292a (obverse and reverse) we have fragments of an opisthographous *stele* on which the Tamiae of Athena and the Other Gods recorded votives of Artemis Brauronia and Athena assembled in the Opisthodomos and Hekatompedon. Another *stele* devoted to articles that were melted down at this time may be identified in *IG*² II 1502 (*below*, pp. 91 f.). A comprehensive view and record of the votives in the temples can have seemed desirable to the new board of Treasurers. At the end of the year the Tamiae handed over to their successors the votives which survived (*IG*² I 290), cataloging them in three inventories and inscribing them on three *stelae* under the captions ἐν τῷ νεῷ τῷ Ἑκατομπέδῳ, ἐκ τὸ Παρθενῶνος, ἐκ τὸ Ὀπισθοδόμο. In the first of the three were entered articles of Artemis Brauronia kept, then or formerly, in chests in the Opisthodomos. Articles of clothing, etc., were omitted. They may have been left all the while in the *hieron* of Artemis, in the stoas there (Hondius, *op. cit.*, p. 67). Such articles were inventoried again by the *epistatae* of this shrine after *c.* 342/1 B.C.; but then we have to do mostly with replacements. The earlier *kosmos* had doubtless become "rotten and unusable" long since.

It is also possible, I think, that we have to do with two identical *stelae*, emanating one from the Tamiae of Athena and the other from the Tamiae of the Other Gods for 407/06 B.C., prepared on behalf of themselves, or "the four archae" of the *penteteris*, in collaboration with their successors — the Tamiae of Athena and the Other Gods for 406/05 B.C.[2] If the identifications of the items in (3) with Parthenon articles are rejected,

---

[1] Kolbe now argues with considerable force that the Erechtheum was known throughout antiquity as the Ancient Temple of Athena Polias (*Ber. Phil. Woch.*, 1931, pp. 101 ff.).

[2] See *above*, p. 64, n. 2.

we shall have to regard all our fragments as portions of an inventory of Artemis Brauronia. Since neither of them is cogent (p. 63, n. 2, 4), this is the solution which I prefer. Accordingly, IG^2 I 291/2/2a (obverse and reverse) should be stricken from the list of inventories of the Parthenon.[1]

The three pairs of years, 410/09–409/08, 409/08–408/07, and 408/07–407/06 B.C., then remain open for IG^2 I 292b. With the usual formulae (beginning with [τάδε h]οι τ[αμίαι] and inserting the name of the Chairman of the board from which the votives were received) and a line of 125 letters, it is possible to restore lines 7–9 so as to suit the conditions required in 408/07: in line 9 we should have the *demotikon* of the Chairman of the board of Tamiae for 409/08, thus [Πα]ια[νιέος]; but there may be other better solutions.

The inventories of the Parthenon may now be assigned to Tablets as follows:

	Year of Obverse	IG^2	Year of Reverse	IG^2
TABLET I	434/3–431/0	276–279	414/3–412/1	286–288
TABLET Ib		vacant	411, 411/0	lost
TABLET 2	430/29–427/6	lost	none	vacant
TABLET 3	426/5–423/2	lost	none	vacant
TABLET 4	422/1–419/8	280–283	none	vacant
TABLET 5	418/7	lost	none	vacant
	417/6	lost	none	vacant
	416/5	284	405/4	289 *
	415/4	285	none	vacant
	406/05	290 *	none	vacant
TABLET 6	410/09 ⎫			
	409/08 ⎬	292b I	none	vacant
	408/07 ⎭	292b II	none	vacant
	407/06			

* We can imagine that there was no blank space on the obverse of Tablet 6; that the Tamiae of 406/05 B.C. had, therefore, to go back to Tablet 5; and that the Tamiae of 405/04 B.C. continued where their predecessors ended — with the reverse of Tablet 5. It is noticeable that the first of the New Style inventories of the Parthenon is out of chronological order. Now that identical writing has been found on both sides of IG^2 I 292a, it is clear that the inventory to which this fragment belongs was not inscribed, as Kirchhoff conjectured (IG^2 I 169, p. 61; cf. Hiller, IG^2 I 291), on the reverse of Tablet I.

[1] This conclusion leaves us with the result that 407/06 B.C. is the only year between 434/3 and 404/03 for which we have no inventories whatsoever in our possession; but the record for 410/09 B.C. is almost as defective.

VII

THE PUBLICATION OF THE INVENTORIES

FOR the sake of completeness (*above*, pp. 54, 68) and convenience of reference we shall insert at this point a general
view of the way in which the Treasurers consigned the inventories of the Pronaos to stone tablets:

	Year of Obverse	*IG²*	*Year of Reverse*	*IG²*
TABLET 1	434/3–431/0	232*–235	none	vacant
TABLET 2	430/29–427/6	236–239	418/7–415/4	244†–247
TABLET 3	426/5–423/2	240–243	414/3	248
			413/2	249
			412/1	250
TABLET 3b		vacant	411	251/252*
			411/0	253
TABLET 4	422/1–419/8	lost	none	vacant
TABLET 5	410/09	lost	none	vacant
	409/08	254 ⎞		
	408/07	255 ⎟		
	407/06	none ⎬	none	vacant
	406/05	none ⎟		
	405/04	255a ⎠		

* A new fragment of *IG²* I 233 is published by Woodward in *JHS*, 1928, pp. 160 ff.;
also a new fragment of *IG²* I 252, *ibid.*, pp. 165 ff.

† I do not know why Woodward (*JHS*, 1928, p. 159) assigns these inventories to
a new Tablet instead of to the reverse of Tablet 2. Kirchhoff (*IG¹* I p. 49) states definitely that Tablet 2 is opisthographous.

Since no trace of writing has been found on the reverse of
Tablet 1, the inventories of the fourth *penteteris* were obviously
inscribed on a new tablet, viz., Tablet 4. It was, accordingly,
in 414 B.C., at the end of the fifth *penteteris*, that the decision
was taken to begin using the backs of the earlier stones for the
inventories of both the Hekatompedon and the Pronaos. In
the latter case the Tamiae left the reverse of the first tablet
blank and began the new series with Tablet 2; in the former
they used the reverse of Tablet 3. It is clear that the inventory
of the Pronaos had grown so much that the reverse of the first

tablet was now too small. The first Hekatompedon tablet had
been big enough to receive the inventories of two *penteterides*
(Woodward, *JHS*, 1911, pp. 37 f.; 1928, p. 168); but the inventory for the fifth *penteteris* occupied more space than those
of the first two taken together, and it is possible that the reverse of Tablet 2, which is lost, was also inadequate for the
record of 418/7–415/4 B.C. In the case of the Parthenon the decision to use the backs of the slabs was deferred another *penteteris*. But with this inventory, too, the Tamiae of 418/14 B.C.
made an innovation: they posted the items for their *penteteris*
in two columns, not, as theretofore and subsequently, in one.
Their successors, having determined to use here also the reverses of *stelae*, had to find room for five inventories instead of
four, since a special inventory was required of the Treasurers
who served during the two months' archonship of Mnasilochos
in 411 B.C.[1] None of the earlier tablets being large enough to
accomodate so unusual a record, and an extra slab of stone being, accordingly, necessary in any case, the first tablet was as
good as any other, and it was back to its reverse that the Treasurers of 410 B.C. went. We have designated this additional
stele Tablet 1b. On its reverse were inscribed the inventories
for 411 and 411/0 B.C., as is shown by the fact that the bottom
of Tablet 1, reverse, was reached with the end of the inventory
of 412/1 B.C. The same treasurers faced a similar problem in
publishing the inventories of the Pronaos and the Hekatompedon. They solved it differently in each case. For the Hekatompedon they were precluded from employing an unused
reverse by the action of their predecessors. For had they gone
back of Tablet 3, the inventories would not have followed one
another in chronological order. Hence they used a new tablet,
and, this being the case, they provided one large enough for all
five inventories. For the Pronaos they decided, naturally
enough, to use the reverse next in order to the one already used

---

[1] The accounts for 414/3 B.C. (*IG*² I 297) were inscribed on the reverse of the
stone containing on its obverse the accounts of 432/1 B.C. (*IG*² I 296). Where the
accounts for 413/2 (*IG*² I 307), 412/1, and 411/0 B.C. were posted we do not know:
those for the extra *arche* of the *penteteris* (411 B.C.) were inscribed on the right margin
of this same stone (*IG*² I 298). It is probable that what remained of its reverse when
*IG*² I 297 was cut was used for the intervening years (Meritt).

for the fifth *penteteris*, thus making it necessary to add a new piece, which we have designated Tablet 3b. This time an effort was made to inscribe four inventories on the original tablet, if we may infer thus much from the fact that the length of the line was raised from *c.* seventy-six letters to *c.* ninety at the beginning of the inventory for 411 B.C. But either the attempt was begun too late, or some other reason exists for the lengthening of the line at this point, since it was abandoned almost immediately [1] and it was on the new slab that the fourth inventory was finished. The fifth inventory, that for the archonship of Theopompos, followed. It occupied only part of the stone, the rest being left partly unused and partly unsmoothed.

Since there was no inscription on the other side (obverse) of Tablet 3b of the Pronaos, it appears that the new tablets remained blank on the front. We may assume that they were integrated with the old so as to form really a single surface. The practice was a familiar one in Athens. "As in all previous building accounts, e.g., those of the Parthenon, the Propylaea, and probably also the original work on the Erechtheum," writes Dinsmoor (*AJA*, 1913, p. 251; quoted by Caskey in Paton, *The Erechtheum*, p. 323), "it was intended that the accounts should be inscribed on the obverse and reverse of a single slab; with the gradual lengthening of the prytany accounts, however, both obverse and reverse had been occupied while yet two prytanies, perhaps, remained to be inscribed. There was no alternative but to set up a second *stele*, to the left of the first with an *anathyrosis* joint between, and to continue on its reverse the accounts of the final prytanies, while the obverse remained blank." The *stelae* were probably let into sockets in their pedestals and fastened with lead (*The Erechtheum*, p. 281), and the joint between two *stelae*, placed one above the other, could be made so inconspicuous that a line of letters, subsequently incised, might be set right on top of it (*ibid.*, p. 648, fig. 236).

The case of 410/09 B.C. presents some peculiarities. It is clear from *IG*² I 254 that the inventory of the Pronaos for

---

[1] Woodward (*JHS*, 1928, pp. 166 f.) has shown that the lengthening was confined to the prescript.

410/09 B.C. was not inscribed on the same stone with the inventories of the two following years of the seventh *penteteris*. We might imagine that it would occupy the obverse of the new slab added to Tablet 3; but this would bring it into a position to the left, that is to say, ahead of the inventory for the year 414/3 B.C., and, as already remarked, the stone which gives us IG^2 I 252/3 is not opisthographous, or, perhaps we should rather say, not prographous. The inventory for 410/09 B.C. must have been incised on a separate slab. It can be imagined that this was set on top of the stone containing the inventory of 409/08 B.C.; but this had a vacant space of 0.06 at the beginning; and, though vacant spaces occur not infrequently in these inventories during the fifth century, they were either left in the expectation, which was not realized, that they would be filled in later, or (as in IG^2 I 255 after line 323) to indicate a break in the continuity of the inventories. Neither condition exists here, so far as we can see. But a *lacuna* following (and preceding) the joining of two slabs is intelligible. It is simpler, perhaps, to imagine the inventory for 410/09 B.C. on a separate slab. Judging from the case of Pronaos Tablet 3b, we may conclude that the obverse of Parthenon Tablet 1b was not used for the inventory of the Parthenon for 410/09 B.C. Had this been done, the record for 410/09 would have preceded the record for 430/26 B.C.

We need not assume that the inventory of the Pronaos for 410/09 B.C. was set up at the end of that year and the second slab with the later inventories of the *penteteris* some years afterwards. It suffices to assume that the "four archae" of 410/09–407/06 B.C. (after the experience of their predecessors) determined not to seek out one large slab, but to piece one together to the dimensions needed out of two or more slabs by the use of *anathyrosis*, dowels, etc. They can have done this in 407/06 B.C. But the other alternative exists, explains more satisfactorily the use of more than one *stele*, and is to be preferred for other reasons. As already remarked, the inventories of the Pronaos became set in 413/2 B.C. No further dedications were accepted for display in that portion of the Temple. These inventories could, therefore, be prepared in advance and inscribed in advance, room being left at the top of each, as in *IG²* II 1377, 1378, and 1421, for the insertion of the names of the new Treasurers when they had been elected and had completed their term. It is conceivable that in these circumstances *IG²* I 254 and 255 were cut simultaneously with the lost inventory for 410/09 B.C. during the month of July, 409 B.C., when the Treasurers for 409/08 were known and those for 408/07 unknown. Hence the *lacuna* of 0.07 left between 254 and 255 for the prescript of 408/07. It was assumed that the Treasurers of the fourth "arche," acting for "the four," would have the names of their predecessors inserted and their own inventory added in its proper place on the balance of the stone. And this is indeed, in all probability, the way in which this Tablet came into being.[1] But the Treasurers of 407/06 B.C. did not carry out their part of the transaction. They neither filled in the names of their predecessors nor inscribed their own inventory. The fact seems to be that neither they nor their successors (now Treasurers of Athena and the Other Gods) had an inventory of the Pronaos inscribed at all. This we infer from the postscript added by the Treasurers of 405/04 B.C. What the ten Tamiae there listed handed over to the Hellenotamiae was τὰ χρέματα τῆς θεῶ as they were set forth in the inventory of 408/07 B.C. — as they had been set forth, for that matter, in all the inventories of the Pronaos since 413/2 B.C. Had there been an inventory published for 407/06 and another for 406/05 B.C. it is surely at the end of the latter that the postscript should have been placed. As is well known, the new regime of Treasurers of Athena and the Other Gods ceased altogether to issue inventories of the Pronaos. Since it was not till after Hekatombaion 28th, 405 B.C., that the Pronaos was denuded of its *anathemata*, the Tamiae might have posted inventories for 407/06 and 406/05 B.C. as usual, had it seemed worth while; but the reason for thinking that they did not do so is valid. They probably

---

[1] Woodward (*JHS*, 1928, pp. 175 ff.) postulates a vacancy of two lines at the beginning of the inventory for 411/0 B.C. in Tablet 4 of the Hekatompedon. Here too there had been a sequence of at least four years without *epeteia*, so that the inventory for the last year of the *penteteris* could have been inscribed safely in advance of the election of the last Tamiae and Secretary, those for the archonship of Theopompos.

had no obligation in the matter. After July, 406 B.C., the contents of the Pronaos were kept in their place, not because they belonged thereafter to the competence of the Tamiae, but simply because the Hellenotamiae were unready to remove them. After the vote of the *demos* they were at the disposal of the Hellenotamiae at any moment. Their tardy removal to the mint may be due to the fact that they were practically all of silver. The one article of gold in this place of deposit was not touched. Gold money could be turned out twelve times as quickly as silver, once the dies were made. It is to be noticed that in 405/04 B.C. the Attic money disbursed by the Tamiae was wholly in gold (*IG*² II 1686).

If the *stele* containing the inventory of the Pronaos for 410/09 B.C. was placed on the left side of that for 409/08–408/07, it must have been unusually narrow. It would be interesting to know whether the left margin of *IG*² I 254/5 shows dowel holes and *anathyrosis*; equally so to know whether these signs of a join appear on the top of the stone. However it may have been in the case of the Pronaos, the inventory of the Hekatompedon for 410/09 B.C. was not inscribed on a *stele* calculated to accommodate it alone (*above*, pp. 47 ff., 55, n. 2). In regard to that for the Parthenon we have no knowledge; but the presumption is that its *stele* was designed to serve for all the records of the *penteteris*, especially if it had the length of line suggested above (p. 68).

VIII

THE ACCOUNTS OF THE TAMIAE FOR THE YEARS 406/04 B.C.

THE Treasurers' accounts for the year 407/06 B.C. (IG^2 I 304B) date the items by the days of the month and the days of the prytany. If we omit two isolated instances, both taken from the records furnished to the *logistae* by the Treasurers of the Other Gods for 423/2 B.C. (IG^2 I 324: Meritt, *Athenian Calendar*, Plates), this double dating is unique in this class of documents.[1] In the accounts assigned to 406/05 B.C. (IG^2 I 305) the Tamiae date the items by the days of the month alone (Meritt, *op. cit.*, p. 96), following the example set by the Tamiae of the Four Hundred (IG^2 I 298) and adhered to perhaps by the Tamiae of the Five Thousand.[2] IG^2 II 1686 and 1687 date entries by the days of the prytanies alone — the usual practice of the Tamiae.

The dating of IG^2 I 305 [3] in 406/5 B.C. is primarily an inference from the use of the Ionic script. It cannot belong to 407/06 B.C., or 409/08, or 410/09, since we already have accounts for

---

[1] It appears in the accounts of the *poletae* in 414/3 B.C. (IG^2 I 328).

[2] Apart from inventories the only official document we possess for the Five Thousand is the decree of the Council indicting Antiphon and his associates for treason ([Plut.], *Lives of the Ten Orators*, p. 833 E). It is dated with a precision unparalleled in this class of documents prior to 368 B.C. — by the day of the prytany. The reformers of 411 B.C. obviously made innovations in the dating of public records. They had reasons, doubtless, for using days of the month in accounts and days of the prytany in decrees.

[3] IG^2 I 306 has now become IG^2 I 324, frg. o (Meritt, *op. cit.*, Plates). IG^2 I 307 has been tentatively joined with IG^2 I 301 (Woodward, *JHS*, 1914, p. 280, n. 22); but I, at least, cannot fit it anywhere in the body of that text. Moreover, there was obviously no expenditure of 61,697+ staters recorded in IG^2 I 301 (Wade-Gery, *Num. Chron.*, 1930, pp. 37 f.). The most natural time for an outlay of so large a sum in staters is 413/2 B.C. (*above*, pp. 23 f.). Till then Athena's reserve of electrongold was drawn on sparingly, as was natural since reserves of silver existed. Afterwards it was unequal, probably, to so large a draft. It is conceivable that in 413/2 B.C., before they resorted to the extreme measure of broaching the special naval reserve of 1000 talents, the Athenians drew out of the Opisthodomos most of its stock of staters. (Meritt

these years. Nor can it belong in 411/0 B.C., because it posts expenditures made for the Panathenaia. There were no Panathenaia in the archonship of Theopompos and the outlays for the Panathenaia of 410 B.C. are entered in IG^2 I 304A. We have the accounts for the archonship of Mnasilochos (IG^2 I 298). Of the years which can be considered as possible, apart from 406/04 B.C., 408/07 alone remains, and the use of pure Ionic in accounts of this year would be extraordinary (Appendix I). Moreover, if it belonged to 408/07 the stone would have to be the reverse of the one which gives us IG^2 I 301 (*above*, p. 33); and since its left margin is preserved in part, we should expect it to contain the ends of the lines of which the beginnings are in our possession (IG^2 I 301B). This, however, seems not to be the case. 408/07 B.C. is, accordingly, excluded. But on the score of script alone 405/04 would be equally open with 406/05 B.C.

In line 8 appears the entry ἀθ[λ]οθ[έταις ἐς τὰ] Παναθήν[αια. Since it was preceded by entries reaching back at least to the month Elaphebolion (l. 3), we have to do with the ending and not with the beginning of an account. Hence the Panathenaia in question are the fête of July, 405 B.C., or July, 404 B.C., according to the date given to the document. Records of payments for the Panathenaia of 405 B.C. present no difficulty. A month or two had yet to elapse before Aegospotami. But the Panathenaia of 404 B.C., if they were celebrated at all, fell three months after the surrender of Athens to Lysander. They belonged to the Thirty. That need not exclude them perhaps;

informs me that the letters agree closely with those of IG^2 I 297; cf. *above*, p. 70, n. 1.) IG^2 I 308 and 294 belong to IG^2 I 299 (Wade-Gery, *JHS*, 1930, pp. 288 ff.). IG^2 I 309 is, I think, unidentified as yet. IG^2 I 309a is part of IG^2 I 296 (Wilhelm, *SEG*, III, 33). Two accounts published by Kirchner in Vol. II of the *Editio Minor* (1686 and 1687) are doubtless pre-Eukleidean accounts of the Tamiae. 1686 is ascribed (*below*, pp. 77 ff.) to 405/04 B.C. 1687, with the phrase [στα]τῆρας Ἀττ[ικῶ χρυσίο], is involved in the controversy as to whether Attic gold staters were coined in 406/04 B.C. (Woodward, *JHS*, 1914, pp. 286 ff.; Gardner, *History of Ancient Coinage*, p. 293; *below*, p. 86, n. 1). I feel certain that it belongs in 406/04 B.C. Staters, like talents and minas, may be units of money, not coins (Köhler, *Zeit. f. Numismatik*, 1898, p. 7). A sum of 100 drachmas can have consisted wholly of tetradrachms or triobols. Accounts of this sort would be unexampled in 394/3 B.C. or, for that matter, anywhere after 403 B.C. (*below*, p. 128). Can it form part of IG^2 I 305? An examination of the stones might help.

but the item immediately preceding the entry dealing with the Panathenaia (ll. 7 f.), dated in the last decade of Hekatombaion, records a payment of 30 talents. It is hard to believe that the Tamiae of 405/04 B.C. were in a position to make an expenditure of that magnitude in July, 404 B.C. Athens was then in the thick of the tyranny. There cannot be much question that the Panathenaia of *IG*² I 305 are the Panathenaia of 405 B.C., as universally held; and that this document contained first the record of expenditures from the *epeteia* and then, after a summary, under the caption τάδε ἐκ τοῦ Ὀπ[ισ]θοδόμο[υ παρ]έδομε[ν, the record of an expenditure (dated Munychion 27th) or expenditures (of that date and later) from the balance left in the treasury.

There is now *IG*² II 1686 to be considered. This set of accounts belongs before the abolition of the Hellenotamiae (404/03 B.C.), and after the issuance by Athens of a gold currency. If it originates with the Tamiae, it can belong to no other year than 405/04 B.C. Its attribution to the Tamiae would, I think, be unquestioned if we possessed the record from the obverse of the stone alone (*IG*² I 1686A). It is the account from the reverse that raises doubts and Kirchner lists the entire document among the *Fragmenta incerta*. It is certain that the accounts on the reverse belong to the same board of magistrates as the accounts on the obverse. We have many instances from both the fifth and the fourth centuries where the reverses of *stelae* were used by the officials who had used the obverses, or by their successors; none where a different board of magistrates utilized for their own purposes space of this sort, which, of course, did not belong to them. Decrees appear back of decrees or under one another; inventories were placed behind other inventories, and accounts of Treasurers behind accounts of the same board of Treasurers; accounts of Commissioners (ἐπιστάται) behind accounts of the same board of Commissioners; but neither decrees, inventories and accounts, nor accounts and inventories of different magistrates impinged on one another's tablet-space.[1]

---

[1] For the seeming anomaly of an account appearing on the reverse of a stone containing an inventory on its obverse (*IG*² II 1492A and B, 305/04 B.C.), see *below*, p. 133.

The prescripts of both accounts recorded in *IG²* II 1686 are lost. It was in them that the officials, whose statements followed, were named; and in the statements they were more likely to refer to officials to whom they had made payments, or with whom they had other dealings, than to themselves. Consequently, the appearance of the names of officials in oblique cases argues against, rather than for, these officials being responsible for the record. In the text on the obverse the Hellenotamiae were mentioned—in what connection we do not know (*IG²* II 1686A, l. 11: δὲ Ἑλληνοτ[αμι-]). *Epistatae* appear twice (l. 10: τ]ῶν ἐπιστατ[ῶν; l. 36: [ἐπι]στάταις ε). The officials responsible for the accounts, whoever they were, did something with silver articles, undoubtedly *phialae*,[1] each being identified, seemingly, by the name of the dedicator. With this entry our fragment begins. Then follows a section of nine lines of which the first two and the last two ended with the words ἐκ τὸ Παρθενῶνος - - - τούτων ἀφηιρέθη. The rest of the main account consisted of outlays of Attic gold and a summary. It was followed by the second part of the account (*IG²* II 1686A frg. b) recording payments made during the same period as those entered in the first part, but drawn from different sources.

Considering the circumstances and the context, there can be little doubt that the *epistatae* are the *epistatae* of the Mint.[2]

Since something like six-sevenths of each line of *IG²* II 1686A

It is a different matter when a board of magistrates like the *curatores navales* incorporate in their inventory a decree authorizing the *traditio* to the *oikist* Miltiades of ships and tackle (*IG²* II 1629, ll. 165 ff.); or when a special inventory, of the Chalkotheke for example, is appended to the decree requiring it to be made (*IG²* II 120; cf. *IG²* II 1440); or when the Tamiae quote in their accounts (*IG²* I 302, ll. 5 ff.) the text of a decree changing the destination of certain funds already appropriated (Meritt, *AJA*, 1930, p. 150, Plate II).

[1] A pair of [silver *phialae*] appears in line 6; cf. φιάλα ἀργυρᾶ ‖ in the inventories of the Parthenon, no. 43; also φιάλα ἀργυρᾶ δύο in the inventories of the Pronaos, no. 8.

[2] This title appears in the Athenian decree requiring the allies to use Attic silver money. It is used in all probability to designate local officials (Ziebarth, *Beiträge zur Gesch. des Seeraubs und Seehandels im alten Griechenland*, pp. 82, 135; cf., however, Hiller, *Zeit. f. Numismatik*, 1925, p. 220); but if it was common to all the federated states, it was doubtless used by Athens also. On the other hand, if we are to assume, as seems likely, that the name of the magistrates in charge of the mint varied from city to city throughout the Empire, the natural thing for the Athenians to do was to apply generally their own terminology.

is lost, a restoration is hopeless; [1] but from the repetition of the phrases ἐκ τὸ Παρθενῶνος - - - τούτων ἀφῃρέθη, with practically the same interval between Παρθενῶνος and ἀφῃρέθη in each case (thus suggesting the repetition of a formula), we are warranted in concluding that the ἀφαίρεσις was at the same time a segregation: some things were taken and others left. As we have seen (above, p. 57), the votives in the Parthenon not suitable for minting were listed in the inventory for 406/05 B.C. Consequently, the separation of mintable from non-mintable preceded 405/04. The things "taken away" were given to the Hellenotamiae (IG² I 255a). It seems likely, therefore, that the articles noted in this account as taken away "from those formerly in the Parthenon" — in a sense an account is now the complement of an inventory — are the articles disposed of by the Tamiae in 405/04 B.C.: to a general definition of the source (the identical formula between Παρθενῶνος and ἀφῃρέθη) was added a specific enumeration of the objects disposed of; and on the analogy of IG² I 255a we should expect the parties to whom they were handed over to be the Hellenotamiae — for consignment to the epistatae of the Mint. Since τῶν ἀργυρῶν follows in the next line after the first ἀφῃρέθη, we may conclude that the second ἀφαίρεσις concerned articles of gold, especially since it was preceded by a reference to Nikae, the purport of which is, however, quite obscure.[2] Preuner (IG² II 1686, p. 329, note) suggests that the silver phialae first mentioned were those taken from the Pronaos; and, if the votives there were taken away at the beginning of the year 405/04, that is possible. But there are alternatives. The objects of silver may be recent dedications, i.e., epeteia, as is suggested by the specification of the dedicator; or, since the Tamiae are the Tamiae

[1] In view of the fact that a shorter as well as a longer formula was used to designate the prytanies (cf. lines 19 and 22 with line 21), I do not see how we can calculate even approximately the number of letters to the line or ascertain precisely the number of prytanies during which payments were made. Normally the accounts of the Tamiae had about 84 letters to the line. There need not, I think, have been more than seven prytanies. That is to say, the expenditures can all have fallen before the surrender of Athens on Munychion 16, 405/04 B.C. (Plut. Lys. 15).

[2] For a separation of gold from silver in this way, see IG² I 91/2, ll. 18 ff.; 301B (409/08 B.C.); II 1415 ff.

of Athena and the Other Gods, they may have been assembled from shrines outside the Acropolis.

In line 16 began the record of expenditures. In every case (so far as can be determined) the payments were made in the new gold coinage.[1] On the assumption that the Tamiae are the actors we may restore the formula of transition, *exempli gratia*, as follows: [παραδεξάμενοι δὲ παρὰ τô ἀργυροκοπισ]τῆρος[2] Σιβυ[ρτίου - - παρέδομεν - -]ος Μελιτεῖ ἐπὶ [τῆς — ίδος πρυτανείας, κτλ. In any event, we have to account in some way for the gold when coined getting back into the hands of the Tamiae.

IG[2] II 1686A frg. a is intelligible as an account made by the Tamiae (of Athena and the Other Gods) of the objects of silver and gold originating in the Parthenon and of silver *phialae*, possibly originating elsewhere, which they handed over for minting in 405/04 B.C.; and of disbursements of Attic gold coins to some official or officials during several prytanies of the year. It corresponds in its position on the stone to the accounts of expenditures from *epeteia* made by the Tamiae during the preceding year; and we may, I think, assume that the Attic gold staters expended were received by the Tamiae in the course of the year and hence posted as *epeteia*. *IG*[2] II 1686A frg. b will then be the account of expenditures from the balance left them by their predecessors. This included the sum of 3470 + drachmas of silver. Its disposition was recorded and probably also its source. The balance also included the yield in coin (gold or silver?) of objects originating in the Hekatompedon. They had apparently been handed over directly or more probably indirectly (by the agency of the Hellenotamiae) to the *epistatae* of the Mint. It is to be noticed, therefore, that this account, with its division between articles formerly in the Parthenon, [from the Opisthodomos], and from the Hekatom-

[1] The last words preserved are σταθμὸν XX. Since there was no need to give the weight of Attic coins, there probably was some expenditure either of foreign staters or drachmas or of specie (cf. Wade-Gery, *Num. Chron.*, 1930, p. 21).

[2] I can find no Athenian name ending in -τηρ or -τηρος except Σωτήρ, which occurs only once in the Prosopographia Attica, and that as late as the middle of the second century B.C. (*PA*, 13396; Sundwall, *Nachträge*, s.v.). I imagine it was used as a proper name only after it had become familiar as a cult name of rulers. Instead of [ἀργυρο-κοπισ]τῆρος we may restore [χαρακ]τῆρος (Koerte, *Hermes*, 1929, pp. 70 ff.); but this use of the word is rare.

pedon, agrees with the classification of votives in the inventories issued by the Tamiae between 406/05 and 386/5 B.C.

It remains to consider whether this account can be connected equally well with any other board of magistrates — the Hellenotamiae for example. In 411 B.C. the Hellenotamiae obtained the treasury of the *kolakretae* (*above*, p. 3); but the duties and traditions of this office did not bring them into contact with silver *phialae* or warrant the issuance of accounts like those we have just analyzed. After the reorganization of the financial boards made in 411 B.C., the Treasurers of Athena continued to grant military subsidies to the Hellenotamiae, and, as we have seen (*above*, p. 34), they were put in the way of acquiring a new reserve for emergencies. But from 411 B.C. on they also included in their accounts moneys disbursed for domestic purposes — to the *athlothetae* for the Panathenaia, to the *hieropoii* for a hekatomb, to the *logistae* for what object we do not know.[1] These payments, theoretically at least, were advances to the state which should be repaid some day. So were the subsidies granted to the Hellenotamiae for the *diobelia*. Otherwise they would not appear in these accounts. For it should be borne in mind that the accounts of the Treasurers of Athena were recorded on stone, not because they were accounts — all Athenian magistrates who handled money presented accounts, of receipts as well as expenditures, for auditing at the end of their term, but they had no thought of recording them publicly. It was

---

[1] Cf. *above*, p. 31, n. 2. It seems to me clear that these accounts for the period following 411 B.C. contained "advances" to the state made by the Tamiae on their own responsibility from the private funds of Athena; that is to say, without specific vote of the *demos* authorizing each payment and without a preliminary vote of *adeia*. One general vote empowering the disbursement of the *epeteia* to the magistrates entitled to receive them is all that *IG*[2] I 304A, l. 3 demands; and it is quite incredible that the *demos* voted separately on the petty sums expended by the Tamiae of 407/06 B.C. On this hypothesis we can explain the making of payments during the days when the Panathenaia were being celebrated (*IG*[2] I 304A, ll. 5 ff., cf. West, *Class. Weekly*, 1929, p. 62; *IG*[2] I 305, l. 10, cf. *below*, p. 145, n. 1), notwithstanding that no meetings of the Assembly were held during festivals (Arist. *Ath. Pol.* 43 3; [Xen.] *de rep. Ath.* 3 2).

On the other hand, it is likely that disbursements from the reserve in the Opisthodomos had to be authorized, after as well as before 411 B.C., by specific votes of the Assembly in each case; and that we have herein an additional reason why the Tamiae between 409/08 and 405/04 B.C. kept a separate account of these disbursements, when there were any.

because they were statements of loans made by the Goddess to the Athenian people (*IG*² I 324 and 302, l. 56; Meyer, *Forsch.*, II, p. 135, n. 1, and p. 124, n. 1; cf. *above*, p. 16, n. 1; but also Francotte, *Finances*, p. 189) that the "accounts" of the Tamiae were published. The Hellenotamiae did not publish *their* accounts: what they published was the record of the *aparche* offered to Athena. If *IG*² II 1686a were a record of the Hellenotamiae, it would be absolutely unique. The crisis of 406 B.C. passed without affecting in any observable particular the general position and reciprocal relations of the Tamiae and the Hellenotamiae. We have therefore no warrant for supposing that the Hellenotamiae exercised a function of the Tamiae in 405/04 B.C.

Once we have identified the *epistatae* of this document as the Commissioners of the Mint, it becomes impossible to think of them as the authors of the document. If I understand him aright, Kirchner suspects that the *epistatae* are the ἐπιστάται Ἐλευσινόθεν, who were wont to record publicly an account of the first fruits of barley and wheat offered to Demeter and Kore. At any rate he refers to *IG*² I 76, 311; II 140 and 1672, ll. 263 ff.; and has been understood in this sense by Körte (*Gnomon*, 1928, p. 240). But just as certainly as the *epistatae* of the Mint can have had nothing to do with the accounts on the reverse, the *epistatae* of Eleusis can have had nothing to do with the accounts on the obverse of *IG*² II 1686. Assuming that both accounts originated with the Tamiae, how shall we explain the extraordinary character of those of the reverse?

This document is of course as defective as the one on the front; that is to say, something like six-sevenths of every line is lost. But its general character is easily perceived. It is a reckoning of distributions of barley and wheat made on specified days during each of at least three (consecutive?) prytanies. At the end of several items for each prytany the total for the prytany was added. The givers (cf. παρέδομεν, l. 64) are not mentioned in the fragment. The receivers are some official (on one occasion ['Ἀρι]στοφῶντι Αἰθαλί[δει]) or officials and his or their colleagues (καὶ ξυνάρχοσιν). In one instance the destination is the dikastery ([ἐ]ς τὸ δικαστ[ήριον]). The amounts (in

minimal figures) range from a few tens of medimni to 4510+.
On one day the [Tamiae] handed over 314 medimni, one hekteus
of barley and an unknown quantity of wheat, on another over
4510 measures of grain. These are impressive figures. Their
magnitude will be appreciated when it is noted that on a single
day nearly eight times as much grain was given out as the total
of the first fruits of Eleusis collected from all the ten *phylae*
in the entire year 329/8 B.C. (*IG*² II 1672, ll. 263 ff.: the total
for the year from all sources was 1189 medimni, 1 hekteus, 3
choinikes, cf. ll. 279, 283).

Near the bottom of the fragment the word "silver" appears
([κεφάλαιον?]ἀργυρί[ο]), showing that payments of silver money
were also noted. But what have the Tamiae to do with distributions of grain? In ordinary circumstances their outlays
were in coined money, exceptionally in bullion, and latterly,
as part of the process of getting coined money, in gold and silver
plate.[1] But what about the time of the great siege of 405/04
B.C.? When Lysander had closed the harbor and Agis and Pausanias had invested the walls, the only hope Athens had of de-
ferring the harsh necessity of surrender was in husbanding its
stock of grain. There can be no question that the public authorities seized all the barley and wheat they could get their
hands on, as Klearchos had done in Byzantium in 408 B.C.
(Xen. *Hell.* I 3 19); and we have no difficulty in assuming that
they stored it for safe-keeping [2] against the starving multitude
on the Acropolis in the charge of the Tamiae. Instead of money
for the *diobelia* these officials now doled out grain.[3] There was

[1] The only commodity in kind regularly put on the Acropolis in the custody of the
Treasurers of Athena was the oil from Athena's sacred olive groves (Arist. *Ath. Pol.*
60 3).

[2] The Temple on the Acropolis was the depot in which the Thirty kept the arms
taken from the citizens not on the roll of the Three Thousand (Xen. *Hell.* II 3 20).
See also *below*, p. 129, n. 1, and the inventories of the Chalkotheke.

[3] It is probably owing to the loss of all but the concluding fragment of the stone that
there is no ascertainable reference to the *diobelia* in *IG*² I 305; for in its year (406/05
B.C.) the institution still flourished under the conduct of the demagogue Archedemos
of Pelex (Xen. *Hell.* I 7 2). The rôle of Kallikrates of Paiania (Kirchner, *PA*, 7975),
who, according to Aristotle (*Ath. Pol.* 28 3), "abolished" (κατέλυσε) the *diobelia* and "was
the first to promise to add another obol to the two," is obscure. Line 78 of *IG*² I 304B
seems to run: λογισται E. TONO.ΟΛΟΝΧΗΙΙΓ·· [λ]ο[γ]ισται[- - (Meritt). May

no purpose in giving men two obols a day or wages for work on the Erechtheum when there was no longer food to be bought.[1] Naturally the dikasts were not forgotten. It may be conjectured with a good deal of plausibility that the intermediaries were the Hellenotamiae. *Sitonae* had not been thought of as yet (Busolt, *Griech. Staatsk.*, I, p. 433; II, pp. 1067, 1121).

*IG*² II 1686 are the last accounts published, to our knowledge, by the Tamiae. From them we learn the rôle played by the Treasurers of Athena and the Other Gods, as custodians of the Acropolis, in the terrible final scene of the Peloponnesian War. They also enable us to understand the disappearance of Cleophon's device for sustaining the will to war of the impoverished population of Athens. The payment of money became a distribution of grain. At the end of the siege this was discontinued and the *diobelia* was not revived.

we conclude that late in 407/06 B.C. the *diobelia* was supplemented by an *obelia*? The *diobelia* existed during the month Hekatombaion, 406/05 B.C. (*IG*² I 304B, l. 90, Meritt) and later (Xen. *Hell.* I 7 2). Like *IG*² I 301 (*above*, p. 40), *IG*² II 1686 is so badly mutilated that expenditures may have been recorded in it for the *diobelia* without our knowing it. We should expect to find them, if anywhere, in the accounts on the obverse. The three prytanies of the reverse coincide approximately with the "three months and more" during which Theramenes was detained by Lysander. Xenophon alludes four times to the shortage of food in Athens at this epoch and its fatal consequences (*Hell.* II 2 10, 11, 16, 21; cf. also *Lysias*, XIII 11).

[1] *IG*² II 1654, ll. 23 ff. (Paton, *The Erechtheum*, XXVIII, p. 420) must be regarded as the account of payments made for the repair of the Erechtheum before the siege began, during the first prytany or two of the year 405/04 B.C. (*above*, p. 49).

IX

THE CONVERSION INTO MONEY OF ATTIC
TEMPLE PROPERTIES

THE policy of drawing on the offerings to the gods and the furnishings of the temples in case of extreme necessity was enunciated by Pericles at the opening of the Peloponnesian War (*Thucy.* II 13 4). Besides the 6000 talents of coined silver at hand on the Acropolis, "there was," Thucydides makes him say, "uncoined gold and silver in public and private dedications, and all the sacred vessels used in the processions and games, and the Persian spoils and other treasures of like nature, worth not less than five hundred talents. And he estimated, besides, the large amount of treasure to be found in the other temples.[1] All this would be available for their use, and, if they should be absolutely cut off from all other resources, they might use even the gold plates with which the statue of the Goddess herself was overlaid. The statue, as he pointed out to them, contained forty talents' weight of pure gold, and it was all removable. This treasure they might use for self-preservation, but they must replace as much as they took."[2]

In reporting Pericles to this effect, Thucydides had unquestionably in mind the arrival, in the later stages of the war, of the emergency which called for the sacrifice of these precious properties of the gods. The extreme necessity of stripping the Goddess herself of her golden plates did not, indeed, arise. The statue of Pheidias remained intact, as the inventories of the fourth century prove (*IG*² II 1407, note on l. 5); and it was not till over one hundred years later, when Athens was again

---

[1] The phrase used, καὶ τὰ ἐκ τῶν ἄλλων ἱερῶν προσετίθει χρήματα, suggests that we have to do with the treasure which was assembled in the Opisthodomos in 434 B.C. Had the *kosmos* and sacrificial articles left behind in the several shrines been meant, ἐν τοῖς ἄλλοις ἱεροῖς might have been used. Cf. Kolbe, *Sitz. Ber. Akad.* 1927, p. 321.

[2] Translation by Smith in the *Loeb Classics*.

in dire financial straits and "absolutely cut off from all other resources," that, as the comic poet Demetrios said, γυμνὴν Ἀθηνᾶν τότ' ἐποίησε Λαχάρης (Kock, III, p. 357, cf. *Hellenistic Athens*, p. 134; *Pap. Oxy.*, XVII, 2082, cf. *Class. Phil.*, 1929, pp. 1 ff.). We may, I think, assume that the rest of Pericles' program was carried out.

As already pointed out (*above*, p. 24), the first attack on the private properties of Athena of which we have knowledge was made in 409/08 B.C. At that time "silver" was taken from the Parthenon. Our imperfect record next acquaints us with the expropriation for conversion into coin of "the golden Nikae." This we learn from Hellanicos and Philochoros as quoted in the *scholia* on Aristophanes' *Frogs*, 720: τῷ προτέρῳ ἔτει ἐπὶ Ἀντιγένους Ἑλλάνικός φησι χρυσοῦν νόμισμα κοπῆναι· καὶ Φιλόχορος ὁμοίως τὸ ἐκ τῶν χρυσῶν Νικῶν. As Beloch points out (*Griech. Gesch.*, II, 2, p. 242), it is not strictly said that Philochoros dated in 407/06 B.C. the minting of the golden Nikae; but if he did not trace to this source the gold from which the gold coins were struck, the scholiast would hardly have cited him at all. Beloch also questions the reliability of Hellanicos' date; and with partial justification, as we shall show presently.

Before gold could be coined in Athens, special dies and anvils had to be made; for the city had issued theretofore no coins of this metal. This apparatus (οἱ χαρακτῆρες καὶ ἀκμονίσκοι [ἐφ' ὧν τὸς χρυσὸς ἔ]κοπτον) [1] appears in the Opisthodomos in inven-

---

[1] Cf. Koerte, *Gnomon*, 1928, pp. 237 f.; *Hermes*, 1929, p. 72. If we accept Gardner's view (*History of Ancient Coinage*, p. 294) that χρυσοῖ means staters, and that no staters were struck in 406/04 B.C., we may restore the line [ἐπὶ (or διὰ) ὧν τὰ χρυσία ἔ]κοπτον. The only gold coins of this epoch which have reached us are the drachm, hemidrachm, diobol, and obol, and since the anvils were four in number, one for each denomination probably, we may infer that staters were not struck at this time. Gardner contends that this minting apparatus belongs to a second coinage of gold made c. 393 B.C.; but the new date of *IG*² II 1408 excludes this. Köhler (*Zeit. f. Numismatik*, 1898, p. 14), followed by Head (*Hist. Nummorum*², p. 375), dates this second coinage in c. 339 B.C., connecting it with an alleged melting down of gold votives made during the regime of Lycurgus. The inventories yield no evidence on the point; and had an expropriation of this sort, which accords ill with the religiosity of Lycurgus, occurred, we should probably have heard of it. The minting of gold at Athens was inseparably connected with the melting down of votive offerings; and it was not till 301–295 B.C. that the conjunction of 406/04 was repeated. The second issue of gold is definitely assigned to Lachares by Svoronos (*C.R. Ac. Inscr.*, 1919, pp. 34 ff.; *Jour. intern. d'arch.*

tories of the Treasurers of the epoch 398/7–367/6 B.C. (IG^2 II 1388+1408, 1409, Ἀρχ. Δελτίον, 1927/8, p. 128, col. I, ll. 119 f.; cf. *below*, p. 129, n. 1). In 409/08 B.C., as we have seen (*above*, p. 41), the Tamiae handed over to the Hellenotamiae gold bars (φθοῖδες) from Skaptesyle, the value of which in silver was entered in their accounts. The presumption is that this was sold for what it would bring.[1] Certainly it was unminted when it left the hands of the Treasurers; but that proves nothing, since it was the business of the Hellenotamiae to attend to the minting (*above*, p. 79). The probability that it was not minted at all rests on the well-known passage of the *Frogs* of Aristophanes (717 ff.). In January, 405 B.C., the gold currency was described as καινόν, the silver as ἀρχαῖον, and both are held up as models in contrast with the πονηρὰ χαλκία recently struck. It seems to me difficult to suppose that the gold would be characterized as "new" if it had been in circulation for three years. In 408/07 B.C. the Tamiae of Athena made an arrangement whereby they set aside in the Opisthodomos 2000 drachmas of gold bullion as security for 3 talents, 2000 drachmas of silver money borrowed from the temple at Eleusis. The exchange was ordered by vote of the *demos* (IG^2 I 313, ll. 173 ff., cf. 314, ll. 14 ff. and *above*, p. 27, n. 1). This transaction is intelligible on the assumption that in 408/07 B.C. Athens was not yet contemplating the issuance of a gold currency. Had the "dies and little anvils" been already in operation, the gold could have been used more profitably for coining money.[2] As we

---

numismatique, XXI, pp. 159 ff.) and Newell (*The Coinages of Demetrius Poliorcetes*, p. 133, n. 4), who very kindly informs me that he is absolutely convinced of the correctness of this attribution.

[1] The Commissioners of the chryselephantine statue of Athena bought and sold gold in Athens (IG^2 I 354–362). The word [ἐ]πράθε has been deciphered in line 113 of IG^2 I 301 by Wade-Gery (*Num. Chron.*, 1930, p. 27).

[2] Since the 20,000 drachmas borrowed were already deposited on the Acropolis (ἐμ πόλει), doubtless with the Tamiae, the affair was largely a matter of bookkeeping. The money borrowed was practically all the cash which Demeter and Kore then possessed. According to Wade-Gery's brilliant restoration of IG^2 I 301, ll. 119 f., [λελογισμένον δ]εκαστάσ[ιον] (*Num. Chron.*, 1930, p. 24), the ratio of gold to silver current in 409/08 B.C. was 1 to 10, and this was also the ratio at which the exchange was effected in 408/07 (Sardemann, *Eleusinische Uebergabeurkunden aus dem V Jahrh.*, p. 38); but Wade-Gery surmises that some gold was sold in 409/08 B.C. ἐνδεκαστάσιον. Gardner (*History of Ancient Coinage*, p. 292) and others (cf. Köhler, *Zeit. f. Numisma-*

have seen (*above*, p. 12), it was in the archonship of Kallias (406/05 B.C.) that the Athenians voted to convert the votive offerings of Athena into money. We have also seen that the Tamiae for 406/05 B.C. handed over to their successors, as regards the Parthenon, the attenuated list of dedications which, with some exceptions,[1] meets us in the post-Eukleidean records. The sorting of this collection for conversion into money may have begun before Hekatombaion 28th, 406 B.C.; but it was probably not till after that date, in 406/05 B.C., that the minting played havoc with it, and it was not till after Hekatombaion 28th, a year later, that the articles in the Pronaos were taken away by the Hellenotamiae for consignment to the melting pot. In the failure of the Tamiae of 407/06 B.C. to publish an inventory of the Pronaos we have, perhaps, an intimation that they knew that the *ex-votos* were to be converted into money. But it was in the archonship of Kallias (406/05 B.C.) that Athens began to issue the bronze coins plated with silver which belong to the same system of monetary expedients as the issue of gold coins made from dedications (Aristoph. *Frogs*, 725 and the *scholion:* ἐπὶ γὰρ Καλλίου χαλκοῦν νόμισμα ἐκόπη).[2] We

---

tik, 1898, p. 7; *JHS*, 1914 pp. 276 ff.) believe that the coins issued in 406/04 B.C. reveal by their weights the equivalence of 1 part of gold to 12 parts of silver; but cf. Segrè, *Metrologia*, p. 242. The difference would have more than offset the cost of minting. In the latter half of the fourth century the ratio of the two metals, as determined by the equivalence in silver of gold vases (*IG*² II 1496, note on p. 100), by the accounts of the Tamiae for 306/05 B.C. (*IG*² II 1492B, ll. 101 ff.), and other statements of equivalences collected by Reinach (*L'histoire par les monnaies*, pp. 53 ff.) and Segrè (*Metrologia*, pp. 244 f.), was still 1 to 10; and it was the same in 189 B.C. (*Polyb.* XXI, 32 8).

[1] The pair of gold necklaces ([hορμίσκ]ọ δύο) listed in *IG*² I 289 (405/04 B.C.; cf. *above*, p. 61), for example.

[2] Gardner (*History of Ancient Coinage*, p. 295) and Segrè (*Metrologia*, p. 230) affirm that bronze was first struck in the archonship of Kallias, but the texts they cite (*schol.* on Aristophanes, *Frogs*, 725, 730) do not justify this conclusion. Svoronos (*Jour. intern. d'arch. numismatique*, XIV, 1913, pp. 123 ff.) argues that a genuine copper currency had been introduced in the time of Pericles, on the initiative of Dionysios, surname Chalkos (cf. also Kirchner, *PA*, 4084; Busolt, *Griech. Staatsk.*, I, p. 595, n. 3). The issue of 406/05 B.C. was token money (for an example see *CAH*, *Plates*, vol. II, p. 5e); and it is because it was a debased silver currency that it was attacked by Aristophanes (cf. also *Ecclesiazusae*, 815 f.). If, as Segrè contends (*Metrologia*, pp. 230 f.), the issue of 406 B.C. was really small change in copper, it was the silver-plated coins, which he terms *falsificazioni private o di stato*, that occasioned the contemptuous comment of the comedian. Seeing that "thousands of examples" of them have been found

may conclude, therefore, that while it was certainly in the archonship of Kallias that the vote of the *demos* was passed authorizing the transfer to the Hellenotamiae of the sacred properties of the gods (*IG*² I 255a), the part of this archonship which comes in question is that which overlapped with the term of office of the Tamiae for 407/06 B.C., viz., the period between the 1st and 28th of Hekatombaion, 406 B.C.

This conclusion would be confirmed if it was the Tamiae who handed over the golden Nikae for the melting pot. But we can, I think, show that such was the case. In the fourth century the one Nike which escaped the minting was in the custody of the Tamiae (*IG*² II 1371, note). How many Nikae there were prior to 426/5 B.C. we do not know; but one at least was made before that date. Its parts, weighed separately, were listed in the mutilated lines at the beginning of the inventory of the Nikae *IG*² I 369.¹ After it were entered two more, which the ἐπιστάται τοῖν Νίκαιν, to whom the state had delegated the task of having this pair made, consigned to the custodians of the Nikae in 426/5 B.C. (*IG*² I 368; *SEG*, III 40). From *IG*² I 368 we learn that this pair of golden Nikae belonged, as we should expect, to Athena Nike; and, since this is so, their custodians must have been the Tamiae of the Goddess. We may, therefore, conclude with Foucart (*BCH*, 1888, pp. 283 ff.) and Meyer (*Forsch.*, II, p. 110, n. 1) that the custodians by whom the fifth-century inventories of the Nikae were issued were in fact the Treasurers of Athena (cf. Arist. *Ath. Pol.* 47 1), and not some board of officials whose year coincided with that of the Archon.

Hellanikos very probably found, or said, that the golden Nikae were consigned to the melting pot on action of the *demos* by the Tamiae of Antigenes' archonship; but he either failed to observe, or the scholiast who quoted him failed to notice, that it was in the archonship of Kallias that the vote of the people

(Svoronos, *ibid.*, XXI, p. 158), they were issued in such great quantities that it is impossible to regard them as private forgeries.

¹ Since the stone is broken at the beginning, there may have been more than one. Kolbe (*Sitz. Ber. Akad.*, 1927, pp. 426 f.), interpreting *IG*² I 92, l. 34, traces the inauguration of the plan of making golden Nikae back to 434 B.C. See further, *below*, p. 122, n. 2.

was passed. A mistake, perhaps, but a venial one.[1] It enables us to understand further why he also entered under Antigenes' archonship the grant by the Athenians of freedom to the slaves who served on the fleet at Arginusae (*schol.* on Aristoph., *Frogs*, 694). The tender of this reward was obviously made in advance; and it, too, can have been voted on by the *demos* between the 1st and 28th of Hekatombaion. It is, however, manifestly an error when the scholiast on Aristophanes' *Frogs*, 33, dates the battle of Arginusae itself in Antigenes' year. That the engagement occurred in Kallias' year is made certain by Aristotle (*Ath. Pol.* 34 1) and Athenaeus (V 218a). The victory of the eight generals was gained shortly before the celebration of the Apaturia in Pyanepsion (October) 406/05 B.C., as Xenophon shows (*Hell.* I 7 8). The fleet put to sea thirty days after word reached Athens of Conon's situation (*ibid.*, I 6 24). It is to be presumed that the vote to expropriate the *anathemata* and to emancipate the slaves followed closely on the receipt of the news from Mytilene. I am inclined to think that we should date the arrival of Conon's message nearer the 28th than the 1st of Hekatombaion, because the Generals Leon and Erasinides, who took office on Hekatombaion 1st, were blockaded in Mytilene with Conon (Xen. *Hell.* I 6 16; Beloch, *Griech. Gesch.*, II, 2, p. 242).[2] On this basis we arrive at a date toward the close of Metageitnion for the setting out of the fleet, and in the early part of Boedromion (September) for the battle of Arginusae. A brief delay in coining the new money of gold and bronze is intelligible in view of the need to make new minting apparatus; and, for that matter, the urgent need for money began after the fleet put off rather than earlier, seeing that the ships manned were old triremes, not new constructions (Meyer, *Gesch. d. Alt.*, IV, p. 643); but we cannot doubt that the Tamiae

---

[1] The accounts of the Tamiae for Antigenes' archonship (*IG*² I 304B) continue beyond Hekatombaion 1st, 406/05 B.C., without mentioning the change of Archon. In official documents the Tamiae were recorded at this time as serving for the year of the Archon during whose term they entered office (see *below*, p. 138, n. 2).

[2] We hear nothing further of Leon. Erasinides probably commanded the ship which escaped to carry to Athens the news of Conon's predicament. He subsequently led a squadron at Arginusae.

in office at the moment the decree was passed took the first steps needed to put it into effect.

The evidence we possess is best served when we conclude that shortly before Hekatombaion 28th in the year 406 B.C. the *demos* decided by one and the same vote to expropriate for minting the golden Nikae of Athena Nike and the objects made of precious metals in the Pronaos, Parthenon, and Hekatompedon. It cannot have been many days before Hekatombaion 28th that this action was taken; but it was sufficiently in advance of the expiry of the term of office of the Tamiae for 407/06 B.C. to permit the election for the coming Panathenaic year of the new board of Tamiae of Athena and the Other Gods, the creation of which was organically connected with the despoiling of the temples (*below*, pp. 105 ff.).

As has been said, the first of the pair of Nikae dedicated in 426/5 B.C. (*IG*² I 369, ll. 9 ff.) appears in the inventories of the Hekatompedon after 403 B.C. (*below*, p. 118, n. 1). *IG*² II 1502, which Kirchner publishes among the *Fragmenta Incerta*, with the note that it is written in "good letters of the opening of the fourth century,"[1] begins, so far as it is preserved, with an inventory of golden Nikae. The last to be catalogued (ll. 5–9) is one that existed before 426/5 B.C. (*IG*² I 369, ll. 2–6). Its total weight was 1 talent, 5987 drachmas. It was preceded by a Nike which has not been identified. Its total weight was 12,201 + drachmas.[2] We do not know the weight of the second

---

[1] We are, of course, unable, on the basis of the letter forms alone, to distinguish an Attic document of the last six years of the fifth century from one of the first decade of the fourth.

[2] The total weight of the Nike dedicated in 374/3 B.C. (*below*, p. 137) was 11,894 drachmas, 4 obols; that of the one carried over into the fourth century from the fifth was 11,964 drachmas, 3 obols, in 398/0 B.C. In 369/6 B.C. it was a figure ending in 16 drachmas, 3 obols ('Αρχ. Δελτίον, 1927/8, p. 126, col. I, l. 41), if this line has been correctly restored as κεφάλαιον (it may be something else); the items were 2044 dr., 2 ob.; 1948 dr.; 1939 dr., 3 ob.; 18 (?) 94 dr.; 4035 dr., yielding a total of 11,860 drachmas, 5 obols; but they are derived from three inventories of successive years ('Αρχ. Δελτίον, 1927/8, p. 128, col. I, l. 18; *IG*² II 1425, l. 16; 'Αρχ. Δελτίον, 1927/8, p. 126, ll. 29, 32, 35), and are in part due to restorations. Obviously the amount of gold assigned for the making of each Nike was 2 talents (cf. *below*, p. 115, n. 1), of which the equivalent in silver money was 20–24 talents. The seven Nikae melted down in 406/04 B.C. (*below*, p. 122, n. 2), therefore, produced money worth 140–168 talents. We might think that

of the pair of 426/5 B.C.; the two may be the same or different.
The important thing in the present connection is that this inventory, containing, as it does, two Nikae, must precede 403/02
B.C., when only one existed. The date of *IG*² II 1502 is, therefore, earlier than the archonship of Eukleides; and, since it is
written in the Ionic script, it is *prima facie* later than 407/06
B.C. If it was an inventory of Nikae alone, we might take it to
be another of the series to which *IG*² I 369 belongs; but this
is not the case. For the Nikae were followed by an object of
gold which an *epistates* dedicated when he founded or consecrated the Artemision (χρυσ[- - ὃ ὁ δεῖνα ἀνέθηκεν ὅτε ἵδρ]υ-
σεν (or [καθίδρ]υσεν) τὸ Ἀρτεμίσιον ὃ ἐπεστάτε, σταθμὸν Τ-. This
conjunction of articles proves that the officials responsible
for the inventory were the Tamiae of Athena and the Other
Gods, since prior to 406 B.C. the golden Nikae belonged to the
jurisdiction of the Treasurers of Athena while Artemis [Brau-
ronia (?)] was one of the deities served by the Treasurers of the
Other Gods (*IG*² I 324, ll. 72, 89: Meritt, *Athenian Calendar*,
p. 22).¹ It seems to me probable that *IG*² II 1502 is an inventory made after the articles to be saved from the minting,
notably one Nike, had been transferred to the Hekatompedon
or packed in "the chests of Artemis Brauronia" ² (cf. *above*,
pp. 64 ff.).

We are now in a position to appreciate the full significance
of the words of Thucydides quoted at the opening of this section. The expropriation of sacred objects voted in July, 406 B.C.,
was not confined to the Temple of Athena begun in 447/6 B.C.:
it included *ex-votos* of Athena deposited elsewhere and those of

---

the object weighing 2 talents dedicated in the Hekatompedon in 410/09 B.C. (*IG*²
I 274a; *above*, pp. 48, 53) was a Nike, and connect its making with the victory of
Cyzicus, were it not for the gender of the demonstrative pronoun ([τοῦτ]ο) by which it
is indicated and for the further fact that a separate series of inventories existed for the
Nikae. The importance of the golden Nikae for minting purposes may be gauged by
the fact that the total value in silver of all the votives in the Pronaos, Hekatompedon,
and Parthenon was less than 15 talents.

¹ I know no justification for Bannier's exclusion of Artemis Brauronia from the
circle of the Other Gods either in the fifth century or in the fourth (*Rh. Mus.*, 1926,
p. 193). The Tamiae of Athena had nothing to do with any Artemis.

² The articles contained in the chests of Artemis Brauronia were unmintable. See
the list in *IG*² II 1388B.

the Other Gods as well. Incidentally it must be noted that a large part of the dedications listed in the inventories of the Pronaos, Parthenon, and Hekatompedon were added after 434/3 B.C.; and that the articles which appear in the first inventories (IG^2 I 232, 256, 276) are neither so numerous nor of such a character as to be inexplicable as dedications made to be placed in Pericles' temple between 438, when the cult image was completed, and 434 B.C. There is no warrant for the opinion that on the opening of this temple earlier dedications to Athena were transferred to it.[1] Such there were, of course. In fact, they were much the most important part of the whole. In 431 B.C. Thucydides evaluates the votives and sacred vessels, apart from those of the other gods, at 500 talents. As we have pointed out, the Nikae, most of which were dedicated after the opening of the Peloponnesian War, were worth at the outside 168 talents and the votives in the Temple, 15 talents. Thucydides singles out for specific mention the "Persian spoils." They were doubtless left where they had been placed when dedicated; and if we had inventories of Athena's properties in addition to those of the Pronaos, Parthenon, Hekatompedon, and the golden Nikae, we should find that they too went into the melting pot in 406–04 B.C. The vote of 406 B.C. envisaged all the gold and silver properties of the Attic gods. The *kosmos* and sacrificial vessels of Demeter and Kore (see *below*, p. 116), and the like articles of the thirty or forty other gods and goddesses, were gathered in, so far as they were not assembled already, and melted down.[2] Unmintable things

---

[1] Meyer (*Forsch.*, II pp. 109 f.) contends that, so long as work was in progress on our Parthenon and workmen were going and coming, dedications such as appear in the inventories for 434/3 B.C. and later cannot have been set up in the Pronaos, Hekatompedon, and Parthenon. But the work continued throughout 434/3 and 433/2 B.C. (IG^2 I 352, 353), when such articles were already in place. And even if the articles of the inventories, not dedicated in 434/3 B.C. and subsequently, were stored elsewhere till 434/3 B.C., they can represent the accumulation of only a few years, if *epeteia* arrived before the year 434/3 with the same rapidity as after it. It seems to me unthinkable that the articles with which our Parthenon was adorned in 434/3 B.C. represent more than the merest fraction of the offerings made to Athena during the generations and generations of the past. See *below*, p. 154.

[2] IG^2 I 324 does not disclose whether or not the Goddesses of Eleusis were included among the Other Gods: of the thirty-five deities mentioned in it ten are unknown (Meritt, *Athenian Calendar*, p. 22) and Demeter and Kore may be among

were, of course, eliminated in 406 B.C.; also certain objects of
gold or silver (the *karchesion* of Zeus Polieus, the solitary gold
crown left in the Pronaos, the gold leaves from the crown of the
Nike which stood on the hand of the statue of Pheidias, one
golden Nike of Athena Nike, for examples) were held back;
above all the chryselephantine statue of Athena was left in-
violate. But it may well be that these articles were spared,
not through the will of the *demos*, but because of the abrupt
termination of the war.

For it is now evident that the operation of minting was extended over at least two calendar years (406/05 and 405/04
B.C.). The occasion for the general expropriation was undoubtedly the crisis of Arginusae; but the need for the sacrifice
of the *anathemata*, though in some degree lessened by the victory
gained by the Athenians under the leadership of the eight
Generals, and the freedom and faculty it furnished of collecting again the harvest of the Empire, was about as great for the
campaign which ended with disaster at Aegospotami (August–
September, 405 B.C.) as for the campaign which issued successfully at Arginusae. The minting of the Nikae was still in process in 405/04 B.C., if we may trust the indication of line 13 of
*IG*² II 1686 (see *above*, p. 79). Silver from the Parthenon was on
its way to the melting pot in that same year. The dedications
of the Pronaos (with one single exception) were handed over to

them. So too in *IG*² I 310 the money and income of many deities are listed whose
names are lost. Yet these records indicate that the jurisdictions of the Tamiae of the
Other Gods and the *epistatae* of Eleusis were not mutually exclusive. In 324, l. 91, a
loan from the Mother in Agrae is recorded, and in 310, l. 132, 212 drachmas, 4 obols,
are credited to this deity; yet in the account-inventory of the *epistatae* for 408/07 B.C.
(*IG*² I 313/4) acknowledgement is made of the receipt in income of 45 drachmas,
1 obol, "from the Mysteries at Agrae" (l. 146). Moreover, this same record shows
that money, plate, and specie of the Eleusinian deities were kept on the Acropolis
(ἐμ πόλει) — in the Opisthodomos presumably, in the custody of the Treasurers of the
Other Gods. But while this is fairly clear, it is also clear that the *epistatae* of 408/07 B.C.
had in their charge not only a lot of stuff (σκεύε) both in the Eleusinion in Athens and at
Eleusis but also sacrificial vessels and other *kosmos* of Demeter and Kore in both places.
The former was, of course, not included in the account-inventory of the Tamiae: the
latter may have been (*below*, p. 97, n. 2). In any event, the appearance in the Hekatompedon inventory after 403 B.C. of articles belonging to Demeter and Kore (*below*, p.
116) shows that the sacred properties of Eleusis were involved, directly or indirectly,
in the expropriation of the votives made in 406/04 B.C.

the Hellenotamiae in 405/04 B.C.; and if our record were more complete, we might trace in more detail the consignment to the melting pot, group by group, of the properties of the Other Gods, and "all the sacred vessels used in processions and games, the Persian spoils, and other treasures of like nature, worth not less than five hundred talents." And as the dedications passed over to the Mint, gold [and silver (?)] coins into which they were converted passed back into the hands of the Tamiae of Athena and the Other Gods to be put into circulation.[1] They were a novelty in January, 405 B.C.; they were disbursed by the Tamiae to the practical exclusion of all other money in 405/04 B.C. Since every gold coin had ten or twelve times the value of silver of like denomination, it was natural that, once the decision was taken to sacrifice the votive offerings and the requisite dies were made, the process of minting began with the objects of gold (*above*, p. 74). The despoiling of the Temple probably commenced with the Hekatompedon (cf. *above*, p. 80), which was especially rich in articles of that metal. There was urgent need of as much money as possible. After the siege of Athens commenced, the need of grain was greater. How long the Athenians continued to mint gold we do not know. Had the Thirty Tyrants denuded the temples yet further of their dedications, the fact would doubtless have appeared in our copious record of their infamies. By 399/8 B.C. the "dies and little anvils with which the gold was struck" were already dedicated to Athena; that is to say, their period of use was ended.[2] The "copper" currency which began to be issued in 406 B.C. was demonetized in or before 393 B.C. (Aristoph. *Ecclesiazusae*, 821 f.).

[1] It can, I think, be assumed that the Tamiae received only a quota of the new coins, the rest being expended by the Hellenotamiae directly.

[2] Through the kindness of Mr. West I have had some advance information regarding the far-reaching work of Mr. Woodward and himself in joining together and dating more precisely the fragments of the inventories of the Tamiae published in *IG*² II 1370 ff. I have thus been enabled, at the last moment, to avoid some errors (cf. *above*, pp. 9, 66, 86; *below*, pp. 112, 115, 119, 129, 150), though, doubtless, not all (cf. pp. 114, n. 1; 132, n. 1).

X

THE "FOUR ARCHAE"

IN the fourth century the *athlothetae*, who had charge of the Panathenaic procession and games, who saw to the making of Athena's *peplos* and the Panathenaic vases, and apportioned to the victorious athletes the oil from Athena's sacred olive groves, served for four years (Arist. *Ath. Pol.* 60 1), from one Great Panathenaia to the next, doubtless (*ibid.* 62 2). A *penteteric* tenure of office was made possible by the inauguration in 566/5 B.C. of the Great Panathenaia. It is likely that the *athlothetae* had not existed theretofore (*PW*, II, 2, p. 2064). Tamiae, on the other hand, were very old officials (Busolt, *Griech. Staatsk.*, II, pp. 819, n. 2, 1135); and the presumption is that their term of office became annual at the same time as that of the Basileus, Polemarch, and Archon (683 B.C.?), running, however, from Panathenaia to Panathenaia.

In 434 B.C. the four boards of Tamiae of Athena for a Panathenaic period (αἱ τέτταρες ἀρχαί) were combined for certain purposes in a single unit (*IG²* I 91, ll. 57 ff.; *below*, p. 98). Simultaneously the Other Gods were consolidated and given Tamiae of their own. The year of these Treasurers also began and ended at the Panathenaia. Did they, too, form a group of four boards? It is affirmed by Beloch (*Rh. Mus.*, 1888, p. 121; *Griech. Gesch.*, II, 2, p. 347) that they acted thus collectively; and notwithstanding the collapse of his major contention — that it was not till 418 B.C. that the board of *ten* Tamiae of the Other Gods was created — the rôle of the "four archae," both in their case and in the case of the Tamiae of Athena, needs further definition.

Since it is unthinkable that the Tamiae of the first three years of a Panathenaic *penteteris* remained ὑπεύθυνοι, and hence ineligible for any other office, till the entire *penteteris* was completed,[1] we have to assume that they submitted their accounts for auditing yearly (cf. *below*, p. 99, n. 1) and that the collective responsibility of the "four archae" was a minor one. As we have already pointed out, the complete accounts of the Tamiae of Athena were not publicly recorded, certainly not in any records which have reached us. What *was* inscribed on stone *stelae* and set up on the Acropolis was in the first place records of the "loans" made by the Tamiae to the state (which, following general practice, we have called "accounts"), and in the second place records, commonly called inventories, of the *ex-votos* of the Pronaos, Parthenon, and Hekatompedon, and of the golden Nikae of Athena Nike. On the other hand, the complete accounts of the Treasurers of the Other Gods *were* published, and for one year, 429/8 B.C., they have reached us, though in a badly mutilated condition. They were issued annually; and, unlike the so-called accounts of Athena, they included the annual receipts (ἐγκυκλ[ίο] καρπô ἐκ [τôν] ἱερôν, *IG*[2] I 310, l. 209) and doubtless also the expenditures (Col. I).[2] The "accounts" were at the same time an inventory of the section

---

[1] Pythodoros of Halai, Tamias in 418/7, was elected General for 414/3 B.C. (*Thucy.* VI 105 2; cf. Beloch, *Griech. Gesch.*, II, 2, p. 266) before the "four archae" to which he belonged had completed their term.

[2] A new, much improved, text of *IG*[2] I 310 has now been published by Johnson (*AJA*, 1931, pp. 31 ff.), who notes (pp. 35, 39 ff.) that the records on Face D of the stone (Col. I) are different in composition and content from those on Face A (Col. II and III) and Face B (Col. IV). He thinks it possible that the entire stone contained the "accounts" of many years, Face D those of 434/3–430/29 B.C., Face A those of 429/8 B.C., and Face B those of three or more years. But it seems to me that the view taken in the text of the composite character of this document is required by *IG*[2] I 91, ll. 24 ff. (where a single annual *stele* listing property on hand together with receipts and expenditures is clearly envisaged), and by the preserved titles and indications of the record itself: Face A is the inventory (of the Opisthodomos?), followed in frg. V by the receipts of the year — so entitled; Face B (beginning in frg. IV) contains a statement (κεφάλαιον) of the articles left in the separate temples; Face C may be a continuation of Face B and contain, in addition, the receipts of the individual shrines for the year; Face D is the account of expenditures, which were all in Attic silver, as was proper, the *hieropoii* and the Hellenotamiae figuring (doubtless as recipients, with παρέλαβον or something similar supplied), and the payments being credited to the various deities, who accordingly appear as often as their funds were drawn upon. The change from the genitive to the dative in posting the names of the deities whose moneys were expended (ll. 291 ff.) is paralleled by *IG*[2] I 304A, ll. 5, 6, and *IG*[2] I 304B, ll. 43, 59; 305, l. 11; cf. Wilamowitz, *Arist. u. Athen*, II, p. 212, n. 2. *IG*[2] I 313/4 furnish an analogy for a document thus composite in character.

of the Opisthodomos reserved for the Tamiae of the Other Gods (IG^2 I 92, ll. 52 ff.). Since the solitary copy of these accounts-inventories which has reached us does not belong to a Panathenaic year, we do not know whether the "four archae" were concerned with it or not. But there is no warrant in IG^2 I 91/2 for supposing that they were. The instructions given them by the *demos* (ll. 18 ff.) at the time of their first appointment make no mention of collective action by four boards: the instructions given to the Tamiae (ll. 57 ff.), in which "the four archae who submitted their accounts successively from Panathenaia to Panathenaia"[1] were directed to collaborate with the office-holders of the moment in counting and weighing the ἱερὰ χρέματα then uncounted and unweighed, were addressed exclusively to the Tamiae of Athena, for the simple reason, pointed out by Meyer (*Forsch.*, II, pp. 95 f.), that theretofore no Tamiae of the Other Gods existed (Kolbe, *Sitz. Ber. Akad.*, 1927, pp. 322 ff.). On the other hand, it is to the Tamiae of the Other Gods alone that the order is given to incorporate with their inventory in the *stele* which they are required to set up the statement of annual receipts and expenditures which they were to submit to the *logistae* for audit. An inventory alone is all that is required of the Tamiae of Athena; and, as we have seen already (*above*, p. 16, n. 1), that was all they published, for even if the so-called accounts of these Tamiae were issued by them in collaboration with the *logistae*, and not by the *logistae* alone, they had been issued before 434 B.C. and did not begin to be issued quadrennially till 430/29 B.C. (*below*, p. 99).

There is no question that the inventories of the Treasurers of Athena were issued for or by the "four archae." The "four archae" are expressly mentioned in the inventories themselves

---

[1] As Kirchhoff (*Abh. Ber. Akad.*, 1864, pp. 10 ff.) first pointed out (cf. Meyer, *Forsch.*, II, p. 95, n. 1), the inclusion of ἀεί in this formula shows that not only the last four boards of Tamiae, i.e., those for 438/7–435/4 B.C., but also all earlier boards in addition were drawn into the business. I doubt, however, whether there were any earlier boards in a position really to collaborate. It seems to me improbable that dedications were placed in the shrine which we call the Parthenon before the chryselephantine statue of Athena was finished in 438/7 B.C. (*above*, p. 93). According to subsequent practice the "four archae" for the *penteteris* 438/7–435/4 would be the proper parties to collaborate.

in the Great Panathenaic years at the heads of the groups of four into which they fall (IG^2 I 232, 256, 276; 236, 260; 240; 264, 280; 244, 268; 248, 272, 286). But as regards the "accounts" of these officials the evidence is conflicting. In 430/29–427/6 and 426/5–423/2 B.C. not only was the *penteteris* of the "four archae" the period covered by the published accounts, but an auditing by the *logistae* was done for each quadrennium as a whole at its termination, and finally in 422 B.C. for the entire period of eleven years for which the debts were then outstanding (IG^2 I 324; Meritt, *Athenian Calendar*, Plates).[1] Similarly, the accounts published in IG^2 I 302 cover the *penteteris* from 418/7 to 415/4 B.C. On the other hand, IG^2 I 295 is an account for one single conciliar year (433/2 B.C.), and IG^2 I 296 is an account for another (432/1 B.C.); and we may, I think, surmise that a third annual account was issued for the year 431/0 B.C. (IG^2 I 294/299/308?).[2]

It seems to me that we are bound to conclude that the accounts of the Treasurers of Athena were prepared for publication annually till 430/29 B.C.[3] and quadrennially thereafter.

---

[1] This does not preclude its being also done for each year separately, in connection with the yearly auditing of the complete accounts of the Tamiae. This fact has, I think, been overlooked by Meyer (*Forsch.*, II, p. 131). IG^2 I 324 is not only unique in that in it alone the *logistae* appear as the subject, but also in that it includes, along with a detailed statement of the loans made in the final quadrennium, summaries of the total amounts of all loans outstanding and computations of interest. Elsewhere each year's transactions are entered separately; there are no quadrennial summaries, even when four years' expenditures are inscribed on a single Tablet; and there is no reckoning of interest. IG^2 I 324 is also unique in combining in one statement the accounts of both boards of Treasurers. The interest was doubtless computed as well as published, not annually, but quadrennially (IG^2 I 324, ll. 98 ff.). "The former *logistae*" of this document are those, not of the preceding year, but of the preceding *penteteris*. It thus appears that the accountants, like the Tamiae, constituted at this time for certain purposes a board of four *archae*.

[2] Since IG^2 I 301 is an account for a single year, there is no place open for it in this epoch (see *above*, p. 19, n. 1). If IG^2 I 300 belongs prior to 426/5 B.C., as seems probable, it can be taken as part of the *penteteric* record for 430/29–427/6 B.C. It is improbable that the *penteteric* record for 426/5–423/2 B.C. was inscribed on stone twice. [West (*Trans. Amer. Phil. Assoc.*, 1930, pp. 235 f.) gives some further reasons for dating IG^2 I 294/299/308 in 431/0 rather than 430/29 B.C.]

[3] At the time of the Samian War (441–439/8 B.C.) accounts were posted for an episode collectively (IG^2 I 293); but the Panathenaic *penteteris* was not observed. At the end of the year 430/29 B.C. changes were made in the method followed thereto-

We have lost the account for the *penteteris* 422/1–419/8 B.C. That for 414/3–411/0 was inscribed in part at least and probably in its entirety on the reverse and left margin of the stone which gives us *IG*² I 296 (*above*, p. 70, n. 1); that for 410/09–407/06 is largely in our possession (*IG*² I 304A, 301, 304B). But the rôle of the "four archae" in making and inscribing the "accounts" is not palpable. Indeed the grouping of the accounts into fours may be the work of the *logistae* and not of the "four archae" of Tamiae at all. After 411/0 B.C. the accounts were all *posted* annually; for even when the accounts of two years appear on a single stone, notwithstanding that they belong to the first and last years (410/09 and 407/06) of one *penteteris*, they were inscribed, in part at least (cf. ll. 77–93 of *IG*² I 304B), in a totally different script; hence at different times. So, too, the accounts for one of the intervening years of this same *penteteris* (409/08, *IG*² I 301) were a separate issue (see *above*, pp. 33 f.). After 407/06 B.C., when the accounts show no signs whatsoever of having been manipulated by the *logistae*, and were, doubtless, published as they were drawn up by the Tamiae, they cover in each case the transactions of a single year — from Panathenaia to Panathenaia; as do, for that matter, the accounts of 407/06 B.C. itself. When we ascribe the *penteteric* grouping of the "accounts" to the *logistae*, the rôle of the "four archae" is circumscribed to participation in making the inventories of the Pronaos, Parthenon, and Hekatompedon. How long was it maintained?

In the fourth century, as is well known, the Tamiae of each year were completely independent. No trace of the "four archae" is to be found. The last occasion on which, in our record, the "four archae" acted as a single body was in the archonship of [Glaukippos],[1] when they handed over a com-

---

fore in assigning to *phylae* the Secretaries of the Tamiae of Athena and possibly also of the Hellenotamiae (*above*, p. 10, n. 1). It was either then that the decision was taken to post the accounts of the past year, not immediately, but when the *penteteris* was completed, or a year earlier, at the end of the Panathenaic *penteteris*.

[1] The Archon's name is restored, but it suits the space and is otherwise probable. This bronze differed from all the other tablets included in the inventory in that it alone is described as a gift ὑπὸ τῶν τεττάρων ἀρχῶν. The significance of this specification is clear if the dedication was made in the archonship of Glaukippos; for during the pre-

memorative tablet of bronze to be set up on the Acropolis, where it was found when commissioners appointed on the initiative of Lycurgus were making an inventory of the bronzes on the citadel (*IG*² II 1498). Since the "four archae" for 410/09–407/06 B.C. were not yet in existence in Glaukippos' archonship, the reference must be to the "four archae" of the preceding *penteteris*. Hence this text contributes nothing to our knowledge on this point, since we know from *IG*² I 248, 272, and 286 that the "four archae" (five rather) for 414/3–411/0 B.C. published their inventories collectively.

Unfortunately the prescripts of all three inventories for 410/09 B.C., the opening year of the following *penteteris*, in which the formula αἱ τέτταρες ἀρχαί was due, have been lost. But since the inventories of the next two years of the *penteteris* (409/08 and 408/07 B.C.) have the usual non-initial prescripts of the past (*IG*² I 254, 274, and 275, 255: there is room in the *lacuna* only for the common prescript), we should expect the lost inventories of Glaukippos' year to begin as usual with τάδε παρέδοσαν αἱ τέτταρες ἀρχαί. But this does not mean that in this case the four boards of Treasurers, acting in conjunction with the Tamiae elect for 406/05 B.C., published the three sets of four inventories all together in 406 B.C. We have already seen reasons for the belief that the inventories of the Pronaos, now stereotyped, for 410/09, 409/08, and 407/06 B.C. — the latter minus the prescript, which was to be filled in later — were cut on stone in July, 409 B.C., ready, when the Treasurers for 407/06 B.C. had added their quota, for the *stele* of the last three years (the inventory for 410/09 B.C. had a *stele* of its own, which was doubtless set up when inscribed) to be erected by the "four archae" at the end of the *penteteris*. But in consequence of the events of July, 406 B.C. — the expropriation of

ceding *penteteris* there had been five *archae*, not four. The Tamiae of the Four Hundred had no part in the gift, and the other Tamiae took pains to exclude them in the dedicatory inscription. So, too, notwithstanding that the inventory of the revolutionary Tamiae was published along with the other four, the *traditio*, of which the five inventories were the record, is credited to *the* "four archae" alone. The ostracism of the Tamiae of the Four Hundred is also disclosed by the fact that their accounts (*IG*² I 298) were relegated to the margin of the *stele* which, it seems, contained the accounts of the other boards of the *penteteris*.

the *ex-votos* by the state, and the amalgamation of the Treasurers of Athena with the Treasurers of the Other Gods into one board — the task left unfinished in 409 B.C. was never completed.

As we have already seen (*above*, p. 47), the inventory of the Hekatompedon for 409/08 B.C. (*IG*² I 274) resembles somewhat the final section of the "accounts" of 407/06 B.C. (*IG*² I 304B, ll. 77 ff.), so that it can be thought to have been inscribed by the Tamiae of 407/06 B.C.; and what holds for it is doubtless true for the inventories of 408/07 and 410/09 B.C., though they may not have been incised by the same stonecutter.[1] The inventories of the Parthenon for 410/09–407/06 B.C. are so microscopical that we forbear to make any conjecture as to their time and mode of publication; but since the Parthenon, like the Hekatompedon, received *epeteia* during the years of this *penteteris*, its inventories could not have been inscribed in advance. After 407/06 these inventories were obviously inscribed annually, one by one.

The conclusion seems clear that the collaboration of the "four archae," already weakened during the *penteteris* 410/09–407/06 B.C., came completely to an end at its expiry. And if the grouping of the "accounts" was the work of the "four archae," and not of the *logistae*, their activity in this connection ceased simultaneously. The consolidated board of Treasurers of Athena and the Other Gods at once proceeded to cut on stone and set up on the Acropolis their inventories and their accounts at the end of their annual terms of office. The "four archae" are never heard of again.[2] But the Panathenaic *pen-*

---

[1] The new model drawn up in 410/09 B.C. (*above*, pp. 53, 59) was not adhered to as slavishly as the old model it replaced: variations occur in script (*above*, p. 47), in the spelling out of numerals (*above*, p. 55), and in prescript (*above*, p. 50, n. 1, l. 187).

[2] Something analogous is found in the requirement that "the Tamiae of the Goddess who held office since Molon's archonship should be present" at the making of the inventory of the Chalkotheke (*IG*² II 120); for Molon's year was the first of a Panathenaic *penteteris* (362/1 B.C.: Ol. 104 3). If the Tamiae of the four years concerned (334/3–331/0 B.C.) were associated with the quadrennial Commission of Lycurgus in preparing the statement published in *IG*² II 1496, as seems probable, we have again something like the "four archae"; but here the *penteteric* continuity belongs to the Commission. None the less, it did affect the four boards of Tamiae. Since the beginning and end of the stone are lost, we do not know what period was covered by the

teteris persisted as a unit in the operations of the Tamiae during the fourth century (*above*, p. 14), and under Lycurgus (334/3–323/2 B.C.) *penteteric* posting, not perhaps of the *corpus* of the *anathemata*, but of accessions made to it, was introduced (*below*, p. 124) — an approximation, like other reforms of the epoch, to Periclean practice.

"accounts" of the Tamiae published in *IG²* II 1492B. Like those of *IG²* I 293 they may have dealt with an episode, the Four Years' War (*Hellenistic Athens*, pp. 112 ff.) — thus including the record for 307/06 B.C. as well as those of 306/05 and 305/04 (*below*, p. 125). In that event they were not *penteteric*. But they can have covered the quadrennium 306/05–303/02 (Ol. 118 3–119 2).

THE AMALGAMATION OF THE TWO BOARDS

THE question left pending in the opening section of this study (*above*, p. 7), as to whether it was in 406 or 405 B.C. that the amalgamation of the two boards of Treasurers into a single *collegium* of Tamiae of Athena and the Other Gods occurred, has now been settled; and it remains simply to assemble the evidence. We have seen (*above*, p. 92) that the inventory *IG*² II 1502 was issued by the Tamiae of Athena and the Other Gods; yet, since it lists the Nikae that were minted and these were converted into money in 406/05 B.C. (*above*, pp. 89 f.), it has to be dated in 406/05. Already in 406/05 B.C. we encounter the attenuated inventory of the Parthenon issued by the joint board (*above*, p. 57). It can be safely assumed that the *collegium* which used the new type of record originated it. We are struck by the disorderly publication and abrupt termination of the accounts of the Tamiae of Athena for 407/06 B.C. (*IG*² I 304B) and shall not err probably in connecting it with the abrogation of this board in Hekatombaion, 406 B.C. (*above*, pp. 32, 89). We note the novel form of the accounts for 406/05 and 405/04 B.C. (*above*, pp. 34 f., 80 f.). And finally we interpret in this sense the cessation in 407/06 B.C. of *peneteric* posting of inventories and accounts, and of the issuing of inventories of the Pronaos. We note further that the Treasurers for 405/04 (*IG*² I 255a; *above*, p. 13) designate themselves Tamiae simply. It was only when there was a single board, and hence no chance of ambiguity, that they named themselves thus compendiously.[1] This was the case before 434 B.C. During the sixth and early fifth centuries the Treasurers were frequently addressed as Tamiae without further determinative (*IG*² I 393, 3/4, 75, 355,

---

[1] In *IG*² I 324 the reference to Tamiae of the Other Gods in lines 54 ff. enabled the *logistae* to use the simple title for the Tamiae of Athena in lines 1 ff. *IG*² I 378 (430/29 B.C.) is too fragmentary for use in this connection.

358; Arist. *Ath. Pol.* 4 2, 7 3, 8 1), or as Tamiae ἐκ πόλεος (*IG²* I 359–361). So, too, in 434 B.C. (*IG²* I 92, l. 39), in instructions issued before Tamiae of the Other Gods had been chosen, the brief title Tamiae suffices.[1] This was also the case in the fourth century after 342/1 B.C., when the two boards were again amalgamated. Then they regularly issued their inventories as Tamiae simply (*IG²* II 1455, 1456, 1462, 1466, 1468, 1469, 1471, 1491; cf. Arist. *Ath. Pol.* 60 3).[2] Not only did the Treasurers call themselves Tamiae simply in 405/04 B.C., but in that year they observed the practice which the Treasurers of Athena and the Other Gods followed during the whole period of their subsequent existence (Kolbe, *Philologus*, 1930, p. 262) of prefixing the names of the entire board to their inventories. Finally, as we have already pointed out (*above*, pp. 57 ff.), the inventories issued in 406/05 and 405/04 B.C. resemble closely the inventories used by the Treasurers of Athena and the Other Gods, not merely in the items they include, but also in the phrases by which they are described and the order in which they follow one another. There was a distinct breach in the continuity of the inventories in style and arrangement at the end of 407/06 B.C., none at the end of 406/05 or at the beginning of 403/02 B.C. The main point, however, is this. Once it has been shown that the creation of the amalgamated board antedates 405/04 B.C., we are bound to go back to 406 B.C. for an appropriate occasion for the change.

There cannot, I think, be the slightest doubt that it was in July, 406 B.C., that the decision was reached to amalgamate the two boards of Treasurers; and in all probability the same decree [3] of the *demos* which expropriated the dedications placed

[1] The context of ταμίαι in line 30 shows that the Tamiae of the Other Gods are meant.

[2] Exceptionally (*IG²* II 1458, 1629, l. 215, and Arist. *Ath. Pol.* 47 1) and not in prescripts where we have official utterances of the Tamiae themselves, they are called Tamiae of the Goddess or Tamiae of Athena. They began to call themselves Tamiae of Athena in 307/06 B.C. (*IG²* II 1484, 1493). See *below*, p. 118.

[3] There was no time for *nomothetic* action. Since the amalgamation was virtually the suppression of the board of Tamiae of the Other Gods, with attendant transfer of their duties to the new *collegium* (*below*, p. 141), *ekklesiastic* action alone was demanded; for it was by *psephisma*, and not by *nomos*, that a separate board of Treasurers of the Other Gods had been created (*IG²* I 91/2).

the control of all the ἱερὰ χρήματα in the hands of a single *colle-gium* of Tamiae, as was planned in 411 B.C.

This being so, a causal connection between the two decisions must have existed. The instructions issued in 434 B.C. for the guidance of the Treasurers of the Other Gods just created in-cluded an order to assemble in the Opisthodomos articles of gold and silver belonging to the other gods and goddesses of Attica. The one inventory-account of the new board which we possess shows that this was done (*IG*² I 310). From the ac-counts of the *logistae* for 426/5–423/2 B.C. (*IG*² I 324) we see that the moneys at the disposal of the Tamiae of the Other Gods belonged to at least thirty-five deities. The inventory-account discloses that the articles of gold and silver in their keeping belonged to an equally large number of shrines. It also reveals that the jurisdiction of the Tamiae of the Other Gods extended to *kosmos* and sacrificial vessels or money of the Other Gods left in the local shrines; for the first part of Col. III of *IG*² I 310 contained a statement of the value of such articles headed by the caption κεφά[λαιον τõν ἐν τοῖς] νεõͅς. Included in it were objects or sums of gold and silver alone. Obviously some line was drawn in 434 B.C. between articles which could be as-sembled fittingly in the Opisthodomos and articles which could not be removed from the local shrines. The line drawn was probably double: value for conversion into coin, and local need for worship.

The shrines of the Other Gods were situated, many of them, outside the city, at points like Sunion, Zoster, Pallene, Muny-chia, Phaleron, Salamis. After the occupation of Decelea by the Spartans (413 B.C.) the Treasurers of the Other Gods must have found it difficult to include in their inventories-accounts the *epeteia* of many of the shrines within their jurisdiction (Meyer, *Gesch. d. Alt.*, IV, pp. 533 ff.). They doubtless had to leave the control in some cases to the local authorities, so far as the articles in question were not in, or gathered for safe-keeping into, neighboring fortresses. The jurisdiction of the Tamiae was thus in fact circumscribed to a much smaller group of shrines. But, since their primary function was the custody of the money, and gold and silver in bullion and plate, assembled in the Opisthodomos, the more important shrinkage in the duties of the Tamiae of the Other Gods was occasioned by the withdrawal by the state for its war needs of the total accumulation of ready money in the Opisthodomos. This was a *fait accompli* by 411 B.C.

The decision taken in 411 B.C. to consolidate the two boards of Treasurers into one may have been motivated wholly in a desire to simplify management. Such an impulse underlay the entire scheme of administrative reform put forward by the moderates in that year (*CAH*, V, p. 339). Or the Theramenists may have envisaged already the necessity which arrived in 406 B.C. In any event the proposal to amalgamate was rejected by the *nomothetae*. But once the people came to the conclusion that no means existed for carrying on the war farther except by laying hands on all the objects of value in all the shrines of the country, the project was revived. A single board would be more efficient for the task contemplated; and easier to deal with. Consolidation would forestall questions as to the order in which the two groups of shrines and their individual members should make the sacrifice of their sacred objects. The secularization of religious properties that were used in worship or consecrated in the shrines to serve as monuments of the piety of individuals and of the glory of the people, its colonies, Council, priests, or private citizens came easily within the purview of enlightened men like Pericles and Theramenes and his associates; but it must have gone against the grain of a large portion of the population of Attica as well as of the personnel attached to the various shrines.[1] Even fifty years later Demosthenes concluded one of his orations (XXII 69–78) with an eloquent denunciation of the outrage done to the piety, pride, and sense of gratitude of the Athenians by his adversary (Androtion) in having the *ex-votos*, with all their historic sug-

---

[1] The care taken to avoid offending religious sensibilities is disclosed by the euphemism employed by the orator who drafted the resolution. Cf. Demetrius, *de eloc.*, 281: ὁ τὰς Νίκας τὰς χρυσᾶς χωνεύειν κελεύων καὶ καταχρῆσθαι τοῖς χρήμασιν εἰς τὸν πόλεμον οὐχ οὕτως εἶπεν προχείρως, ὅτι κατακόψωμεν τὰς Νίκας εἰς τὸν πόλεμον· δύσφημον γὰρ ἂν οὕτως καὶ λοιδοροῦντι ἐοικὸς ἦν τὰς θεάς, ἀλλ' εὐφημότερον, ὅτι συγχρησόμεθα ταῖς Νίκαις εἰς τὸν πόλεμον· οὐ γὰρ κατακόπτοντι τὰς Νίκας ἔοικεν οὕτως ῥηθέν, ἀλλὰ συμμάχους μεταποιοῦντι. Also *Quintil.* IX 2 92.

gestiveness, converted into more massive, less perishable, and doubtless more serviceable articles (*phialae, amphores*) of temple furniture. Androtion had, of course, less imperious necessity for his iconoclasm than the politicians of 406 B.C. But he had not effected secularization at all (*below*, pp. 118 ff.). It can have been thought that the work of demolishing the sacred vessels would proceed more smoothly in 406/04 B.C. if it were in the hands of one board instead of two.[1] And, once the plate was melted down and the coins of gold and silver manufactured from it came back to the hands of the Tamiae, they could be disbursed as part of a single stock. Indeed it must have been no longer possible to say to which particular deity specific coins belonged. The articles in many of the lesser shrines were so few and small that they were doubtless melted down together. The complexity of bookkeeping entailed in accounting for the last remnants of the money in the Opisthodomos disbursed according to the statement appended by the Treasurers to their accounts for the year 406/05 B.C. (*IG*² I 305, ll. 13 ff.; cf. *above*, pp. 29, 77) contrasts with the simplicity of designation (χρυσίο Ἀττικô στατῆρας) used in the records drafted in the new style (*IG*² II 1686, 1687). Once the last resources of the state were pooled through the agency of the melting pot, it was desirable to entrust the handling of them to a single board of Tamiae.

But, while giving due weight to these advantages to be gained by centralizing authority in a single board, we shall doubtless not err in recognizing as the decisive motive for the amalgamation a reform instituted simultaneously in the administration of the *ex-votos* which escaped expropriation. Sadly depleted by the removal of what had the greatest intrinsic value, they were no longer left dispersed in the Pronaos, Parthenon, Hekatompedon, Opisthodomos, and wherever the golden Nikae had been kept. One chamber of the Temple sufficed for the remainder. Naturally the one chosen was the *cella* of the Goddess herself. Its bareness would have been otherwise depressing

---

[1] On other occasions when the melting down of votive offerings occurred the work was entrusted to extraordinary Commissioners (*IG*² I 379; Philoch. in *Harpocr. s.v.* πομπεῖα, cf. Kirchner, *PA*, 915; *below*, p. 113, n. 2; *IG*² II 1493, 1534B, 1539).

to Athena and her worshippers. In the Hekatompedon, accordingly, the *ex-votos* were assembled, irrespective of whether they belonged to Athena or to the Other Gods. The task of watching over them, correspondingly lessened, was entrusted appropriately to ten Tamiae of Athena and the Other Gods. With this view as to the prime cause for the consolidation of the two boards accords the current opinion as to the reason for their separation again. By 385 B.C. the number and value of the *anathemata* had so increased as a result of new offerings that the care of keeping and cataloguing them called for the creation once more of Tamiae of the Other Gods. The *cella* of the Temple, too, must have become seriously congested by that time.

XII

THE LATER HISTORY OF THE TEMPLE PROPERTIES [1]

AS is well known, the Tamiae of Athena and the Other Gods issued three inventories annually of the sacred articles in the Hekatompedon. In one were listed dedications that belonged in the *cella* of the Temple itself; in another, objects which had been taken to it from the Parthenon; and in the third, objects which had been taken to it from the Opisthodomos. The one gold crown left in 405/04 B.C. in the Pronaos was not included, naturally, in these inventories; and, since it would have been absurd to devote to it a separate inventory, and since the practice of dedicating objects in this part of the Temple had been given up in 412 B.C., no inventory of the Pronaos was issued by the amalgamated board of Treasurers. There is, however, one exception to the general rule that only articles actually in the Hekatompedon should be inventoried. Objects left behind in the Opisthodomos, some then or formerly in chests, one of which is designated as the property of Artemis Brauronia, while others were certainly hers even though not so designated, were included in the first inventory along with the objects in the Hekatompedon not transferred to it from the Parthenon or the Opisthodomos. Logically they should have appeared in a fourth inventory under the caption ἐν τῷ ’Οπισθοδόμῳ; and after 386/5 B.C., in so far as they belonged to the Other Gods, they were inventoried separately.

Apart from the properties of Athena, and a drinking cup of Zeus Polieus which had been in the Hekatompedon scine 428/7 B.C., the objects listed in these New Style inventories belonged, in all cases where ownership is noted, to Artemis Brauronia,

---

[1] Hans Lehner's justly esteemed work *Ueber die athenischen Schatzverzeichnisse des vierten Jahrhunderts* (Strassburg Diss., 1890) furnishes the basis for the study of this subject. It has been antiquated, but not superseded, by the labor of Kirchner and his associates on the Editio Minor of *Inscriptiones Graecae*.

Demeter and Kore, the Anakes, Aphrodite, and Poseidon from Sunion (IG^2 II 1401, note). There is no trace of any more of the thirty-five deities whose money had been borrowed by the state prior to 422 B.C. (IG^2 I 324: Meritt, *Athenian Calendar*, p. 22) and the equally large number whose properties had been catalogued by the Tamiae of the Other Gods in 429/8 B.C. (IG^2 I 310). Nor does a larger number of deities appear in the inventories published by the Treasurers of the Other Gods [1] after they were set up again as a separate board in 385/4 B.C. The deities concerned were substantially the same:[2] Poseidon disappears,[3] but Meter is added (IG^2 II 1445, l. 24).

After 386/5 B.C. the Treasurers of Athena issued one inventory alone. In it the articles were listed irrespective of their place of origin and place of deposit. Some attempt was made to group them according to their character (Bannier, *Rh. Mus.*, 1911, p. 43; IG^2 II p. 24, note); but it was not carried beyond the beginning of the inventory, since in its major portion all kinds of votives follow one another in the wildest confusion. This disorder may have been lessened somewhat by the insertion, over certain groups, of a specification of place of deposit (IG^2 II 1414, l. 28: ἐν τῷ Ἑ[κατομπέδωι (?)]); but the checking up of the objects by an inventory thus drafted must have been a tedious operation if it was conducted conscientiously. At some date to be determined later (*below*, p. 118, n. 1) a change was made, the effect of which is manifest in the inventories of the ensuing years [4] (IG^2 II 1415; 1421/4, 1423, 374/3 B.C.; 1422, 371/0 B.C. [?]; Ἀρχ. Δελτίον, 1927/8, p. 128, 369/8 B.C.; IG^2 II 1425, 368/7 B.C.; 1426; 1428 = Ἀρχ. Δελτίον, 1927/8, p. 126, 367/6 B.C.; 1429 ff.).[5] The articles in the Hekatompedon, whether native there or in the Parthenon and Opisthodomos,

---

[1] That this was their title is shown by IG^2 II 1541.

[2] It is uncertain what became of the *phialae* and *karchesion* "from the Anakeion" (IG^2 II 1400, l. 44) after 386/5 B.C.

[3] Only one article "of this god" is concerned and it was a παρακαταθήκη, or temporary deposit.

[4] Minor changes, stylistic in character, were made in 374/3 (the arrangement of the inventory in columns) and at *c*. 370 B.C. (IG^2 II p. 37).

[5] Line 9 of IG^2 II 1426 should be restored ἐν τῷ [ὀπισθοδόμῳ τῆς χαλκοθήκης]; cf. IG^2 II 1471, ll. 60, 63. The phrase ἐν τῇ χαλκοθήκῃ αὐτῇ, which appears in IG^2 II 120 and 1440, is explicable when it is seen that articles were also stored in its *opisthodomos*.

were catalogued as one *corpus*, according to the materials of which they were made (gold; silver; bronze, ivory, wood, etc.), a special category being reserved for the miscellaneous objects taken (mainly) [1] "from the Parthenon" in 406 B.C. The properties of Athena in the Opisthodomos, those in the Ancient Temple (the Erechtheum), and those in the Chalkotheke and its *opisthodomos* were included in the same inventory, but they were recorded each in a list by itself under appropriate captions. Theretofore the articles in the Chalkotheke alone had been segregated (*IG*² II 1414, ll. 38 ff.); those in the Opisthodomos had been entered in the main catalogue (*IG*² II 1412, l. 28; 1414, ll. 19, 21; cf. Ἀρχ. Δελτίον, 1927/8, p. 128, col. I, ll. 115 ff.), without seemingly a specific designation of place such as is found before 385/4 B.C. (*IG*² II 1388 + 1408, ll. 11 ff., 1409, ll. 5 f.); and so had those in the Ancient Temple (*IG*² II 1407, ll. 28; 1414, l. 26; cf. Ἀρχ. Δελτίον, 1927/8, p. 128, col. III, ll. 68 f., 71 f.).[2]

After their reconstitution as a separate board in 385 B.C. the Treasurers of the Other Gods inventoried the articles in the Opisthodomos which belonged to these deities (Lehner, *op. cit.*, p. 77; *IG*² II p. 63), that is to say, the contents of the chests of Artemis Brauronia, and the other objects there; also some of which the provenience is not recorded (one came [ἐκ τ]ὸ Μητρώιο, *IG*² II 1445, l. 24).[3] The limitation of the authority of the

---

[1] The special dating of the πήληξ χαλκῆ in Ἀρχ. Δελτίον, 1927/8, p. 126, l. 206, is to be connected somehow with the fact that this article is absent in the fifth-century inventories of the Parthenon. It probably appears in *IG*² II 1380 (*c.* 400 B.C.).

[2] Few identifications are possible — in the case of the Opisthodomos because the Tamiae of Athena had few articles on deposit there, in the case of the Ancient Temple because nearly all the articles there were dedicated after 378/7 B.C. The earliest votive in this shrine to which a precise year can be assigned was offered in 394/3 B.C. This accords with Kirchner's date (*IG*² II 1654, note) for the completion of the work on the Erechtheum; but now that we have seen that *IG*² II 1655 belongs either before 406/05 or after 386/5 B.C. (*above*, p. 49), there is little probability that *IG*² II 1654 belongs in 395/4 B.C. (cf. Kolbe, *Ber. Phil. Woch*, 1931, pp. 102 f.).

[3] They are not found in the earlier inventories. Most of them belonged to the Eleusinian Deities and Artemis Brauronia. They may be dedications made in the local shrines between *c.* 398 (*IG*² II 1388) and 386/5 B.C., and not taken at once to the Hekatompedon. At some point prior to the end of 398/7 B.C. (*IG*² II 1388, ll. 51 ff.) the inventory of the Hekatompedon received an addition entitled ἄγραφα καὶ ἄστατα ἐπέτεια, which was carried on as a separate category till 385/4 B.C., when it, and another group of *epeteia* (*IG*² II 1388, ll. 64 ff.) — those of the year 398/7 B.C. itself — were distributed

Tamiae of the Other Gods to the Opisthodomos is a return to the situation that existed before 406 B.C.[1]

Each board of Treasurers included in its inventory *epeteia* made in the several places of deposit.

At some epoch before 350/49 B.C. (*IG*² II 1436) — to be determined later as *c.* 358/5 — the inventory of the Treasurers of Athena was again remodelled, the articles being now grouped according to their character, the gold crowns coming first. A separate list was made for the Chalkotheke and its *opisthodomos* alone. This followed the model set by a new inventorying of this edifice executed on decree of the *demos* passed in 358/4 B.C. (*IG*² II 120, 1440). Thereafter no significant change was made till the reunion of the two boards of Tamiae in 342/1 B.C. (*IG*² II 1455).

The most noteworthy additions made in the early fourth century to the dedications in the charge of the Tamiae were silver *hydriae*. By 391/0 B.C. Athena Polias possessed twenty-seven of these vessels (*IG*² II 1400), whereas in *c.* 400 B.C. (*IG*² II 1385) their number was nineteen or twenty.[2] To them were added

in the body of the inventory (Bannier, *Rh. Mus.*, 1911, p. 48). The first group represents an assemblage of *epeteia*, of Athena and Artemis Brauronia mainly, made during the preceding years and hitherto "uninventoried and unweighed." As was suggested to me by my pupil, Mr. Robert Louis Stroock, recently deceased, they were doubtless kept distinct in the inventories till 385/4 B.C. because of the disposition of the items in the "book" of the *paradosis* (*IG*² II 1455, l. 44; 1457, l. 22; 1458, l. 3) used by the Tamiae in the process of checking up the articles in the Hekatompedon. We may assume that by 385 B.C. another lot of such articles had accumulated, which, so far as they did not belong to Athena, were then transferred to the Opisthodomos. Accordingly, they appear thereafter in the inventories of the Tamiae of the Other Gods.

[1] We cannot expect to find in the inventories of the fourth century the *phialae*, *karchesia*, *lebetes*, *thymiaterion*, etc., catalogued in *IG*² I 310 and 313/4, since they doubtless went into the melting pot in 406–04 B.C., and, in any event, were not described in such a way as to enable us to identify them. Bannier (*Rh. Mus.*, 1911, p. 45) proposes the identification of one of the *oinochoae* of *IG*² I 313, ll. 46 f.; 314, ll. 53 f. with the *oinochoe* listed in *IG*² II 1400, ll. 36 f., which he in turn identifies with the *oinochoe* ἱερὰ Δήμητρος of *IG*² II 1445, l. 9; but the weights are different.

[2] It seems to me likely that these *hydriae* belonged to the πομπεῖα made with the confiscated property of the Thirty (Philoch. in *Harpocr. s. v.*). It is suggested by Foucart (*BCH*, 1888, p. 288), following Michaelis and Köhler, that a golden Nike was included in the *pompeia* made from the goods of the Thirty; but our ancient texts always treat the Nikae and the *pompeia* as separate things (*IG*² I 92, l. 34; 379; II² 1493, ll. 8 ff.; [Plut.], *Lives of the Ten Orators*, 852A ff.; *Paus.* I 29). Hence when Philochoros specifies *pompeia* he excludes Nikae.

later — besides three new ones of Athena Polias and four of
Athena Nike — seven of Artemis Brauronia, three of the
Anakes, five of Demeter and Kore, and one of Aphrodite.[1] The
weight of Athena's first twenty-seven was approximately 1000

---

[1] The date of these accessions needs revision. It has been fixed by Lehner (*op.
cit.*, p. 91; cf. Kirchner, *IG*² II 1428, note) between 385/4 and 367/6 B.C. The date
ante quem must be put back at least eleven years. Since these additional *hydriae* appear already in *IG*² II 1412 and 1413, inventories of the period of disorderly arrangement, whereas *IG*² II 1421/4 (374/3 B.C.), in which it can be presumed that they were
listed at the end of col. III, belongs in arrangement to the succeeding epoch, the year
ante quem should be moved back to 376/5 B.C.; and indeed, since neither *IG*² II 1412
nor 1413 can be dated in either 376/5 or 377/6 B.C., which belong to *IG*² II 1411 and
1410, it must be moved back to 378/7. Moreover, it is by no means certain that they
were absent in 385/4 B.C. They can have appeared in the later (lost) portion of *IG*² II
1407, in a position corresponding to that in which they appear in *IG*² II 1412 and 1413.
Consequently the date *post quem* is 390/89 B.C. (*IG*² II 1400). This conclusion would
be vitiated if Lehner's observation were correct, that only part of the new *hydriae*
was listed in *IG*² II 1412, 1413. The restorations of these inventories given below,
(Appendix II) show, however, that they were all present. It remains uncertain, therefore, whether they were dedicated before or after 385/4 B.C. In favor of the earlier
date it may be urged that if those of them which belonged to Artemis Brauronia, the
Anakes, Demeter and Kore, and Aphrodite had been dedicated after the Tamiae of
the Other Gods had been set up anew, they would perhaps have gone to the Opisthodomos. Between 398/7 (*IG*² II 1388, 1393) and 390/89 B.C. (*IG*² II 1400) the treasures
of Demeter and Kore were enriched by 120 silver *phialae*. These went to the Opisthodomos in 385/4 B.C. (*IG*² II 1445, ll. 31 ff.). But there was possibly some reason connected with their use in religious ceremonies for keeping the *hydriae* all together in the
Hekatompedon. In any event, there is no ground for associating the making of the
new vessels with the melting down of *anathemata*, in 378/7 B.C.

I have taken *IG*² II 1421 and 1424 to be parts of the same inventory. Now that
Kolbe (*Philologus*, 1930, pp. 261 ff.) has shown that *IG*² II 1421 is dated in 374/3 I
do not see any alternative; for the date of *IG*² II 1424 also is manifestly 374/3 B.C.
(Hondius, *Nov. Inscr. Attic.*, p. 58; Kolbe, *Ber. Phil. Woch.*, 1926, p. 1159). The differences of style noted by Kirchner (*IG*² II 1421, p. 37) in the two pieces are illusory.
Since the left margin of the stone is preserved, *IG*² II 1424 must have been a continuation of col. I of *IG*² II 1421. In 'Αρχ. Δελτίον, 1927/8, p. 128, the stonecutter abandoned
the practice, adhered to otherwise except in lines 70–86 of col. I, of beginning a new item
with a new line when he came to the third or miscellaneous portion of the inventory. In
*IG*² II 1425 he did the same. In *IG*² II 1421/4 he maintained it longer (he was obviously
cramped for space at the right in col. IV) and abandoned it only when he turned back
to the lower part of col. I to find room for the list of articles in the Ancient Shrine. At
this point he had left a blank. Since the new Nike of 374/3 B.C. was reserved for mention
after the inventory of the Ancient Temple and the recent accessions (*IG*² II 1424, ll. 31
ff.), *IG*² II 1421, col. I is continued directly by *IG*² II 1421 col. II, so that, without *IG*²
II 1424, col. I must have been appreciably shorter than col. II and col. III (when continued, as this should be, by the list of the *hydriae*) and col. IV. The original portion of
col. I was sufficiently wide for both weights (outset at the left) and text. The addition

drachmas each [1] — the same value as was fixed by law on occasions for crowns voted by the *demos* (*IG²* II 1496, l. 52, note). It seems clear that they were made to conform to a standard set by public authority. The weights of the twenty-three new *hydriae* fluctuate from what seems to have been a norm in three cases (Athena, the Anakes, and Aphrodite) of 900 drachmas, in the fourth case (Artemis) of 950 drachmas, and in the fifth (Nike) of 1000 drachmas. But their conformity to set sizes is also unmistakable. That they were all, unlike crowns, etc., public offerings is indicated by the complete failure of the records to connect any of them with specific donors. The place of deposit of all these *hydriae* was the Hekatompedon, and their custodians were the Tamiae of Athena even after the reëstablishment in 385/4 B.C. of a separate board of Treasurers of the Other Gods. These officials did not receive charge of those of them which belonged to the Other Gods, as might have been expected. They could have got them only if they had been diverted to the Opisthodomos.

The division of authority between the two boards made in 386/5 B.C. thus worked to the disadvantage of the Treasurers of the Other Gods; and since the *ex-votos* of the Other Gods collected in the Opisthodomos between 434 B.C. and 406 B.C., through being objects of gold and silver that were convertible into money, did not survive the crisis of 406–04 B.C.; and since the policy of assembling such articles on the Acropolis was not resumed in 403 B.C., or resumed only half-heartedly (*above*, p. 112, n. 4), the Tamiae of the Other Gods had a comparatively restricted charge. After 406 B.C. the supervision of the votives in the great majority of the shrines of the Other Gods must have rested, as before 434 B.C., in the hands of the local authorities.[2] At the end of the Peloponnesian War the local shrines were probably impoverished. Seeing that the Boeotians took the

---

had no weights to record. It was therefore natural that its text should have lines long enough to fill the column; and, consequently, that new items should be begun in incomplete lines. [Woodward restores *IG²* II 1421/3/4 with three columns only; cf. *above*, p. 95, n. 2.]

[1] The fact that each group averages something less than the norm may be attributed to deductions to cover the cost of manufacture.

[2] *Epistatae* of the Asklepieion in the Piraeus appear in *IG²* II 47, ll. 28 f. in *c.* 400 B.C.

opportunity after 413 B.C. of transferring to their own country even the doors and tiles of the village houses and stables, they doubtless did not spare the movable property of the undefended shrines. At Eleusis the *epistatae* may have had to recognize the concurrent jurisdiction of the Tamiae during the last period of the war (*above*, p. 93, n. 2). The presence of articles belonging to Demeter and Kore in the Hekatompedon between 403 and 385 B.C. and their augmentation even thereafter are explicable only on the basis of such concurrence; but there cannot be much doubt that in the early fourth century the Commissioners of Eleusis gained their complete independence.[1] From *IG*[2] II 1541 we learn that between 361/0 and 357/6 B.C. the Tamiae of the Other Gods transferred to them a lot of objects which they had received in 363/2 B.C. from Leptines of Koile (cf. Kirchner, *PA*, 9046), to whom the people had doubtless entrusted some extraordinary commission. The articles were miscellaneous in character, of no great intrinsic value, and many of them defective (Lehner, *op. cit.*, pp. 80 ff.). They obviously belonged to Demeter and Kore, and Leptines conceived the Opisthodomos to be the proper place for them. We do not know why they were taken from the custody of the Tamiae of the Other Gods. It may have been simply a question of finding storage room for them; but the transfer may be significant of a general policy of decentralization, which persisted till the reforms of Lycurgus. In this light we can interpret another occurrence. At some date not narrowly determinable, possibly 342/1 B.C., the Treasurers of the Other Gods were reduced in function by the creation of a standing board of Commissioners (*epistatae*) who

[1] The extant *tabulae* of the *epistatae* of Eleusis (*IG*[2] II 1540 ff.) go back beyond the middle of the fourth century. At this time the *penteteris* for which they served began with the first year of the Olympiad; in 422/1 B.C. (*IG*[2] I 311) it began with the third and ran from Great Panathenaia to Great Panathenaia. In or about 411/0 B.C. their term became annual (*IG*[2] I 313/4; cf. Sardemann, *Eleusinische Uebergabeurkunden*, p. 12). Between 403 and 401/0 B.C. Eleusis was independent of Athens (Arist. *Ath. Pol.* 40 4). We may connect the limits of the fourth-century *penteteris* with the fact that the first *epistatae* after the reunion began to serve in 400/399 B.C., Ol. 95 1. In the carved relief which surmounts the inventory of the Tamiae of Athena and the Other Gods for 400/399 B.C. (*IG*[2] II 1374, note; cf. Lehner, *op. cit.*, pp. 121 ff.) the matronly figure who grasps the hand of Athena is doubtless Demeter, and the subject of the scene the reunification of Athens and Eleusis.

took charge of the offerings made in the shrine of Artemis Brauronia.[1]

The Tamiae of the Other Gods probably existed for forty-four years as a separate board. If *IG*² II 1454 is restored correctly, as seems to me probable,[2] they are still found in 343/2 B.C. They had ceased to exist in 341/0 B.C. (*IG*² II 1455). As the fourth century advanced, offerings made to the local gods must have enriched the local shrines and reduced by comparison the value of the objects concentrated in the possession of the central board. Nor did these Tamiae have exclusive control of the Opisthodomos. The Tamiae of Athena had charge of a few articles deposited there ('Αρχ. Δελτίον, 1927/8, p. 128,

---

[1] The date assigned by Hondius, 376–373 B.C. (*Nov. Inscr. Attic.*, p. 67), rests on quite insecure foundations (*below*, p. 130, n. 1). The extant inventories of the *epistatae* belong after 350 B.C. For all I can see the Commission can have been established in 342/1 B.C., when the Tamiae of the Other Gods ceased to exist.

[2] The restoration ταμίαι τῶ[ν τῆς θεοῦ] is possible epigraphically; but if the boards were already recombined this title would be exceptional, since the title invariably used in the prescripts of inventories prior to 307/06 B.C. for the reamalgamated board was ταμίαι simply (*above*, p. 105, n. 2). If they were not combined, what have Tamiae of Athena to do with *anathemata* ἐν τῷ 'Αφροδισίῳ? As late as 346/5 B.C. (*IG*² II 1442) the Treasurers call themselves [τα]μίαι τῆς [θεοῦ]. The last certain reference to Treasurers of the Other Gods occurs in 361/0–357/6 B.C. (*IG*² II 1541). But in 352 B.C., when Demosthenes delivered the oration against Timokrates, the two boards were probably distinct, since otherwise we should have expected some intimation that the two distinct boards there mentioned belonged to the past (*Dem.* XXIV, 136; cf. *below*, pp. 129 f.). No trace of votives of the Other Gods, such as appear in *IG*² II 1455 (341/0 B.C.), are found in the inventories of the years 350/49 B.C. (*IG*² II 1436) or 344/3 B.C. (*IG*² II 1443), or of the intervening years, which, though fragmentary, might be expected to reveal their presence, if they were really there. Moreover, in *IG*² II 1443, ll. 139 ff. (344/3 B.C.) appear some gold *phialae* τῶν ἄλλων θεῶν. The grouping of the *ex-votos* in this way may be taken to indicate the existence of the grouping of the deities under a separate administration. The entry of these articles in an inventory of the Tamiae of Athena, and not in an inventory of the Tamiae of the Other Gods, is in order. Like the silver *hydriae* of Artemis, the Anakes, Demeter and Kore, and Aphrodite, the gold *phialae* of these deities were put in the Hekatompedon in the charge of the Tamiae of Athena (*below*, p. 122, n. 1). It may be noted further, as indicative of state interference with the *anathemata* in 342/1 B.C., that it was at this time, with a priest of the *phyle* Erechtheis, that the second of the comprehensive inventories of the Asklepieion began (*IG*² II 1533; cf. Dinsmoor, *Archons of Athens*, pp. 450 ff.: Appendix C). 342/1 B.C. was the year of the Great Panathenaia; hence appropriate for a change (*above*, p. 14). Finally, the inventory assigned to what, on this hypothesis, was the last year of the separate existence of the Tamiae of the Other Gods (343/2, *IG*² II 1454) shows peculiarities (Köhler, Kirchner, note) consistent with the idea that the votives of the Other Gods were then overhauled preparatory to the contemplated fusion of the two boards.

col. I, ll. 115 ff.); and, as we shall see presently, they had maintained throughout rights of entry to this chamber: they used it as a place of deposit for money. Now that on two occasions (378/7 and *c*. 358/5 B.C., *below*, pp. 118 ff.) old and minor articles of gold and silver had been converted into fewer, more substantial vessels, it is imaginable that the Tamiae of the Other Gods had come to seem superfluous. That what happened in *c*. 341 B.C. was their virtual absorption by the Tamiae of Athena is shown by the fact, already alluded to (*above*, pp. 104 f.), that the single board, once more restored and again in charge of the dedications of the deities thitherto grouped as the "Other Gods" as well as those of Athena, was known, not merely as Tamiae, but also as Tamiae of the Goddess (*IG*² II 244, l. 38, 337/6 B.C., cf. 1458, 1484, 1629, l. 215; 1492B, 1493), and that its duties are defined by Aristotle (*Ath. Pol.* 47 1) under the title Tamiae of Athena. From him we learn that "the Treasurers of Athena took over the statue of Athena, the Nikae, the rest of the *kosmos*, and the χρήματα in the presence of the Council." They were again, we must assume, as before 434 B.C., ταμίαι ἐξ Ἀκροπόλεως; and after 307/06 B.C. they styled themselves in the prescripts of inventories, Tamiae of the Goddess (cf., however, *IG*² II 1491).

At two points during the period between 386/5 and 341/0 B.C. the votives in charge of the Tamiae of Athena were subjected to a general overhauling, first in 378/7 B.C.[1] (Ol. 100 3) and again

---

[1] Now that we have a practically complete inventory of the Tamiae of Athena for the epoch 375/3–367/6 B.C. (Ἀρχ. Δελτίον, 1927/8, p. 128), we can observe that various articles present in *IG*² II 1400 (390/89 B.C.), 1407 (385/4 B.C.), and 1410–1418 are no longer inventoried. The most important omissions are the gold crowns. The point at which they disappeared can be inferred from the point of departure of the crowns listed in the later inventories. Beginning with the Panathenaia of 377 B.C., a gold crown was dedicated to Athena every year. In the years of the Great Panathenaia (378/7, 374/3, and 370/69 B.C.) it came to Athena as an *aristeion*; in the other years (377/6, 376/5, and 375/4 B.C.) it came to the Ancient Temple as a gift of the Council. Seemingly no crowns were dedicated in 373/2–371/0, but after 371/0 the practice was followed with yearly regularity (*IG*² II 1436). There were also private donations of crowns, notably those of Timotheos, Philippos, and Kallikleia, the wife of Thukydides, in 374/3 (*IG*² II 1424). It appears, therefore, that in 378/7 B.C. all the gold crowns then existing (cf. *IG*² II 1400, ll. 14 ff.; 1407, ll. 27 ff.), with the exception, naturally, of the crown on the head of the Nike that stood on the hand of the statue of Pheidias, and of a few crowns recently dedicated in the Ancient Temple (Ἀρχ. Δελτίον, 1927/8, p. 128,

in *c.* 358/7–356/5.[1] On each occasion articles disappeared from the inventory. After 378/7 B.C. we miss many of the objects of gold and silver theretofore in the Hekatompedon, inventoried

col. III, ll. 67 ff.), were disposed of, including the *aristeia* of the Great Panathenaia for the period following 402/01 B.C.

To this same year as the epoch of a general overhauling of the *anathemata* we are led by other data. A decree of 346/5 B.C. (*IG*² II 216/7; *below*, n. 1; Kolbe, *Philologus*, 1930, pp. 265 ff.) fixed 377/6 B.C. (archonship of Kalleas) as the starting point for the revision of which Androtion had charge, that is to say, Hekatombaion 1st or, more probably, 28th, 377 B.C.; and, in fact, the crowns which Demosthenes mentions as having been melted down by him run back to that point and no farther (Kolbe, *Philologus*, 1930, pp. 265 ff.; cf. *below*, p. 121. It need hardly be added that 378/7 B.C. was an appropriate year for an overhauling of this sort. It was the end of a Panathenaic *penteteris* (cf. *above*, p. 14). It is marked not only by the foundation of the second Delian Confederacy and the inauguration of the system of symmories with attendant reassessment of all Athenian property, but it was also the time of other important changes in administration (Glotz, *REG*, 1921, pp. 1 ff.; Calhoun, *Trans. Amer. Phil. Assoc.*, 1919, pp. 190 ff.; S. B. Smith, *Class. Phil.*, 1930, pp. 250 ff.; Bonner and Smith, *The Administration of Justice from Homer to Aristotle*, pp. 359 ff.; *below*, p. 135).

It remains to inquire what was done with the gold secured by the disposal of the crowns. It seems to me clear that it went into the golden Nike dedicated in 374/3 B.C. Ἐπιστάτ[α]ι τ[ῆς Νίκης] are mentioned in *IG*² II 1409. It now appears (West, Woodward, *above*, p. 95, n. 2) that this inventory belongs shortly after 398/7 B.C. Hence we may doubt whether the restoration τ[ῆς Νίκης] is correct. The *epistatae* are five years too late to be connected with the Nike of *IG*² II 1370/71/84 (403/2 B.C.), which, moreover, was dedicated in 426/5 B.C. (*above*, p. 91). No new Nike was added between Eukleides and 374/3 B.C. Commissioners of the Nike were active in 375/4 B.C. (*IG*² II 1421, ll. 12 ff.); and in 374/3 B.C. the Tamiae acknowledged the receipt of the statue. Is not the rapidly moving female figure in the *anaglyph* by which the inventory of the Tamiae of Athena for 377/6 B.C. is adorned (R. Schöne, *Griech. Reliefs*, taf. XV 71) a Nike? That gold secured in 378/7 B.C. was used to make gold *hydriae* of stock size is noted in the text. The silver *pinakes* inventoried in *IG*² II 1415 (375/4 B.C.?) and in the inventories of the period 374/3–367/6 B.C. may also be thought of in this connection — there was one such *pinax* in *c.* 390/89 B.C. (*IG*² II 1401, l. 24). The specimens (δοκιμεῖα) used in testing the gold that went into "the *oinochoe* of Athena, the *oinochoe* of the gods, the *phialae*, and the *thymiateria*" kept in boxes in the Hekatompedon (*IG*² II 1415; Ἀρχ. Δελτίον, 1927/8, p. 128, col. III, ll. 28 ff.) may reveal other activities of the χρυσοχόοι of 378/7 B.C.

[1] The precise year cannot be determined. The outside limits for the new inventory of the Chalkotheke are 362/1 (archonship of Molon: *IG*² II 120) and 351/0 B.C.. (archonship of Theëllos: *IG*² II 1440); but there cannot be any doubt that the period *in quo* should be narrowed from each end. The requirement that the Tamiae, starting with those of Ol. 104 3 (362/1 B.C.), should be present at the making of this inventory suggests that the work was undertaken at the end of that *penteteris* (358/7 B.C.) or in the course of the one next following (358/7–355/4 B.C.). See Kirchner, *IG*² II 120, note. The task designated in the decree prefixed to the inventory *IG*² II 1440, which is simply an adaptation of *IG*² II 120, concerned objects dedicated both in the Chal-

as "from the Parthenon" (*IG²* II 1373, 1376, 1377, 1395, 1418 [after 385/4 B.C.?]; cf. 'Αρχ. Δελτίον, 1927/8, p. 128; and the stock of the Hekatompedon became enriched, if not by twenty-three

kotheke and elsewhere: crowns were listed at the top of the appended inventory, among them one from the cleruchs at Samos, which, judging from its position in *IG²* II 1437, we might conclude was offered in the archonship of Diotimos (354/3 B.C.; cf. Lehner, *op. cit.*, p. 106). Thus we again get 354/3 B.C. as the *terminus ante quem* for the new inventory of the Chalkotheke; and we have at least an intimation that the making of this scrutiny of the articles in the Chalkotheke was part of a larger process. The inventory of the Chalkotheke was, after all, of one piece with the rest of the inventory of the Tamiae and inscribed on the same tablet. It is noteworthy that in the fourth century changes of administration affecting the Tamiae and their treasures occur regularly in the third years of Olympiads (cf. *above*, pp. 14, 118, n. 1); and, since 354/3 B.C. is excluded, we should naturally think of 358/7 B.C. as the year in which the Chalkotheke was reinventoried. But there is no necessity about this. The quadrennium followed in inventorying the chryselephantine statue of Athena ran from the fourth year of the Olympiad (Köhler, *Athen. Mitt.*, 1880, pp. 89 ff.; Panske *Leip. Stud.* 1890, pp. 18 ff.; Lehner, *op. cit.*, p. 42; *IG²* II, pp. 24 f.). A decree, perhaps of the year 385/4 B.C., perhaps four, eight, twelve, or sixteen years earlier, laid down the rule that it should be inventoried at once and reinventoried each fourth year thereafter. The statue appears in the inventories of the Tamiae subsequently either in the fourth years of the Olympiads or in the first — for such retardations see Sundwall, 'Εφ. 'Αρχ., 1909, p. 207; Kirchner, *IG²* II 1407, note. It is not found in 'Αρχ. Δελτίον, 1927/8, p. 128 (Ol. 102 4); but it can have appeared at the top of col. I in *IG²* II 1425 (Ol. 103 1), cf. *below*, p. 179. It is, therefore, permissible to think that some occasion other than the termination of a Panathenaic *penteteris* led to the creation of the Commission of which Androtion was a member. From a comparison of *IG²* II 1436 with 1437 Lehner (*op. cit.*, p. 93) infers that in 354/3 B.C. the datable crowns then existing were arranged for inventorying in chronological order; but the inference, as he himself admits, is largely subjective. And even if we accept it as valid, we may separate this process from an earlier process of separating those to be melted down from those to be left. As we shall see (*below*, p. 143), 355/4 B.C. was probably the first year of the new tribal cycle of the secretaries of the Tamiae. The alteration was doubtless arranged in 356/5 B.C. We may think of this year as an alternate for 358/7 B.C. The *terminus ante quem* for Androtion's activity is 355/4 B.C., the year of Demosthenes' oration in which he is censured. Either of the two years suggested will suit this requirement, which also makes it inadvisable to date the work of Androtion earlier than 355/4 B.C. by more than a few years. Glauketes can have held the post attributed to him by Demosthenes (XXIV 129) in 354/3 B.C.; but we have no reason to connect his alleged misdemeanor with the work of Androtion's Commission.

From *IG²* II 216/7 we learn that in 346/5 B.C. the decree of Androtion regarding the *anagraphe* of the votives was made the basis for some new regulations. 346/5 was at once the last year of the first tribal cycle of the secretaries of the Tamiae of Athena (*below*, p. 144) and the year immediately following the conclusion of a Panathenaic *penteteris*. It is possible that Androtion's disposition of the inventory was tried for ten years and reënacted; but it is more probable that *IG²* II 216/7 was timed with reference to the Great Panathenaia. It was on the occasion of this festival, e. g., in 378, 374, and 370 B.C., that earlier remodellings of this inventory had been made (*above*,

silver *hydriae* (*above*, p. 114, n. 1), by three gold *hydriae* of stock
size ('Αρχ. Δελτίον, 1927/8, p. 128, col. I, ll. 24 ff., 63; *IG*² II 1425,
ll. 19 ff.). Various crowns disappear, notably the one dedicated
by Lysander in 403 B.C. (*IG*² II 1388, l. 32; 1407, ll. 31 f.; cf.
'Αρχ. Δελτίον, 1927/8, p. 128 — where it is lacking). It has been
thought (Johnson, *AJA*, 1914, pp. 10 ff.; Hondius, *Nov. Inscr.
Attic.*, p. 59, n. 13) that in *IG*² II 216, 217 Androtion appears as
the mover of a decree of the year 377/6 B.C. dealing with the
anagraphe of the *anathemata*, and that this crisis is to be connected with the work of the Atthidograph so savagely indicted
by Demosthenes (XXII 69 ff.; XXIV 176 ff.). But this is impossible for three reasons: first, because the activity of Androtion censured in 355/4 B.C. (Diony. Hal. *Ep. ad Amm.* 4,
p. 724) cannot have preceded its arraignment by twenty-two
years; secondly because the crown dedicated by Conon after
the battle of Cnidos, which Androtion is charged with having
had melted down (*Dem.* XXII 72; XXIV 180), was still in
existence in 369/8 ('Αρχ. Δελτίον, 1927/8, p. 128, col. III, l. 67)
and 368/7 B.C. (*IG*² II 1425, l. 284); and thirdly because, as
Kolbe (*Philologus*, 1930, p. 266) has recently pointed out, the
crowns melted down by Androtion were described by Demosthenes as "rotten," yet they included, on the assumption that
his work as ῥήτωρ, χρυσοχόος, ταμίας, ἀντιγραφεύς belongs in
377/6 B.C., crowns which were in one instance — that of "the
allies" — less than one year old and in another instance —
that of Chabrias — nonexistent! It is with the second crisis,
that occurring about 358/7–356/5 B.C., that we are to connect
the activity of Androtion. On his motion and under his super-
intendence crowns that had become damaged ("rotten") were
melted down, new *phialae* and other cult articles (*ekpomata,
thymiateria, amphoriski, chrysides*) were made of the metal.

p. 111 and n. 4; cf. *below*, p. 184). It is also worth noting that in 346/5 B.C. the Tamiae
of the Athenian cleruchy at Samos in charge of the votives of the Heraion prepared an
extraordinary inventory. That this was special is shown by the fact that the παράδοσις
occurred partly in the second and partly in the fifth prytany of the year (C. Curtius,
Inschriften und Studien zur Geschichte von Samos, pp. 10 ff.). The year used in Samos
was the Attic. *IG*² II 216/7 was passed during the seventh prytany.

In 346/5 and 345/4 B.C. an unusually large number of crowns was dedicated in
Athens to Athena (*IG*² II 1443, ll. 89 ff.).

The articles used in processions were repaired.[1] It is noteworthy that in IG^2 II 1436 (350/49 B.C.) and IG^2 II 1438 the
crown dedicated by Conon no longer appears in the catalogue
of crowns. Since the list is drawn up (approximately) in chronological order it must have been posted at the top had it
existed. As we have seen, it was melted down by Androtion.
The crown dedicated as ἀριστεῖον τῆς θεὸ ἐκ Παναθηναίων in
374/3 B.C. ('Αρχ. Δελτίον, 1927/8, p. 128, col. I, l. 64) is also
gone; so are all the crowns inventoried in the Ancient Temple
in 369/8 and 368/7 B.C. Indeed the only crown older than
371/0 B.C. that appears in these inventories made subsequent
to c. 358/5 B.C. is the one dedicated in 378/7 B.C. (IG^2 1436,
l. 11; cf. 'Αρχ. Δελτίον, 1927/8, p. 128, col. I, l. 34; IG^2 II 1425,
l. 29). There was doubtless some special reason for preserving
"the *aristeion* of the Goddess from the Panathenaia" immediately following the formation of the Second Delian Confederacy. The crowns dedicated in the period beginning with 371/0
B.C. were presumably not "rotten" as yet in 358/5. The chief
"enormity" attributed to Androtion by Demosthenes is the
destruction of the crowns.

With the administration of Lycurgus a new epoch in the
history of the dedications on the Acropolis began. His activity
in this connection is noted in IG^2 II 333 and in the decree passed
in 307/6 B.C. on the motion of Stratokles (IG^2 II 457; [Plut.],
Lives of the Ten Orators, p. 852a). In the review there given of
Lycurgus' career it is reported that he "assembled many χρήματα
on the Acropolis, prepared *kosmos* for the Goddess, Nikae of
solid gold,[2] processional vessels of gold and silver, and *kosmos* of

---

[1] The replacements and reparations of Androtion are to be noted in IG^2 II 1437,
col. II (c. 350 B.C.). He had the weights of the votive offerings inscribed on the objects
themselves (IG^2 II 1443, col. II, 344/3 B.C.), if this was not done at the revision of
346/5 B.C. A comparison of IG^2 II 1443, ll. 124 ff. with the inventories of 374/3-
367/6 B.C. shows that in the meantime a large number of gold *phialae* had come into
the Hekatompedon, some of them the property of the Other Gods (*above*, p. 117, n. 2).
They may antedate 346/5 B.C.

[2] The history of the golden Nikae seems to me to run as follows: in 434 B.C. the
plan was adopted of making such statues (IG^2 I 91/2; Kolbe, *Sitz. Ber. Akad.*, 1927,
pp. 326 f.). In 426/5 B.C. two Nikae were added to the one or more already existing
(IG^2 I 368/9; *above*, p. 89). By 406 B.C. eight in all were on hand, of which all but

gold for 100 *canephori*." This phase of his activity is illustrated by the accounts of money received and raised and expended, and of crowns dedicated by private persons and by the state, which are recorded in *IG*² II 1493–1496 (334/3–331/0 B.C.). The authors of the accounts were the Tamiae and a Commission of which Lycurgus was probably Chairman. It appears from *IG*² II 1498 that an inventory was made at this time of the dedications (of bronze?) on the Acropolis which stood (or lay on the ground) out of doors. The regular inventories of the period after 340 B.C. (now inscribed on Hymettian instead of Pentelic marble) are very fragmentary and dateless (*IG*² II 1456–1467). It is impossible to reconstruct anything like a complete record for a single year. But since we do not find in any of them the Lycurgean system of marking articles (grouped in series) with letters of the alphabet (Lehner, *op. cit.*, p. 118; *IG*² II 1469, note),[1] and since they conform in content and arrangement to the model introduced in 341/0 B.C. (*IG*² II 1455), we are warranted in dating them earlier than 334/3–331/0 B.C. All the other inventories preserved to us belong to 321/0 B.C. (*IG*² II 1468) or later; and, what is more, apart from the chryselephantine statue and its Nike (*IG*² II 1468, 1477, 1482), they contained only articles dedicated in 321 B.C. (*IG*² II 1468, l. 13) or subsequently: we are unable to identify in them (leaving those of the Chalkotheke — inscribed on the reverses — out of consideration) any of the articles of the pre-Lycurgean epoch. It can be assumed that Lycurgus converted into Nikae, *kosmos*, *pompeia*, etc., votives of gold and silver previously existing. But where are the many earlier objects not of precious metals?

one (*IG*² II 1371, note; Lehner, *op. cit.*, pp. 24 f.) were converted into money (*above*, pp. 91, 119). The supports (διερείσματα) of the seven which went into the melting pot were preserved in the Chalkotheke ('Αρχ. Δελτίον, 1927/8, p. 128, col. III, l. 129; *IG*² II 1425, l. 382). With gold obtained in 377 B.C. by the melting down of votive crowns and other objects the replacement of one of the Nikae sacrificed in the crisis of Arginusae was undertaken, and in 374/3 B.C. the work was completed (*above*, p. 118, n. 1). Lycurgus replaced others in 334/3–331/0 B.C. (*IG*² II 1493/4/5), perhaps the whole six. They were finally disposed of by Lachares (*below*, p. 126). There is no reason for supposing with Foucart (*BCH*, 1888, pp. 283 ff.) that ten ever existed.

[1] It appears first in his accounts (*IG*² II 1496B) and then in the inventories of the period following *c.* 321 B.C. (*IG*² II 1469 ff.). Its occasional use prior to Lycurgus (*IG*² II 1421, ll. 50 ff.) is a different matter.

where are the new paraphernalia of Lycurgus and the accessions made between 331/0 and 322/1 B.C.?

The answer to these questions may be found in the prescript of the inventory for 321/0 B.C. It is there stated that the Tamiae handed over to their successors the votive offerings "exclusive of such as were engraved on – – –" (πλὴ[ν ὅσα – – – ἀ]ναγέγραπται – – –).[1] Clearly there was another *stele* on which the articles excepted—which the subsequent inventories show to have been the previously existent dedications — were inscribed. In, or before, 385 B.C. the weights of the several parts of the chryselephantine statue of Pheidias had been inscribed on a bronze *stele*, and subsequently the Tamiae had only to certify that they had checked off the *membra* of the image by the *stele* and found everything in order (*above*, p. 119, n. 1). It is probable that Lycurgus had a similar *stele* made as a permanent record of the religious equipment as that existed when the work of his Commission was completed. Being of bronze this *stele* has naturally perished. We can then imagine that accessions were recorded on marble quadrennially, i.e., in 327/6 and 323/2 B.C., and identify *IG*[2] II 1497 with the first of these *penteteric* records. It included *acta* of the Tamiae of 327/6 B.C. and of the two preceding years at least. Clearly it was not an ordinary inventory, yet it cannot be connected with the Lycurgean Commission of 334/3–331/0 B.C. On the assumption that a second such record covered accessions made in 326/5–323/2 B.C. we can explain why, on beginning in 321/0 B.C. to record each year the *epeteia* cumulatively, the Tamiae included in their inventory the crowns proclaimed at the Dionysia of 322/1 B.C. (*IG* II 1468).[2]

The small group of Other Gods whose treasures appear in the fourth-century inventories of the Tamiae remained unchanged,

---

[1] The restoration by means of which the general sense of this prescript is established comes from Preuner (*IG*[2] II 1468, l. 4, note).

[2] It is also conceivable that a second bronze *stele*, bringing the first up to date, was issued in 321 B.C.; but this hypothesis leaves us with *IG*[2] II 1497 on our hands. If we hold that marble inventories of any kind were posted annually between 331/0 and 321/0 B.C., we shall have to assume that but for one small fragment they have all been lost. Neither before nor afterwards does a gap of this magnitude exist in these records. The Panathenaic *penteteris* comes again into prominence during the regime of Lycurgus (*IG*[2] II 333; [Plut.], *Lives of the Ten Orators*, p. 852B; *Diod.* XVI 88).

so far as we can see, till *c.* 321 B.C., except by the addition, in or before 375/4 B.C., of Ammon (*IG*² II 1415; *below*, pp. 131, n. 1; cf. Appendix II, p. 180). Then Zeus (*IG*² II 1492, l. 87), Asklepios (*IG*² II 1474, 1475, 1479, l. 33; 1492, ll. 22 ff.), and Demeter Chloe (*IG*² II 1472, l. 39) were added to their circle. In *IG*² II 1492 is entered at one point a group of silver *hydriae*,¹ the work of Nikokrates of Colonus, to which is attached the name of the Archon for 311/0 B.C.; and at another point one group of two and a second of thirteen silver *phialae* labeled, like the *hydriae*, ἱεραὶ Ἀσκληπίου. The other side of the stone contains the accounts of the Treasurers for 305 and 304 B.C. — probably for the duration of the Four Years' War (*above*, p. 102, n. 2). The presumption is that the inventory is the one for the year 305/4 B.C. The group of two *phialae* was already there in *c.* 318/7 B.C. (*IG*² II 1475). Presumably the other thirteen were dedicated later, i.e., one per year (317/5–305/4 B.C.). We may suspect, therefore, that the practice of placing annually in the hands of the Tamiae a silver *phiale* consecrated to Asklepios was inaugurated after the overthrow of the democracy in 321 B.C. Prior to the end of 318/7 B.C. a silver basket and a gold *phiale* consecrated to Asklepios had also reached the Tamiae. It seems clear, therefore, that during this period the small articles placed in the shrine of Asklepios were being steadily converted into substantial baskets, *phialae*, and *hydriae* and deposited with the Tamiae, especially since this was being done at this time with the *phialae exeleutherae* (*IG*² II 1469) and the small things dedicated in the shrine of Artemis Brauronia (*IG*² II 1479).

Previously (between *c.* 359/8 and 322/1 B.C.) and afterwards (between 297/6 and 248/7 B.C.: Dinsmoor, *Archons of Athens*, pp. 450 ff., 158 ff.) the *ex-votos* of the Asklepieion were allowed to accumulate for periods of about twenty years before being melted down; and the proceeds were used, on one occasion at least (*IG*² II 1534B, ll. 163, 334 ff.), to add to the cult furniture of the temple itself. It is a peculiarity of the epoch between 321 and 304 B.C. that they went to enrich the deposits on the

---

¹ Again (cf. *above*, pp. 114 f.) the weights conform to norms — 1000 or 1500 drachmas.

Acropolis; and since the upper limits of this epoch may be 331/0 B.C., the innovation may be due to the policy of Lycurgus, who is expressly commended (*Lives of the Ten Orators*, p. 852B) for "having assembled πολλὰ χρήματα on the Acropolis." In fact this text is ordinarily interpreted (*IG*² II 1496B, note) to mean that Lycurgus collected the treasure of the local shrines and had it recast (*IG*² II 1496, ll. 200 f.) into more appropriate articles which were left on the Acropolis. In other words it was a revival of Pericles' policy of 434 B.C.; and it is not incredible that the fourth-century financier had the same conception in the back of his mind, viz., to accumulate in the hands of the Tamiae a mass of plate which could be drawn on for the making of money in time of great national need.

The Tamiae make their last appearance in our records in a vote of thanks tendered to them by the *hippeis* in 300/299 B.C. during the regime of Lachares. "They had exerted themselves," so the text runs, "on behalf of the *hipparchs* with the result that the Knights obtained from the state the rations (σῖτος) due them." As is well known, they had to hand over, on Lachares' orders, "the golden Nikae and shields and the gold plates from the chryselephantine statue of Athena" to pay the mercenaries whom "the tyrant" kept in his service and who helped him defend Athens against Demetrius Poliorcetes in 296/5 B.C. (*Pap. Oxy.* XVII 2082; *Class. Phil.*, 1929, pp. 1 ff.); and we can be certain that when these major articles were sacrificed the minor votives were not spared. If the Treasurers' office was not abolished after this unhappy experience, the need for the issuance of annual inventories was ended. The expropriation of the *ex-votos* on the Acropolis in 300–295 B.C. was much more complete than that of 406–04 B.C. If Dinsmoor is right (*Archons of Athens*, pp. 158 ff.), the great inventory of the gold and silver dedications in the Asklepieion (*IG*² II 1534A), made in *c.* 271/0 B.C., began with the *ex-votos* of the year 297/6 B.C. For the preceding epoch, as we have seen, they had been converted annually and at short intervals into *phialae*, baskets, and *hydriae* and had passed into the keeping of the Tamiae — to share the fate of Athena's treasures and those of the Other Gods at the "sacrilegious" hands of Lachares. The

Asklepieion was presumably as bare as the Parthenon in March, 295 B.C. Thereafter there were perhaps no Tamiae to receive for safe-keeping the treasures of Asklepios. In any event, these were once again, as before the time of Lycurgus, or 321 B.C., allowed to accumulate in the shrine till the time came round for recording them on a great tablet of Hymettian marble and converting them into more massive, useful, and beautiful articles of cult furniture. The Tamiae are never mentioned in connection with this periodic work "of taking down from their places, cataloguing, and recasting the *anathemata*" of Asklepios.

Unless it be during the interval between Lycurgus and Lachares, the Other Gods, for whom first the Tamiae of Athena and the Other Gods (406–385 B.C.), then the Tamiae of the Other Gods (385–341 B.C.), and finally *the* Tamiae act in making inventories and looking after the objects inventoried, were the small circle of deities whose *ex-votos* survived, in remnants, in the Hekatompedon and Opisthodomos, the cataclysm of 406–04 B.C. It is interesting in this connection that when a *phiale* was dedicated to Ammon it was put in the temple of Athena in charge of the Tamiae of the Goddess. In other words, Ammon was not one of the Other Gods (*below*, p. 180). In the fourth century, as it happened, the jurisdiction of the Tamiae was confined to the Acropolis and its immediate vicinity, and after *c.* 342/1 B.C., even in this restricted area, it was shared with the Commissioners of Artemis Brauronia until in *c.* 321 B.C. these officials ceased apparently to be appointed.[1] Conversely, the Acropolis and its slopes became set off as a peculiar area of religious administration,[2] and this in turn served to define the personnel of the Other Gods in a sense quite foreign to the original comprehensiveness of the term.

---

[1] The Commissioners existed till some time after 327/6 B.C. (*IG*² II 1527, l. 42). For the reduction and remodelling of the Athenian magistracies in 321 B.C. see *Hellenistic Athens*, pp. 22 ff.

[2] For the Aphrodite who comes in question see *AJA*, 1931, p. 195. The Zeus is doubtless Zeus Polieus.

XIII

THE RÔLE OF THE TREASURERS IN PUBLIC FINANCE DURING THE FOURTH CENTURY

A S has been pointed out already, after 403 B.C. the Tamiae published inventories alone. They no longer issued accounts.[1] The reason for the cessation of accounts is obvious: it was not that the Tamiae now lacked revenues (*epeteia*), or, at least after a certain lapse of time, surpluses; but that, either tacitly or by formal act, the state cancelled its indebtedness to the Goddess, and abandoned wholly the practice of "giving" secular moneys to Athena. Henceforth there was no need of preserving publicly in a permanent record on the Acropolis — Athena's *hieron* — annual or periodic statements of capital, or capital and interest, to be repaid to the Goddess.

It is true that occasionally the Tamiae of the fourth century entered, either in the text of their inventories or as appendices to them, statements that approximate accounts (*below*, p. 133); but, except in one instance (*IG*[2] II 1414, ll. 50 ff., 384/3–378/7 B.C.; cf. *below*, pp. 140, n. 2; 184),[2] these statements are records of public funds which had been deposited with them by the state. They are true accounts, not records of loans. They include receipts as well as expenditures (*IG*[2] II 1443, 1492B). This kind of record was not inscribed on stone in the fifth century. Then receipts and disbursements of this character were doubtless booked. They formed part of the accounts sub-

---

[1] For *IG*[2] II 1493 ff., see *above*, p. 102, n. 2.

[2] As restored by Hicks (*Greek Inscr. British Museum*, I, 32) this statement opened with *epeteia* of sacred money and included the entry τοῖς ἀποδέκτ[αις] between a specification of funds "handed over" to named officials, probably Tamiae, and one of funds "received from [the preceding Tamiae]." Though the stone is too fragmentary to admit of any certainty, it is natural to think that the Tamiae had disbursed some of the sacred money to the *apodektae*. There is no means of knowing whether this was a loan, or a gift, or simply a payment to the Receivers General to cover an advance made by the state to Athena for an expenditure which properly belonged to her.

mitted by the Tamiae and the Hellenotamiae at their *euthyna*, but not of the "accounts" engraved publicly to form a permanent record. The statements incorporated with the inventories of the fourth century do not give us a complete account of the financial transactions of the Tamiae. They do not contain reports of the receipt and expenditure of Athena's own revenues. As in the fifth century, so in the fourth, this latter kind of a record had, of course, to be prepared annually and submitted to the *logistae* and the courts; but it was never inscribed on marble tablets. We are, accordingly, not in a position to win from inscriptions more than the most disconnected and partial view of the Treasurers' financial activities and responsibilities.

From the literary references it seems to me clear that the Opisthodomos was still the bank of the Goddess. Otherwise the Tamiae of the Other Gods would have been held primarily responsible for the fire in the Opisthodomos referred to in Demosthenes' speech against Timokrates (XXIV 136); for at the time of this incident (*below*, p. 130) the Tamiae of the Other Gods had charge of all but a few [1] of the *anathemata* kept in this edifice, whereas Demosthenes mentions the Tamiae of Athena first. Both boards were imprisoned pending investigation of their part in the fire. The text runs: καὶ οἱ ταμίαι ἐφ' ὧν ὁ Ὀπισθόδομος ἐνεπρήσθη, καὶ οἱ τῶν τῆς θεοῦ καὶ οἱ τῶν ἄλλων θεῶν, ἐν τῷ οἰκήματι τούτῳ ἦσαν, ἕως ἡ κρίσις αὐτοῖς ἐγένετο. The meaning of the passage admits of no misinterpretation: there were two boards of Tamiae at the time, and both were so con-

---

[1] The new inventory of the Tamiae published in 1930 by Kyparisses from Meritt's transcription (Ἀρχ. Δελτίον, 1927/8, p. 128) acquaints us with the fact that these Treasurers had charge of a few objects on deposit in the Opisthodomos. Notable among them were a box containing four iron anvils, hammers, and twenty-two dies; also 318 cases of arrows. There were at the same time (369/8 B.C.) eight and one-half cases of arrows in the Hekatompedon, but these had been transferred from the Parthenon, in 406 B.C. probably, and were noted as rotten and unusable. The box of anvils and dies appears in the inventories of the period 398/7–396/5 B.C., where the apparatus is described as that with which the gold money was coined (*IG*² II 1408/1409). There were five other dies in the Chalkotheke in 369/8 B.C. Later, after 321/0 B.C., twenty-one dies and two hammers appear in the inventories of this edifice (*IG*² II 1469, l. 107; 1471, l. 56). The section of the inventory of the Tamiae of Athena entitled ἐν τῷ Ὀπισθοδόμῳ was obviously omitted in 368/7 B.C. (*IG*² II 1425).

nected with the Opisthodomos as to be involved in the charges arising out of the fire.

Demosthenes cites the incident as one among several precedents for the imprisonment, pending trial, of prominent persons charged with misdemeanors. His words, read without prejudice, are capable of only one construction: he dated the fire after 403/02 B.C. The order of citation is as follows (133–136): τοὺς μὲν οὖν πρὸ Εὐκλείδου ἄρχοντος ἐάσω καὶ τοὺς σφόδρα παλαιούς. καίτοι - - -. ἀλλὰ μετ' Εὐκλείδην ἄρχοντα, ὦ ἄνδρες δικασταί, πρῶτον μὲν Θρασύβουλον - - -. ἔπειτα Φιλέψιον - - -. ἔπειτα 'Αγύρριον - - -. καὶ Μυρωνίδης ὁ 'Αρχίνου υἱὸς - - -. καὶ οἱ ταμίαι, κτλ. To argue, as Judeich does (*Hermes*, 1929, pp. 411 ff.), that, while the men mentioned may have been tried after Eukleides, the acts for which they were imprisoned were committed earlier, is to defend an untenable position. Two general amnesties had been issued meanwhile, one in 405/04 (*Andoc.* I 73 ff.) and another in 403 B.C. (Arist. *Ath. Pol.* 39). Precedents taken from the period prior to the issuance of the new law-code in 403/02 B.C. would have had no relevancy in 353/2 B.C. (date assigned by Diony. Hal., *Ep. ad Amm.* 4, p. 725 to *Dem.* XXIV). It was for this very reason that the orator drew the line at the archonship of Eukleides. But, in any case, the existence at the time of the fire of two boards of Treasurers rules out the contention which Judeich's forced construction of Demosthenes sustains — that the fire in the Opisthodomos mentioned by Demosthenes is the fire entered by the interpolator of the chronological data in Xenophon's *Hellenica* under the archonship of Kallias (406/05 B.C.).[1] For we now know that in 406/05 B.C. there existed a single *collegium* of Tamiae. The probability is that Demosthenes' order of citation is chronological and that the imprisonment of the Tamiae occurred some considerable time after 403/02 B.C. The earliest possible date is the separation of the two boards in 385/4 B.C.

[1] The only way I can see of identifying the fire which burned "the old (παλαιός) temple of Athena" (Xen. *Hell.* I 6 1) with the fire in the Opisthodomos (assuming this to be desirable) is to hold that the interpolator confused the Kallias who was archon in 406/05 with the Kalleas (written Kallias in *Diodorus* XV 28) who was archon in 377/6 B.C. His incompetence is so great (*above*, p. 44) that we can easily attribute to him a mistake of this sort. Johnson (*AJA*, 1914, pp. 8 ff.) has given reasons for dating

Wherever or whatever it was (cf. Paton, *The Erechtheum*, pp. 470 ff.), the Opisthodomos possessed apparatus for the orderly keeping of money, bullion, and *ex-votos*. The funds of Athena Polias, Athena Nike, and Hermes could be kept distinct (*above*, p. 21, n. 1). On one side were the treasures of the Tamiae of Athena, on the other those of the Tamiae of the Other Gods. It had numbered cases (θῆκαι) in which bronze caskets could be placed (*IG*² II 314, ll. 14 ff.); in it were wooden chests (κιβωτοί) of various sizes (*IG*² II 1388, ll. 73 ff.). Leathern bags (φασκώλια) containing articles of silver, bronze, and plate could be stored there sealed with the public seal (*IG*² II 1445). It was used in the fourth century as the main arsenal of the state's stock of arrows, of which as many as 318 cases were on hand at one time (*above*, p. 129, n. 1). There were tiers (ρυμοί) of *phialae* in it. Objects in it were included in inventories of the Hekatompedon, in which case they had to be specially earmarked.[1] In 369/8 B.C. (᾿Αρχ. Δελτίον, 1927/8, p. 128) it was a place of deposit distinct from the Ancient Temple, within

in 377/6 B.C. the fire alluded to by Demosthenes; but they are not well grounded in fact (Kolbe, *Philologus*, 1930, pp. 261 ff.; cf. *below*, p. 143, n. 3). The fire of 406/05 B.C. seems established by the accounts of the Erechtheum (Paton, *The Erechtheum*, p. 420, XXVIII, l. 28 = *IG*² II 1654; cf. pp. 460 ff.). All that we can affirm is that the fire of Demosthenes' reference occurred between 385/4 and 353/2 B.C. Cf. Paton, *The Erechtheum*, pp. 462 f. Kolbe (*Ber. Phil. Woch.*, 1931, pp. 82 f.) has come to the same conclusion.

[1] I see no evidence to support the view of Körte (*Rh. Mus.*, 1898, p. 255; cf. *IG*² II p. 24) that the articles taken from the Opisthodomos in 406–04 B.C. had been included theretofore in the inventories of the Parthenon. No trace of them appears there. Some of them were engraved with an image of Zeus or Apollo. We are tempted to think that these belonged to the Other Gods. But in that event they should have been transferred back to the custody of the Tamiae of the Other Gods in 385/4 B.C., which was not the case. The weight of this objection is mitigated by the fact noted by Lehner (*op. cit.*, pp. 59, 62) that quite a number of articles remained with the Tamiae of Athena in 385/4 B.C. which did not belong to them (cf. *IG*² II 1413, l. 29; *below*, Appendix II). Even as late as 369/8 B.C. they had the custody of ἑλικτῆρες of Artemis Brauronia, and collections of *hydriae* and *phialae* remained undivided throughout (*above*, pp. 114 f., 122, n. 1). It should be observed, further, that the Other Gods of 385/4–342/1 B.C. were only a small group of the Other Gods of 434–406 B.C. Their Tamiae may have had no claim on articles that had belonged to Zeus and Apollo. Bannier (*Rh. Mus.*, 1911, p. 43, n. 1) restores [᾿Απόλλ]ωνος in line 6 of *IG*² II 1415; *vix recte*, as Kirchner remarks (cf. *below*, Appendix II). It is, of course, true that some of the articles "from the Opisthodomos" belonged to Athena (*IG*² II 1396, l. 26). We shall have to recognize, I think, that these were left uninventoried before 406 B.C. It

which, consequently, it can, I think, no longer be placed.[1] It can have been continuously in use from before 434 B.C. to long after 376 B.C. — to the (unknown) date of Demosthenes' speech quoted below. It was *the* Opisthodomos on the Acropolis. It was kept locked. An outcry was raised if it was found open: ἀνέῳξαν δήπου πρῴην τινὲς τὸν Ὀπισθόδομον, οὐκοῦν οἱ παριόντες ἅπαντες τὸν δῆμον καταλελύσθαι, τοὺς νόμους οὐκετ' εἶναι, τοιαῦτ' ἔλεγον (*Dem.* XIII 14). It is hard to imagine a situation of this sort arising if the Opisthodomos contained only the *ex-votos* inventoried by the Tamiae. Moreover, we cannot ignore the testimony of the scholiasts on the passage of Demosthenes relating to the fire; for they furnish information not derivable from the context (Johnson, *AJA*, 1914, p. 8), to the effect that the Tamiae "had loaned the money of the state deposited in the Opisthodomos to private bankers;[2] that the bankers failed, and that the Tamiae in their embarrassment set fire to the place so that they could impute the loss to the conflagration." It seems clear, therefore, that in the fourth century, as in the fifth, the Opisthodomos was *the* bank of the Treasurers of Athena (cf. Aristoph. *Plutus*, 1193).

That our lack during the fourth century of Treasurers' accounts in the fifth-century sense is due, not to their total loss,

is conceivable that they had belonged to Athena in Pallenis or Athena by the Palladion, in which case they would have been inventoried in the fifth century by the Tamiae of the Other Gods (Meritt, *Athenian Calendar*, p. 22).

[1] Kolbe (*Ber. Phil. Woch.*, 1931, pp. 76 ff.) has come independently to the same conclusion, likewise Kirchner (*ibid.*); and they have gone farther and inferred that the Opisthodomos was part of our Parthenon. But this does not seem to me to be warranted by the evidence used — the position on the stone of the section entitled ἐν τῷ Ὀπισθοδόμῳ. As I read these inventories, space at the bottom of col. I was regularly filled by material which belonged at the conclusion of the main inventory, in *IG*² II 1421/24, ll. 21–34 (*above*, p. 114, n. 1), and 1425, ll. 117–132, by what were virtually *epeteia*, and in Ἀρχ. Δελτίον, 1927/8, p. 128, ll. 115–122, by the catalogue of the Opisthodomos, which, accordingly, may have appeared on the MS. used by the stone-cutter after the section entitled ἐν τῷ Ἀρχαίῳ Νεῴ; but cf. *above*, p. 112. Kolbe argues that the Opisthodomos was the west porch of our Parthenon.

[2] For an instance where government officials borrowed money from a private banker, see *IG*² II 1672, ll. 39 f. Lycurgus (*Lives of the Ten Orators*, pp. 841D, 852B) is said to have borrowed for the state 250 talents on one occasion, and 650 in all (Dürrbach, *L'orateur Lycurge*, p. 39, n. 3). In Delos the temple funds were regularly loaned by the *hieropoii* to private persons, but this was done openly, for the profit of the temple, and on tangible securities. There is no evidence for such a practice in Athens.

but to their nonexistence, is suggested by the inclusion in the *inventory* for 344/3 B.C. (*IG*² II 1443) of a special deposit, made by the Treasurer of the Military Fund, of silver bullion worth 28 talents.[1] The implication would be clearer if the deposit had been in coined money; but we should look for the entry of such a deposit in the period from 411 to 404 B.C. in the accounts (*IG*² I 301, ll. 114 f.), not in the inventories; and since the inventories acknowledge the receipt of the silver, they must have recorded its withdrawal. Hence we may infer that the inventories alone were available for recording publicly the transaction. In other words, accounts were not published. And if this case is thrown out because the deposit was in bullion and not in money, the case recorded in *IG*² II 1414 (384/3–378/7 B.C.) is unambiguous. Here an account of sacred money (ἱερὸν ἀργύριον) is entered at the close of an inventory of the Tamiae of the Goddess. We arrive at a like conclusion by observing that the accounts of the Tamiae for the sums deposited with them by the state to be used in financing the Four Years' War (*IG*² II 1492B) were published on the reverse of the tablet which contained an inventory on its obverse. They were not a separate record, like the fifth-century accounts, but simply an appendix to an inventory. We have to assume that a similar appendix added to the appropriate inventory recorded the withdrawal of the deposit made by the Treasurer of the Military Fund in 344/3 B.C.

It was obviously only under exceptional circumstances that the state used the Tamiae as their reserve bankers during the fourth century. Our record is so defective that we can determine only a few of these occasions. We have the instance of 344/3 B.C. The money which Harpalos brought to Athens with him, subject to deductions for bribing the politicians, was "carried up to the Acropolis,"[2] for deposit with the Tamiae,

---

[1] Bannier (*Ber. Phil. Woch.*, 1910, p. 831, and Kirchner, note) treat the bullion as gold, thus erroneously enlarging the deposit to 336 talents.

[2] The phrase ἀναφέρειν εἰς τὴν ἀκρόπολιν in the sense "of depositing with the Tamiae in their treasury on the Acropolis" became stereotyped before 434 B.C. Cf. *IG*² I 91, ll. 3 f.; 92, l. 44; *Andoc.* II 7, 8; *Aesch.* II 174 f.; *Hyperid.* I (V), col. 9, 10, and the other texts cited by Bannier (*Rh. Mus.*, 1926, pp. 186 f.). Against the view that the Tamiae were the custodians of the money of Harpalos it may be urged that their accounts for 325/4 B.C. — those submitted at their *euthyna* — must have revealed the

doubtless. And the Tamiae were the bankers for the funds, both those received as gifts from Antigonus, and those raised by Athens by its own efforts and those of its cleruchs,[1] for the prosecution of the Four Years' War against Kassander. If we may generalize the procedure followed on this last occasion, payments from such funds were made on vote of the Council or the *demos* and certified by the Chairman of the prytany for the time being.[2]

The normal rôle of the Tamiae in public finance is more difficult to apprehend and may have changed from time to time. On the abolition of the Hellenotamiae in 404/03 B.C. the state began to defray all its contingent expenses from the funds of the Tamiae; but at the end of about ten years, in *c.* 394 B.C. (Johnson, *Class. Phil.*, 1914, p. 421), it created a new office, the Treasurership of the *demos*, upon which it saddled the charges of this nature met between 411 and 404 B.C. by the Helleno-tamiae (*IG*² II 24, 25, 53, 56). Since the moneys involved passed through the hands of the *apodektae* to the Tamias, the *demos* might give an order to them directly (*IG*² II 29, 387/6 B.C.) "to allocate (μερίσαι) the specified sum, from the revenues received, when they made the allocations prescribed by the laws";[3] or, compendiously, "to allocate so and so many drachmas" for the designated purpose (*IG*² II 31, 386/5 B.C.). It may be doubted whether a decree ordering a contravention of the legal distribution of the public revenues was not liable to be annulled by a *graphe paranomon*. And, in fact, in the first instance it was not till the regular time had arrived at which the *apodektae* drew up the annual schedule (διάταξις) of dis-

amount received, which, though ascertained at the time it was carried up to the Acropolis by Demosthenes and his fellow depositors, was kept secret (Tarn, *CAH*, VI, p. 451); but this difficulty is not removed by assuming that some other officials were its custodians.

[1] A committee of the Areopagus and the Treasurer of the Military Fund raised the money in Athens.

[2] *IG*² 1492B; cf. Arist. *Ath. Pol.* 47 1, and for identical procedure in the Athenian cleruchy at Samos, C. Curtius, *Inschriften und Studien zur Geschichte von Samos*, pp. 10 ff. (346/5 B.C.).

[3] Busolt, *Griech. Staatsk.*, I, p. 630, n. 1. It seems to me difficult to reconcile this procedure with the existence of a fund specially segregated to meet expenditures authorized by decrees; hence I am inclined to agree with Johnson (*Class. Phil.*, 1914,

tributions [1] that the order of the *demos* was to be honored. Probably the law had not yet been passed depriving the Assembly of the right to determine thus in advance the allocation of funds; at any rate at a later date the *demos* gave the order in such cases to the Chairmen of the *nomothetae* to have the laws governing allocations of funds altered (*IG*² II 222, *c.* 344/3 B.C.; cf. Francotte, *Finances*, pp. 223 ff.; Elter, *Ein athen. Gesetz über die eleusin. Aparche*, pp. 9 ff.; Weiss, *Griech. Privatrecht*, I, pp. 108 f.).

After the reëstablishment of a separate board of Treasurers of Athena in 385/4 B.C. the contingent expenses were again transferred to it; but it would appear that an annual sum fixed in 378/7 B.C. at ten talents (*IG*² II 43) was allocated by law to the Tamiae with which to meet expenditures authorized by decrees of the people.[2] A further change was made between 377 and 368 B.C., by which the Treasurer of the *demos* was given charge of this fund; [3] and this official continued to make

p. 421) that *IG*² II 21 and 82, in which the payer is the Tamias and the source the ten-talent fund, belong after *c.* 376 B.C. See, however, Kirchner, *IG*² II 21, Add. p. 656. On the other hand, I see no reason for substituting δõ[ναι τòς ἀποδέκτας] for δό[τω ὁ ταμίας τõ δήμο] in *IG*² II 33 (*c.* 385 B.C.). We can assume that at this time the Tamias paid when he had money; otherwise the *demos* went to the *apodektae* directly; cf. Kirchner, *IG*² II 4 (Index), p. 37. Similarly in *IG*² II 212, ll. 42 ff. (347/6 B.C.): it is here voted that crowns, which were to be conferred quadrennially at the Great Panathenaia on Spartokos and Pairisades Kings of Bosporos, were to be paid for by the Tamias of the *demos* from the contingent fund; but, since it was near the end of the year, and this fund, presumably, was exhausted, *permission* was given to the *apodektae* to hand over the amount required for the first crowns, to be conferred at the approaching Great Panathenaia, from the Military Fund. There were also two Tamiae of the Council to whom came a sum to cover contingent expenses of this body (*IG*² II 120, 358/4 B.C.; 223B, l. 14, 343/2 B.C.).

[1] *IG*² II 844; cf. Francotte, *Finances*, pp. 212 ff.

[2] I see no reason for thinking with Böckh-Fränkel, *Staatshaushaltung* ³, II, p. 47*, n. 296, that this was a loan made by Athena to the state. Francotte (*op. cit.*, p. 217) identifies this fund of ten talents with the fund of ten talents, raised by *eisphorae*, towards which two metics made contributions annually between 347/6 and 323/2 B.C. (*IG*² II 505); and the fund likewise of ten talents, raised by *eisphora*, mentioned in a *nomos* of 337/6 B.C. (*IG*² II 244); but all they have in common is the sum of ten talents. The two latter funds were raised, the one for the building of the shiphouses, the other for the repair of the fortifications, of the Piraeus. Koehler's view (*Hermes*, 1871, p. 12), that the contingent fund of ten talents was allocated from the ordinary revenues, seems to me to be correct.

[3] *IG*² II 40, cf. Add. p. 657, 43 (377 B.C.) and 106, 107 (368/7 B.C.).

payments from it until 307/06 B.C., if not till the office was abolished by Lachares in 301/0 B.C. (Johnson, *Class. Phil.*, 1914, p. 428; *AJP*, 1915, p. 433 ff.).

After 378/7 B.C. one case alone occurs in our record in which the Tamiae clearly disburse money for public purposes which cannot be regarded as a legitimate expenditure of Athena's own property (ἱερὰ χρήματα). The occasion was the dispatch in 325/4 B.C. of a colony to the coast of the Adriatic (*IG*² II 1629, ll. 165 ff.). Sessions of the courts were necessary to settle disputes as to the liability of Trierarchs to service in this connection, and an order was given by the *demos* to the Tamiae of the Goddess "to give to the dikasts their salaries as provided by law" (τὸν δὲ μισθὸν διδόναι τοῖς δικαστηρίοις τοὺς ταμίας τῶν τῆς θεοῦ κατὰ τὸν νόμον).[1] There cannot be any doubt that the state possessed at this time a deposit of public funds with the Tamiae,[2] in the Opisthodomos doubtless, on which it was entitled to draw for paying indemnities for jury service. In the instance alluded to above (p. 133) the money involved was Athena's own and was expressly designated as such (*IG*² II 1414). On other occasions in which the Tamiae expended money it is not clear whether it was their own money or that of the

---

[1] The *kolakretae* had been ταμίαι τοῦ δικαστικοῦ μισθοῦ (*PW*, 21, p. 1068, where the ancient texts are assembled). "Im vierten Jahrhundert," says Ed. Meyer (*Forsch.*, II, p. 137), "zahlt der ταμίας τοῦ δήμου die Kosten der Stelen; wer die übrigen Functionen der Kolakreten hat, wissen wir seltsamer Weise nicht." It is indeed odd that we do not know by whom or from what fund the δικαστικὸς μισθός was paid after 411 B.C. So far as I can find, the passage of *IG*² II 1629 quoted in the text is the only positive statement we possess on the subject (cf. Panske, *Leip. Stud.*, 1890, pp. 31 ff.). It appears that in 325/4 B.C. the νόμοι imposed the duty of paying jurors on the Tamiae; but we cannot be sure when the "law" in question was passed. We naturally think of 403/02 B.C. Wade-Gery's restoration of *IG*² I 301, l. 12 (*above*, p. 24, n. 2), is too uncertain, and the circumstances in which the Tamiae made assignments (of grain) [ἐ]s τὸ δικασ[τήριον] in 405/04 B.C. (*above*, pp. 82 f.) too abnormal, to be used as evidence that after 411 B.C. the Treasurers of Athena exercised the function of the *kolakretae* as paymasters of the dikasts. But after the abolition in 404/03 B.C. of the Hellenotamiae, who had had to provide money for the *diobelia*, and possibly for the other μισθοί as well, it is conceivable that the Tamiae had this charge thrust upon them and that they retained it thereafter. It is curious that Aristotle (*Ath. Pol.* 47 1) has nothing to say on the subject; but he fails systematically to record the financial duties of the specific magistracies, nor does he note the sources or agents concerned with the various μισθοί (*Ath. Pol.* 62 2).

[2] Suidas, *s.v.*, ταμίαι: οἱ τὰ ἐν τῷ ἱερῷ τῆς Ἀθηνᾶς ἐν ἀκροπόλει χρήματα ἱερά τε καὶ δημόσια φυλάττουσι, ἀλλὰ καὶ αὐτὸ τὸ ἄγαλμα τῆς Ἀθηνᾶς.

state that was disbursed. Thus in 374/3 B.C. the inventory of the Treasurers of Athena (*IG*² II 1421, ll. 12 ff.) contains what was doubtless the concluding record of a transaction in which the Tamiae had a part. Commissioners, annually or periodically renewed, had been created in or shortly after 378/7 B.C. to replace the golden Nikae melted down in 406 B.C. The Tamiae had given gold to them for their work. A statue was dedicated in 374/3 B.C. (*IG*² II 1425, ll. 45 f.; cf. 1424, ll. 31 ff.). Some of the gold was not used and this was paid back to the Tamiae in installments. One such repayment — not the first — was made in 374/3 B.C. and acknowledged in the inventory of that year. It is probable that the cost of replacing the Nikae was borne by the Goddess herself: the gold needed was secured by melting down crowns and other votive offerings made during the past twenty-five years. Even objects which survived the cataclysm of 406/04 B.C. were dedicated thus anew. It may have given the Athenians a special satisfaction to incorporate in the monument which symbolized their triumph in restoring the Delian Confederacy the dedication made to Athena by Lysander when he destroyed their first Empire. Neither of these instances requires a standing deposit of public money with the Tamiae. On the other hand, in the case recorded in *IG*² II 1264 (300/299 B.C.) the Tamiae need not have paid out the money that went to provide the rations due to the *hippeis*: all that they are said to have done is to have exerted themselves to get the state to recognize its obligation (*above*, p. 126). This may, of course, have taken the form of securing from the *demos* authorization to make the requisite payment from funds in their possession: and in view of the fact that in 410/09 B.C. (*IG*² II 304A) they were called on repeatedly to disburse money to the Hellenotamiae which went to furnish maintenance for the cavalry (*híπποιs σîτοs*), such was probably the case.

It seems to me likely that in *c.* 394 B.C. the system followed by the *demos* for meeting its contingent expenses between 411 and 404 B.C. was reëstablished, with the difference that the Treasurer of the People took the place of the Hellenotamiae. Thereafter, the Treasurer and the Tamiae occupied between

them the position held by the *kolakretae* prior to 411 B.C. In
a sense, therefore, the Tamiae continued to be the bankers
and the Opisthodomos the bank of the *demos* throughout the
fourth century.[1] In *c.* 377 B.C. the state transferred from the
Tamiae to the Treasurer the regular deposit, then fixed at ten
talents yearly, with which it defrayed its contingent expenses;
but, if we may generalize from one case, the income from fees,
fines, confiscations, etc., by which the cost of the courts was
met, passed through the hands of the Tamiae; and the people
deposited with the Tamiae, when circumstances permitted,
larger sums with a view to military and other like emergencies.
Their normal rôle was circumscribed by the fact that in the
fourth century (as in the fifth) every board of magistrates had
its own private treasury in which it kept, pending disbursement,
the comparatively small sums of money allocated to it; and this
situation was not altered by the creation of the Committee on
the Theoric Fund and the Treasurership of the Military Fund.
These were annual offices (*Hellenistic Athens*, pp. 474 ff.; Busolt,
Griech. Staatsk., II, p. 1055, n. 3), unique in being filled by specially selected men (Arist. *Ath. Pol.* 43 1) and in their right to
oversee the collecting of the revenues (Arist. *Ath. Pol.* 47 2) and
to control their allocation and expenditure (*Aesch.* III 25); like
the Tamiae in that they were held from Panathenaia to Panathenaia.[2] Each had its own treasury doubtless, into which
flowed — into the one during time of peace, into the other during time of war, according to a practice which could be altered
only by constitutional amendment (νόμος) — "the surpluses of

[1] It was from a fund of public money (τῆς πόλεως κοινῇ) that the Councillor Tim-
archos and the Tamias of the Goddess Hegesandros, acting in collusion, embezzled
1000 drachmas in 361/0 B.C., according to Aeschines (I 110).

[2] The view commonly held (Busolt, *Griech. Staatsk.*, II, p. 1135, n. 7), that in the
fourth century the year of the Tamiae was the calendar year, goes back to Böckh
(*Kleine Schriften*, VI, pp. 84 ff.). It rests solely upon the dating of the successive
boards of Treasurers ἐπὶ τοῦ δεῖνα ἄρχοντος. This, however, has no value in this connection. The Tamiae were so dated in the entire period, 413/2–404/03 B.C. (*IG*² II 1498;
I², 255a, *above*, p. 13; 313, l. 174, *above*, p. 27, n. 1). The Tamiae of the Other Gods were
so dated in 429/8 B.C. (*IG*² I 310). The use of the Archon as eponymous of the year,
irrespective of whether this was the calendar year, the conciliar year, or the Panathenaic year, is due to other considerations altogether (Luria, *Hermes*, 1927, pp. 257 ff.;
Meritt, *Athenian Calendar*, pp. 16 f., 95; Dinsmoor, *Archons of Athens*, p. 348). *IG*² I

the financial administration" (τὰ περιόντα χρήματα τῆς διοικήσεως; [*Dem.*] LIX 4).[1] Their relation to the financial advisers to whom, as Aeschines (III 25) puts it, the *demos* gave its confidence (πίστιν), and whom it elected to extraordinary Commissions, tenable for four years at a stretch ([Plut.], *Lives of the Ten Orators*, 841B; *IG*[2] II 1493–1496), — Eubulos, [2] Lycurgus, and others, — is a matter of conjecture and does not concern us here.

In the fourth century Athens replaced in large part, or in

304B (Meritt's text in his *Athenian Financial Documents*, to be published shortly) and 305 (*above*, pp. 30, 81, n. 1) show clearly that in 407/06 and 406/05 B.C. the year of the Tamiae was the Panathenaic year. Hence Bannier's attempt (*Ber. Phil. Woch.*, 1915, p. 1612) to show that in the fifth century their year was the Archon's year is vain. Panske (*Leip. Stud.*, 1890, pp. 20 ff.) was right in holding that the Tamiae held office throughout from Panathenaia to Panathenaia. Not only is there no ground whatsoever for assuming a change, but the frequency with which during the fourth century crises in the administration of the Tamiae are connected with the Panathenaia (*above*, pp. 14, 119, n. 1) emphasizes the significance for their office of the date of the festival.

[1] The books of the state were closed for each successive year at the last session of the Council (Arist. *Ath. Pol.* 48). It is not necessary to suppose that until then the Commissioners and the Treasurer enjoyed only the use of the surpluses of the preceding year: they may have had prospective surpluses allocated to them at the beginning of the financial year and begun to receive surpluses realized by specific magistrates from the moment their allowances exceeded their expenses — at the end of the ninth prytany, for example (cf. *above*, p. 134, n. 2). The reason for having the Commissioners and the Treasurer enter office after the Panathenaia may have been a desire to have their accounts run for the same period as those of the Tamiae (*above*, p. 138, n. 2), though it was a collateral advantage that they gained thereby an extra month in which to expend annual surpluses. That they had their own treasuries is an inference from the general financial practice of Athens. It does not follow from the fact that in 334/3 B.C. (*IG*[2] II 1493) the Treasurer of the Military Fund furnished the Tamiae (and the Commissioners on renovating the *kosmos* of the temples on the Acropolis) with money. Even if the Military Fund had been in their custody, it would have been paid out to them, as to all other parties, by the Treasurer.

[2] From a new reading of the text of the speech of Hyperides against Demosthenes (V (I), frg. VIII, col. 28; cf. Colin, *REA*, 1928, pp. 191 ff.) it appears that Lycurgus was elected Tamias ἐπὶ τὴν διοίκησιν ἅπασαν — an extraordinary office created by decree and hence not dealt with in the νόμοι which Aristotle used as the basis for the descriptive part of his *Constitution of Athens*. Lycurgus can (I think, dissenting from Colin) have served from Hekatombaion 28th, 338 B.C., to Hekatombaion 28th, 334 B.C. and have had dummies elected for the two following *penteterides* (*Lives of the Ten Orators*, p. 841 c), while he himself was Chairman of various commissions — on the Nikae, *dermatika*, public buildings, etc. — after 334 B.C. The basis of his power was the confidence (πίστις) the Athenians had in him. This he lost in 326 B.C., when Menesaichmos (Kirchner, *PA*, 9983) became Tamias, with the ascendancy of the more violent anti-Macedonians.

whole, the sacred properties that went into the melting pot in 406/04 B.C., thus executing the injunction laid upon his fellow citizens by Pericles in 431 B.C. that "they must replace as much as they took." But the people did not try to replace the coined money of Athena and of the Other Gods borrowed to finance the Peloponnesian War. The temper of the age was generally indisposed to recognize such a restitution as a religious obligation.[1] The private resources of the Goddess, diminished by the loss of the *aparche*, the rentals from Lesbos and Euboea and temporarily from Lemnos, Imbros, and Scyros, and the first fruits of the spoils of successful wars, were quite unequal to the task of rehabilitating Athena's reserves. Nor did the receipt by the Tamiae of public money permit the accumulation of a fund. Special deposits were withdrawn almost as soon as they were made. Sums allocated to them by the *apodektae* went to swell the Theoric or the Military Fund, if they were not all spent in the course of the year. After 403 B.C. the Tamiae were primarily custodians of *ex-votos* and other temple properties;[2] and it is intelligible, therefore, that they disappear from our records with the radical expropriation of such articles by Lachares (*above*, pp. 126 ff.).

[1] The restitution required of the Phocians at the end of the Sacred War was due to the exceptional circumstances in which the shrine at Delphi was despoiled. From the point of view of the Amphictyony the Phocians were simply temple-robbers.

[2] The sum mentioned in *IG*² II 1414, ll. 50 ff., was only 2000 + drachmas; but the stone is so badly mutilated that we cannot tell whether it was expenditure, *epeteia*, or balance (*above*, p. 128, n. 2).

XIV

THE TRIBAL CYCLE OF THE SECRETARIES
OF THE TREASURERS: II

THE tenacity with which the Athenians maintained the tribal cycle while selecting the secretaries of the Treasurers of Athena and the secretaries of the Treasurers of Athena and the Other Gods between 411 and 386/5 B.C. is worthy of comment. The official succession of the *phylae* (in reverse order) was not disturbed by the amalgamation of the two boards of Treasurers in 406 B.C. Unless the Secretary of the Treasurers of the Other Gods between 411 and 406/05 B.C. was chosen each year from the same *phyle* as the Secretary of the Treasurers of Athena (*above*, p. 8),—prior to 411 B.C. there was no such coincidence, — the Secretary of the joint board continued the earlier series of secretaries of the board of Athena. Again in 342/1 B.C. the same thing happened. In this year, after a separation of forty-four years, the two boards were recombined; and, as in 406/05 B.C., the secretariat of the board of Athena passed over into the secretariat of the consolidated board without any disturbance of the tribal cycle it was then following (*below*, p. 144). On both occasions the secretariat of the board of the Other Gods (assuming there to have been one between 385/4 and 343/2 B.C.—of which there is no evidence [1]) was simply dropped. In view of the antiquity of the board of Treasurers of Athena and its dominating position both before 406/05 and after 386/5 B.C., it naturally prevailed in this matter over its younger and waning partner. The important thing is

---

[1] The only inventory of the Tamiae of the Other Gods which has reached us with any part of its prescript preserved is *IG*² II 1445 (376/5 B.C.). A comparison of this document with *IG*² II 1411, the inventory of the Tamiae of Athena for the same year, emphasizes the absence of a Secretary in the former. We have inventories of the board of Athena for this period (e.g., *IG*² II 1410, 1428, 367/6 B.C.) which omit the name of the Secretary of the transmitting or receiving board in their prescript; none, I think, which omit both.

that neither in 406/05 nor in 342/1 B.C. was the opportunity of a remodelling of the secretariat taken to start a new tribal cycle or abandon it wholly.

From this point of view it is surprising to find that when in 385 B.C. the Treasurers of Athena were again set up as a distinct *collegium* its secretariat ceased to follow the reverse of the official order and did not adopt the tribal cycle itself which it is found observing after 351/0 B.C. Yet the *phyle* of the one Secretary of Athena known for the intervening period (Εὐθίας Πεισίο Κήττιος, *IG*² II 1410, 1411, 376/5 B.C.), Leontis, shows that such was the case (*Athenian Secretaries*, p. 74).[1] But we can now go farther than was possible at the time the *Athenian Secretaries* was written. In the meantime, I have shown (*Klio*, 1914, pp. 393 ff.)[2] that for the first decade of their existence, prior to their adoption of the tribal cycle in 356/5 B.C., the prytany-secretaries were selected from the ten *phylae*, not indeed in their official sequence, but in such a way that each *phyle* got its turn. The important thing from the Athenian point of view was that the office should pass in rotation among all the approximately equal permanent divisions of the people. For this purpose there was available the time-honored system by which the secretaries of the Council had been assigned to the prytanies and the prytanies to the tenths of the year, namely, sortition. As each *phyle* of the Council was successful in the allotment it was disqualified for the drawing for the secretariat and the prytany during the rest of the year (*Athenian Secretaries*, p. 26). The method in vogue for the distribution of ten offices held successively in the course of a year could be readily applied for the distribution of an annual office throughout a ten-year period. Resort to it was apparently had in the case of the secretariat of the board of Treasurers of Athena in 385 B.C. And it was adhered to for two or three decades — 385/4–

---

[1] Unfortunately the new inventory of the year 369/8 B.C. (Kyparisses, Ἀρχ. Δελτίον, 1927/8, p. 128) lacks the name of the Secretary. The Secretary for 374/3 B.C. was Glauketes (*IG*² II 1421; Kolbe, *Philologus*, 1930, p. 263); but it is impossible to restore his *demotikon*. The reading of *IG*² II 1416, l. 15, ΙΣΝΕΔιεὺς ἐγρα[μμάτευε], is too uncertain to help.

[2] Cf. Dinsmoor, *Archons of Athens*, pp. 357 f.

376/5, 375/4–366/5, 365/4–356/5 B.C. Then the tribal cycle was reintroduced, now in its regular and not in its reverse order. But the beginning was not made with Erechtheis, the first *phyle* in the official sequence. Had that been done, one group of *phylae* would have got the office twice in a decade or another group failed to get it at all.[1] The fixed order of succession had to be resumed where it was left off in 386/5 B.C., and accordingly the *phyle* due to receive the office in 385/4 B.C., Leontis, was given the first place in the new tribal cycle. As to whether the new cycle began in 375/4 or 365/4 or 355/4 there may be some question; but if it began in 375/4 B.C., we should have had two secretaries from Leontis in succession; and since it was in 356/5 B.C. that the official order was first adopted in the case of the prytany-secretary,[2] it is probable that it was at the end of that year, on the completion of the third cycle of allotted succession,[3] that the *phylae* began to hold the secretariat of the board of Treasurers of Athena according to their official

---

[1] The reversal of the process, so that the cycle should proceed forwards instead of backwards, affected only the order in which the *phylae* secured the secretariat within the decade. The abolition of the joint board in 386/5 B.C. cost *phylae* IV–I an assured turn.

[2] And presumably also in the case of the Priest of Asklepios, since he followed the same cycle as the prytany-secretary (*Priests of Asklepios*, p. 131). We do not know why this cycle began with Kekropis. Probably the *phyle* to begin was determined by allotment. Why the reverse of the official order was used consistently prior to 386/5, apart from lists of soldiers who fell in battle (*IG*² I 928 ff.), and the official order was followed with equal consistency after 356/5 B.C. is beyond our knowing. Dinsmoor (*Archons of Athens*, p. 354) notes that 356 B.C. was also the opening year of the fifth Metonic cycle.

[3] Johnson (*AJA*, 1914, pp. 6 ff.) points out that the Treasurers of Athena for 376/5 B.C. (*IG*² II 1410) are not listed in the official order, as usual; and conjectures that the same irregularity of arrangement existed in 373/2 B.C. (*IG*² II 1421) and in the intervening years. But the conjecture rests on the connection of Eurykleides (*IG*² II 1421, l. 4) with the well-known Eurykleides-Mikion family conspicuous in the records of the third and second centuries B.C. — a grave uncertainty. The Treasurers of the Other Gods for 376/5 B.C. are listed in their tribal order. In both cases, though each board falls short of its usual number, the Tamiae were selected κατὰ φυλάς. And, in fact, as Kolbe (*Philologus*, 1930, p. 261 ff.) has shown, *IG*² II 1421 belongs in 374/3 B.C. Johnson's further conjecture, that the secretaries of the board of Athena switched over from the reverse of the tribal cycle to the tribal cycle itself in 386/5 B.C. and (ignoring the period of alleged irregularity, 376/5–373/2 B.C.) adhered to it thereafter, falls to the ground both for the reason just given and because we have now withdrawn all support from my earlier contention (*Athenian Secretaries*, p. 74) that the reverse of the tribal cycle was abandoned in 387/6 B.C. (*above*, pp. 12 ff.).

order.[1] The following table exhibits their rotation so long as it can be traced:

TABLE II

Year	Secretary of Tamiae	No. of IG² II	No. of phyle
355/4			4
354/3			5
353/2			6
352/1			7
351/0	Ἀγάθυμος Ἀδειμάντου Θυμαιτάδης	1436	VIII
350/9			9
349/8	Πιστίδης Θοραιεύς	1436	X
348/7			I
347/6			2
346/5	Ἅγν[ων – Πρασιεύς or Φηγαιεύς][2]	1442	3
345/4			4
344/3	– – Θριάσ]ιος or Φυλάσ]ιος	1443	5
343/2			6
342/1	– – – s	1455	7
341/0	– – ιμάχου Ἐλευσίνιος	1455	VIII
340/9	– – ράτος Τρικορύσιος	1455	IX

Presumably the cycle ended for a time in 322/1 B.C. with Kekropis.[3]

Yet more striking is the non-effect of revolutions on the tribal cycle between 412/1 B.C. and 403/02. Neither the overthrow of the Four Hundred nor the downfall of the Five Thousand; neither the establishment of the Thirty and the Ten nor their ejection and the democratic restoration disturbed the steady succession of the secretaries of the Treasurers in the reverse of the official order of their *phylae*. This is all the more remarkable in that the system was inaugurated by an oligarchic government — that of the Four Hundred. Rotation of office was not exclusively a δημοτικὸν νομοθέτημα, a democratic device: it became democratic only when all citizens, irrespective of birth or property, formed the body among

[1] It was at the same time, perhaps, that Androtion and his fellow *epimeletae* melted down, replaced, and reinventoried the *anathemata* (above, p. 119, n. 1). The epoch coincided with the opening of the regime of Eubulos. It was doubtless in the year 355/4 B.C. (Beloch, *Griech. Gesch.*, III, 2, pp. 258 ff.; *CAH*, VI, pp. 222 ff.) that Commissioners of the Theoric Fund with enlarged powers were created for the first time.

[2] No other name is possible. The *demotikon* may be either Πρασιεύς or Φηγαιεύς.

[3] If - - ἐξ Οἴου γραμματ[εύς is correct (*IG²* II 1477, l. 5, note), which cannot be assured, the cycle was not observed during the regime of Demetrius of Phalerum.

which the offices rotated. Neither extreme nor moderate oligarchs objected to it on principle (*CAH*, V, p. 339; Arist. *Politics* VII (V) 8 5, 1308a). The quarrel of the reformers in Athens was with its unwise application. They regarded it, and its logical sequel, sortition, as a help in filling the routine administrative posts (Arist. *Ath. Pol.* 30 2). And, in fact, the most thoroughgoing enunciation we possess of the principle of rotation of offices is found in the constitution of the Four Hundred (Arist. *Ath. Pol.* 31 3): τῶν δ' ἄλλων ἀρχῶν πλὴν τῆς βουλῆς καὶ τῶν στρατηγῶν μὴ ἐξεῖναι μήτε τούτοις μήτε ἄλλῳ μηδενὶ πλέον ἢ ἅπαξ ἄρξαι τὴν αὐτὴν ἀρχήν, if we except the provision of the pseudo-Draconian constitution which reflects the thought of this same oligarchic movement (Arist. *Ath. Pol.* 4 3): καὶ δὶς τὸν αὐτὸν μὴ ἄρχειν πρὸ τοῦ πάντας ἐξελθεῖν. The inauguration of a system of tribal cycles (its reinauguration, rather; *above*, p. 10) is, therefore, in harmony with the general ideas of the "reformers"; and, as we shall point out presently (*below*, pp. 151 f.), something of the sort was almost dictated by the methods followed by them in filling the purely administrative magistracies.

The Tamiae of the Four Hundred probably served for the two months of Mnasilochos' archonship alone.[1] Since the

---

[1] We cannot define precisely the beginning of the term of office of the Tamiae of the Four Hundred. There are three possibilities: Thargelion 22d, at the moment of the oligarchic *coup d'état*; Hekatombaion 1st, on the assumption of office by the Archon Mnasilochos; and Hekatombaion 28th, at the regular time. The earlier date is ordinarily preferred (Bannier, *Rh. Mus.*, 1915, pp. 405 ff.; Hiller, *IG*² I 251), but on inadequate evidence. Thucydides (VIII 67 3) attributes to the epoch of the Assembly at Colonus, not a change of magistrates, but a change of regime of office-holding; and Aristotle (*Ath. Pol.* 29 5) gives us no warrant for supposing that prior to the establishment of the Four Hundred any offices had been vacated except the Generalships (*Ath. Pol.* 31 2). There is no reason for believing that the Four Hundred on assuming control supplanted any further governing boards except the Council of the Five Hundred; and the right of this body to finish out its year was recognized by its receipt of pay for the unfinished balance of its term (*Thucy.* VIII 69 4). The Four Hundred *did* have magistrates designated to serve from Hekatombaion 1st: the term of Mnasilochos proves it (Arist. *Ath. Pol.* 33 1); the grant to the Four Hundred of authority to supplant its interim Generals by regular Generals chosen "for the ensuing year" (Arist. *Ath. Pol.* 31 2) presupposes it; and the allusion of Lysias (XX 2) to elections by the *phyletae* suggests that the Four Hundred themselves were regularly reëlected (cf. Arist. *Ath. Pol.* 31 1) at some time subsequent to their irregular designation on Pisander's motion at Colonus (*Thucy.* VIII 67 3). The abrogation of indemnities doubtless decimated the civil services after the oligarchic *coup d'état*; but it is unlikely that the Tamiae, who were chosen from the

leaders most influential in establishing the Five Thousand had been themselves members of the Four Hundred, service under the fallen govenment could not of itself be a cause for judicial condemnation. Hence we cannot doubt that the Tamiae of the oligarchy and their Secretary stood their audit successfully. Otherwise their inventories and accounts would not have been

Pentakosiomedimni, were affected by it. Following this line of argument, we should conclude that the Tamiae of the Four Hundred entered office at their regular time, Hekatombaion 28th. But it should be observed that the Four Hundred were empowered not only to appoint magistrates but to modify the oaths of office and deal with the laws governing magistracies as they thought best (Arist. *Ath. Pol.* 31 1). Lysias (XX 14) shows that they used their authority at least so far as the oaths of office were concerned; and they can have used it further to shift back to Hekatombaion 1st the entrance of the Tamiae upon office. We have to consider the fact that the Tamiae of the Four Hundred made a payment of 27+ talents on the 21st of Hekatombaion (*IG*² I 298). This might be taken to indicate that they had, in fact, begun to serve prior to Hekatombaion 28th. Busolt (*Griech. Staatsk.*, II, p. 1055; cf. p. 1135) and Glotz (*La Cité grecque*, p. 257) date the regular entry of the Tamiae about Hekatombaion 20th; but this conjecture is refuted by *IG*² I 305, which shows the Tamiae of 406/05 B.C. still in office on the 27th of Hekatombaion (West, *Class. Weekly*, 1929, p. 63; Meritt, *AJA*, 1930, p. 149; cf. *above*, p. 81, n. 1). There cannot be much doubt that the change of Tamiae occurred regularly just after and not just before the Panathenaia. Yet a payment on the 21st, even though it is credited to the Tamiae holding office after the 28th, can no longer be taken to prove that in the year in question an irregular entry upon office had occurred. Meritt (*Athenian Calendar*, pp. 18 f., 95 ff.) has developed plausibly the theory that in preparing the accounts of the Tamiae for auditing the *logistae* credited to the board which held office for the greater part of their own year the payments made by its predecessor during the brief interval that fell between the close of the preceding conciliar year and Hekatombaion 28th (cf. *IG*² I 324, l. 26). This virtual falsification of the record he attributes to the bookkeeping practice of the *logistae*. I am inclined to think that this explanation is inadequate; and that, granted the fact, we shall have to recognize some sort of joint responsibility as existing during the opening weeks of the fiscal year between the Tamiae in office and the Tamiae elect, as a result of which the Tamiae elect could be properly held to an accounting for the transactions of the whole fiscal year. On this theory the payment made on the 21st of Hekatombaion during the archonship of Mnasilochos can have been made by the Tamiae of the year 412/1 even though it is specifically assigned to the Tamiae of the Four Hundred. But we may query whether in the circumstances this was probable. It seems to me very unlikely that out of deference to a bookkeeping tradition, even though it were justified by a theory of joint responsibility, the Tamiae of the Four Hundred would have been saddled with the onus of accounting for a payment actually made on order of the Four Hundred by the Tamiae for 412/1 B.C. On the other hand, were we to assume that the Tamiae of the oligarchy assumed office on Thargelion 22d, we should have to conclude that during the first two months of their rule the Four Hundred drew no money whatsoever from the treasury of Athena. With this consideration in mind I am inclined to think that in 411 B.C. the Tamiae entered upon office at the same time as the Archon, that is to say, on Hekatombaion 1st.

published. But the view taken of their conduct in September, 411 B.C., was not popular in July, 410. Hence they had no share in the commemorative tablet presented by the other Tamiae of this *penteteris* for erection on the Acropolis (*above*, pp. 6, 100, n. 1), and they were ignored in the prescript of the inventories of the quadrennium notwithstanding that their inventories were included in the record (*above*, pp. 70 f., 100 f.).

The secretary of the Treasurers of Athena for 411/0 B.C. (archonship of Theopompos) is unknown; but the cycle shows that he belonged to the *phyle* Antiochis (*above*, p. 9). All that remains of his name is the final letter of his *demotikon*.[1] The *phyle* Erechtheis had had the secretariat for a very short interval, and in later times it was customary, when an official was replaced during his term of office, to choose his successor from the same *phyle*. This was done, for example, in the fourth century with substitutions in the board of Athenian Amphictyons at Delos (*IG*[2] II 1635; cf. *Class. Rev.*, 1901, p. 38); in the third century in the case of *suffecti* for priests of Asklepios (*IG*[2] II 1534B, ll. 222 ff.; cf. *Priests of Asklepios*, p. 133); and in the second century when for any reason two priests of Sarapis held office in the same year (*Athenian Secretaries*, pp. 46 f.). But, as the appointment of a new Archon shows, the epoch of the Four Hundred was treated as a year in itself.

The cycle also shows that the year 411/0 B.C. did not have a third secretary and board of Tamiae. We have already known that it did not have a third Archon. For Aristotle (*Ath. Pol.* 33 1) tells us that Theopompos was archon for the remaining ten months. Of the Generals in office at the time of the battle of Cyzicus Alcibiades, Theramenes, Eumachos, and Thrasyllos served out their terms, as Xenophon shows (*Hell.* I 1 8; 20 ff.); and indeed it is incredible that the authors of so brilliant a series of naval victories should have been superseded prematurely. The reëstablishment of the democratic Council was doubtless, then as earlier, a demand of Alcibiades (*Thucy.* VIII 86 6), but now that *IG*[2] I 105 is, it appears (*above*, p. 42, n. 1), to be transferred from the archonship of Theopompos to the archonship of

---

[1] *IG*[2] I 253, cf. *JHS*, 1928, p. 177. I do not know for what reason Böckh, Kirchhoff, and Hiller give fourteen spaces for his name and *demotikon*.

Antigenes there is no evidence or reason for supposing that the regime of the Four Councils was set aside till the beginning of the conciliar year 410/09 B.C. (*Andoc.* I 96 ff.). There was, accordingly, no occasion for appointing a third set of officials in 411/0 B.C.; for the battle of Cyzicus probably occurred as late as the end of May or the early part of June, 410 B.C. The tribal cycle of the *phylae* was also adhered to in filling the office of Secretary of the Tamiae for 410/09 B.C. That it surmounted the administrative change of 406 B.C. we have already noted.

The next crisis came on the surrender of Athens to the Lacedaemonians. We have not a single inscription of the archonship of Pythodoros (404/03 B.C.); and if any were incised they were probably destroyed (*above*, p. 57, n. 1). But we know from *IG*² II 1370–1372 that Tamiae existed under the Thirty and the Ten, and that they had a Secretary as usual. If Kirchner is right in restoring lines 20 f. of *IG*² II 1498, [στήλη ταμιῶν τῆ]s θεο[ῦ κ]αὶ τῶν ἄλλων [θεῶν ἐπὶ Πυθοδώρου ἄρχοντος], they set up on the Acropolis the customary commemorative tablet (*above*, p. 6, n. 1; 100, n. 1).[1] Between the fall of Athens (Munychion, 16) and the archonship of Pythodoros an interval of about one and one-half months elapsed. We have known from a reference in Lysias (XIII 20) that the Council of the Five Hundred (ἡ πρὸ τῶν τριάκοντα βουλεύουσα) continued in office for some time after the surrender. Previously it had taken sides actively against Cleophon, who was for holding out even if the multitude perished from starvation (*Lysias* XXX 11). It now lent itself to the party led by Theramenes and Critias, and took vigorous action against the heads of the group which had been formed to prevent the establishment in Athens of an oligarchical government; and in fact its members were in large part reëlected to serve on the Council of the Thirty (*Lysias* XIII 20). There was then no interim Council in the year 404 B.C. Nor was there an interim Archon. Pythodoros succeeded Alexias directly. The cycle shows that there was no interim Secretary of the Tamiae and consequently no interim Tamiae. The date

---

[1] The custom was apparently abandoned on the democratic restoration in 403 B.C. This being the case, the only other possible Archon names (Καλλίου and Ἀλεξίου) are too short.

on which the *demos* adopted Drakontides' motion "to elect thirty men who should frame the ancestral laws according to which public affairs should be handled" (Xen. *Hell.* II 3 2 and 11), and govern the state meanwhile, fell some few days before the opening of the year 404/03 B.C. (Beloch, *Griech. Gesch.*, III, 2, pp. 204 ff.; Meyer, *Gesch. d. Alt.*, V, p. 20; *CAH*, V, p. 366); but the Council and the magistrates whom they appointed, ἐκ τῶν χιλίων? (*Ath. Pol.* 35 1), ὡς ἐδόκει αὐτοῖς (Xen. *Hell.* II 3 11), doubtless entered upon their offices together with Pythodoros. Was he not one of their number?[1] Whatever liberties the Thirty took with the elections,[2] they did not interfere with the arrangement by which the Secretary of the Tamiae for 404/03 B.C. fell to a man from the *phyle* Pandionis. The supplanting of the Thirty by the Ten was obviously not accompanied by changes in the personnel of the administrative offices; Pythodoros was Archon and Patrokles "King" (*Isocr.* XVIII 5)[3] under both; and Pandionis held the secretariat of the Treasurers till the end of the year.

Aristotle (*Ath. Pol.* 39 1) sets the reconciliation between the men of the Piraeus and the men of the City in the archonship of Eukleides (403/02 B.C.). The day of the entrance of the democrats into Athens is given by Plutarch (*De gloria Ath.* 7, p. 349F.; cf. *IG*[2] II 1496, l. 131) as the 12th of Boedromion — nearly two and one-half months after the opening of the calendar year and one and one-half months after the close of the term of the Tamiae of 404/03 B.C. A little later the Council of the Five Hundred was constituted by the usual process of allotment (*Andoc.* I 81). There intervened a period during which there was no Council (*Lives of the Ten Orators*, p. 835F; cf. Arist. *Ath. Pol.* 40 2 and *IG*[2] II 10: *SEG*, III, 70), the government being in the hands of twenty men (*Andoc. loc. cit.*), ten from each faction doubtless.[4] The nonexistence of the Council is noted specifi-

---

[1] Roos' conjecture (*Klio*, 1920, p. 2), that for a period at the opening of 404/03 B.C. there was no government in Athens at all, has been rejected by Beloch (*Griech. Gesch.*, III, 2, p. 208). Aristotle's statement (*Ath. Pol.* 35 1), that the Thirty were established in the archonship of Pythodoros, must not be taken too literally.

[2] They acted as their own *strategi* apparently.

[3] Cloché, *La restauration démocratique à Athènes*, p. 118.

[4] *CAH*, V, p. 373.

cally in the *scholia* on *Aesch.* III 195: οὐδέπω γὰρ ἦν καθεσταμένη βουλὴ μετὰ τὴν τῶν λ' κατάλυσιν. The author of the *Life of Lysias* speaks of "the anarchy subsequent to the return before Eukleides." *IG*² II 1370 and 1371 are too badly mutilated to make it certain that the Tamiae of [Pythodoros'] archonship were the immediate predecessors of the Tamiae of Eukleides' year. As Kirchner points out, the vacancies in lines 6 and 7 of the former will not permit the restoration of the normal *formulae*, παραδεξάμενοι παρά and τῶν ἐπὶ Πυθοδώρο ἄρχοντος. The requirements of space are met by [παραδεξάμενοι ἄγραφα ¹ παρὰ] τῶν προτέρων τ[αμιῶν τῶν ἐν 'Αναρχίαι ἀρξάντων, οἷς Δ]ρομοκλε[ίδης; and we have thus confirmed the opinion already expressed that no inventories were compiled for 404/03 B.C. (*above*, p. 57, n. 1). Officially, then, the Anarchy continued till the entrance of Eukleides upon office. If officials of the Ten replaced on Hekatombaion 1st and 28th respectively the officials chosen by the Thirty, they are nowhere mentioned. We know, however, that after the reconciliation the *phyle* Pandionis was held to have had its turn of the secretariat of the Tamiae in 404/03 B.C., so that the next *phyle* in the cycle, Aigeis, could be given this office in the archonship of Eukleides (403/02 B.C.). In this particular the year of the Anarchy was not treated as if it were nonexistent. The archonship of Pythodoros was counted precisely as the archonship of Mnasilochos had been. It seems to me probable that at the expiry of the year of the Thirty-Ten, that is to say, on or about Hekatombaion 1st, the Ten and their officials went out of office, and that the mysterious second board of Ten which has cropped up so embarrassingly

---

¹ For ἄγραφα see *IG*² II 1388, l. 52; 1393, l. 32; 1400, l. 52. [Xenophon's] statement (*Hell.* II 3 1), Πυθοδώρου δ' ἐν 'Αθήναις ἄρχοντος ὃν 'Αθηναῖοι, ὅτι ἐν ὀλιγαρχίᾳ ᾑρέθη, οὐκ ὀνομάζουσιν, ἀλλ' ἀναρχίαν τὸν ἐνιαυτὸν καλοῦσιν, was surely not invented; cf. *Anony. Argent.* (Keil), p. 69. The next archonless year known to us, 88/7 B.C., was entered in the great Archon List (Ditt., *Syll.*³, 733) as 'Αναρχία (Kirchner, *GGA*, 1900, p. 476; cf. Dinsmoor, *Archons of Athens*, p. 282). The magistrates who compiled this list had earlier precedent doubtless. Official usage was one thing; literary practice another. We have no warrant for restoring Πυθοδώρο in the inventories compiled in 403/02 B.C. in the references to him in Lysias (VII 9), Aristotle (*Ath. Pol.* 35 1), *Anony. Argent.* (Keil), p. 69, Xenophon (*Hell.* II 3 1). Naturally the Tamiae who dedicated the bronze *stele* during his year entered his name on it (*IG*² II 1498, l. 21). [Woodward (*above*, p. 95, n. 2) proposes to retain ἐπὶ Πυθοδώρο ἄρχοντος before οἷς.]

in Aristotle's account of this epoch (*Ath. Pol.* 38 3)[1] assumed control of affairs at this juncture with the definite purpose of coming to terms with the men of the Piraeus, and that in the interim no further officials of any kind were installed.

The strict adherence of the Athenians to the tribal cycle during this period of revolutions and counter-revolutions may be attributed to two special considerations. The introduction of the system and its subsequent maintenance by the oligarchs are to be connected with their fidelity to what they regarded as the ancestral (Solonian) method of election — αἵρεσις or κλήρωσις ἐκ προκρίτων οὓς ἑκάστη προκρίνειε τῶν φυλῶν (Arist. *Ath. Pol.* 8 1; 30 2; 31 1; 35 1; Xen. *Hell.* II 3 2; cf. [*Lysias*] XX 2). For this dual process of selecting officials the *phylae* were yet more important than they were under the democratic system. Even the Thirty seem to have been chosen κατὰ φυλάς (Busolt, *Griech. Staatsk.*, II, p. 912, n. 5). Since the *phylae* were to share equally in the offices, the rotation among them of an annual office like the secretariat of the Tamiae of Athena was in order, and the tribal cycle was a convenient instrument to effect it. The second factor working for the maintenance of the tribal cycle continuously throughout this epoch was the constant overlapping of regimes. The inaugurators of the Five Thousand were members of the Four Hundred. Those responsible for the broadening again of the franchise and the restoration of the Council of the Five Hundred were headed by the Generals of the Five Thousand, Alcibiades and the rest.

[1] This board, to which Aristotle gives the credit for the reconciliation, but which Xenophon ignores, can be identified with the ten representatives of the men of the City on the managing committee of Twenty (*above*, p. 149; cf. Cloché, *op. cit.*, p. 184, n.). While he was a member of the first Ten, Phinon joined others outside it (*Isocr.* XVIII 5 ff.; cf. Cloché, pp. 112 ff.) in getting into touch with the men of the Piraeus (*Ath. Pol.* 38 3; cf. *CAH*, V, p. 371). The intervention of Pausanias made clear to the Three Thousand the desirability of being headed by men who had not worked hand and glove with Lysander (Xen. *Hell.* II 4 37). The second Ten were presumably envoys rather than magistrates. As Beloch remarks (*Griech. Gesch.*, III, 1, p. 12, n. 1), the Ten cannot have acted for the City in negotiations which resulted in their own exclusion from the amnesty. Those who did, naturally joined with a like group from the Piraeus in installing the new regime. Aristotle (*Ath. Pol.* 38 3) antedates, or, rather, seems to antedate, the "deposition" of the first Ten. The second Ten are, however, regarded as unhistorical by Meyer (*Gesch. d. Alt.* V, p. 40), Cloché (*op. cit.*, pp. 170 ff.), Sandys (*Aristotle's Constitution of Athens*, p. 149), and others.

The Council of the Five Hundred for 405/04 B.C. was transformed with only a partial change of personnel and little change of attitude — the democrats alleged that they had been corrupted — into the Council of the Five Hundred of the Thirty. The democratic regime of 403/02 B.C. was a compromise arranged by Pausanias between the moderates of both factions, in which the point of view of the Three Thousand was strongly sustained and safeguarded (*CAH*, V, pp. 372 ff.). And there was at each transition an overlapping of administration. The sharpest breach of continuity in office-holding occurred on the fall of the Four Hundred in 411 and the dislodgement of the Ten in 403 B.C.; but even then there was a *liaison* between the old and the new. The *katalogeis* of the Four Hundred drew up the list of the Five Thousand and the constitution of the Five Thousand itself was of one piece with the constitution of the Four Hundred. The same general who commanded the fleet of the Four Hundred at Eretria, Thymochares, commanded the first fleet sent out from Athens by the Five Thousand; and Theramenes was *strategos* under both regimes. And in 403 B.C., as we have seen (*above*, p. 151, n. 1), the administrative *lacuna* which coincided with the first few weeks of Eukleides' "year" was bridged by the installation of the second board of Ten and its amalgamation with Ten from the Piraeus to form the board of Twenty which set the democratic machine in motion. Rhinon, a member of the first board of Ten, the organiser of the second, was *strategos* in 403/02 B.C.

The two episodes which interrupted the flow of development were the usurpation of power by the extremists among the Four Hundred and the lawless violence of Critias and the Thirty; and both of them were ended on the initiative of their own supporters. Even in this disastrous period the Athenians were not unworthy of their reputation for political sagacity. Athens was not like other cities, says Aristotle (*Ath. Pol.* 40 3), a reluctant witness to democratic continence; far from dividing among themselves the property of the rich in their moments of victory, the democrats of Athens gave of their own possessions for the common weal. That should be put in the balance against the judicial persecutions of the well-to-do during the epoch of Cleophon (*CAH*, V, pp. 348 ff.).

XV

THE ATHENIAN WAR–FUNDS

THE financial procedure of Athens for the coming years was
laid down in 434 B.C. in the famous decree of Kallias
(*IG²* I 91/2; Kolbe, *Sitz. Ber. Akad.*, 1927, pp. 319 ff.). Into
the earlier history of the war-fund entrusted to the Tamiae of
Athena I do not intend to enter, further than to indicate the
conclusions to which I have come through evaluating the evidence collected by the many scholars who have written on this
theme. I do not see how 9700 talents can have been accumulated in the treasury of the Goddess at any time, or 6000 talents
in 431 B.C., except by the *addition* of the surpluses from the
tribute and the private possessions of Athena. Neither of
these sources of savings alone can have sufficed to roll up such
a total. In other words, I think that Meyer (*Forsch.*, II, pp.
88 ff.; *Gesch. d. Alt.*, IV, pp. 31 ff.) errs in postulating devastat-
ing borrowings from the Tamiae prior to 454 B.C.,[1] and that
Beloch (*Griech. Gesch.*, II, 2, pp. 324 ff.) and his school under-
estimate the resources of the Goddess: they depreciate unduly
the increment due to gifts, fines, confiscations, booty, etc.,
during the long past history of the shrine. Since the Other
Gods had *c.* 700 talents of coined money in 433 B.C., Athena

---

[1] From the fact that there was admittedly some money in the treasury at Delos in
454 B.C. Kolbe (*Sitz. Ber. Akad.*, 1929, p. 279) infers that Athens had not borrowed
theretofore from the Goddess. Such may be the case; but this argument does not suffice
to prove it. As pointed out below (pp. 162 f.), the Athenians borrowed money from the
Other Gods when the Treasury of Athena was well stocked and from Athena when the
Hellenotamiae had money in deposit on the Acropolis in abundance. There is, however, another argument which weighs more heavily. In 423/2 B.C. the only moneys
due Athena were those borrowed in 433/2 B.C. and subsequently. Manifestly the huge
drafts on Athena's funds made for the Parthenon, the chryselephantine statue, the
Propylaea, etc., were not loans: these embellishments of the Acropolis were Athena's
no less than the silver and gold with which they were made; they were the Periclean
equivalent of the Nikae, sacrificial vessels, and πομπεῖα into which at various times in
the fourth century crowns and other votive offerings were converted. I do not see how
Athens can have been seriously in debt to Athena in 454 and square in 433 B.C. unless
we do violence to *IG²* I 91, ll. 3 f., and *Thucydides* II 13 3.

must have had many times that amount exclusive of the accumulation of surpluses from the tribute. In both cases votives of silver had probably been converted at some past time into money.

The problem of explaining how the 9700 talents came to be reduced to 6000 notwithstanding that 3000 talents over and above the ordinary revenues of the Goddess were added simultaneously — in other words, of explaining how 6700 plus *c.* 700 talents came to be disbursed between the zenith point and 431 B.C. — has been solved by Cavaignac (*Études*, pp. 107 ff.) by assuming, doubtless erroneously (Beloch, II, 2, p. 341), a corruption in the text of Thucydides, and by Meyer and Beloch by assuming an arithmetical slip on the part of the historian; in effect, by reducing the maximum of 9700 talents by an allowance of 2000–3000 talents for money counted twice. This latter solution rejects the report of a critical contemporary, minded to know and in a position to know the facts, which were not difficult of ascertainment, in favor of estimates of the Treasurers' expenditures between 454 and 431 B.C. based on general considerations and data imperfectly published and extraordinarily fragmentary. Meanwhile the labor of Dinsmoor, Hiller von Gärtringen, and others, incorporated in the *Editio Minor* of *IG* I, has given us a sounder record for such estimates; and recently Kolbe (*Sitz. Ber. Akad.*, 1929, pp. 273 ff.) has demonstrated the possibility, which is all that is needed, not to say the probability, that in fact the Tamiae disbursed the required amounts between the zenith point of their treasury (according to him $\div$ 450 B.C.) and the outbreak of the Peloponnesian War in 431 B.C.

I agree with most scholars who have dealt with the subject recently (e.g., Stevenson, *JHS*, 1924, pp. 1 ff.) in thinking that at least as early as 454 B.C. the profits of the Empire and the treasures of Athena were fused in a single reserve, of which the Goddess was regarded as the owner. But I hold that a new departure of real significance was made in 434 B.C. Once the money given to Athena had reached the desired height, that is to say, when the 3000 talents, voted in 444/3 B.C. perhaps (Kolbe), had been "carried up to the Acropolis" in its entirety, and once the debt to Athena and the Other Gods had been repaid in full (these accounts were square in 434/3 B.C., as IG^2 I 324 shows; in other words, the Samians had already made good the sums borrowed from Athena in 441/39 B.C., and the 200 talents borrowed from the Other Gods were already in the Opisthodomos), the time was ripe for creating a reserve on which the state could draw without borrowing and paying interest. That this is the significance of the crucial lines of IG^2 I 92 (50–52) has been recognized generally; for example, by Meyer (*Forsch.*, II, pp. 113 ff.; *Gesch. d. Alt.*, IV, pp. 281 f.), Francotte (*Finances*, p. 206), Dittenberger (*Syll.*[3], 91, n. 13), and Beloch (*Griech. Gesch.*, II, 2, p. 349). Stevenson's argument to the contrary (*loc. cit.*, pp. 6 f.; cf. De Sanctis, *Atthis*[2], p. 490) is not conclusive: there *were* separate compartments in the right-hand chamber of the Opisthodomos where Athena's money was deposited, and the χρέματα kept there by the Tamiae of Athena included moneys belonging to different funds (*above*, p. 21, n. 1). Since the Tamiae kept a separate account of each of these funds, debiting withdrawals to Athena Polias, Athena Nike, and Hermes as the case might be, they did not need special instructions about storing separately the future yield of the *phoros*: that would follow as a matter of course in the absence of orders to the contrary. Thenceforth the proceeds of the tribute, it must be observed, were to be "deposited on" (κατα-τιθέναι) not "carried up to,"[1] the Acropolis as theretofore, much less "repaid" to the Goddess. What I shall try especially to show in this section is that this purely secular reserve, created by decree in 434 B.C., was created in fact after the Peace of Nicias.[2]

The conditions which made possible "the carrying up to the Acropolis" of 3000 talents in the years preceding 434 B.C. made it equally possible to accumulate a similar amount in the years of comparative peace after 421 B.C. The tribute yielded an-

---

[1] This was the term generally used; cf. *above*, p. 133, n. 2. Kallias must have had a reason for not using it at this point. A simple desire to vary the expression is not an acceptable motive in this kind of document.

[2] The contrary view is expressed tersely by Meyer (*Gesch. d. Alt.*, IV, p. 282, n. 1): "Zur Ausfürung ist diese Anordnung nie gekommen, da schon im nächsten Jahr der Krieg ausbrach."

nually much more in the later period than in the earlier; for, though West (*AJA*, 1925, pp. 135 ff.) has, I think, made out a case for a reduction of this levy in 421 B.C. from its height during the preceding four years, his own figures do not warrant the conclusion that the reduction was a return all round to the Aristidean level; and he finds it necessary to conclude that the *phoros* was raised again in 417 B.C.[1] If Athens gave to the Goddess *c.* 300 talents of imperial money annually between 445 and 434 B.C. notwithstanding the military expenditures of these years, she can have deposited double that sum with the Tamiae annually between 421 and 419 / 8 B.C.; and the moneys thus accumulated suffice to bring the reserve (exclusive of the 1000 talents set apart for a naval crisis) up to the figure (3000 + talents) reached at the time of the Sicilian Expedition (*IG*² I 99), seeing that, under the system then in vogue (*below*, pp. 161 ff.), additions to the reserve can have been made in the years 418/7, 417/6, and 416/5 B.C. also.[2]

Some points in the financial procedure laid down in the decree of Kallias demand elucidation. An essential provision approximated Athena's reserve (inclusive of additions, i.e., unexpended balances of the Goddess' own revenues, that might be made to it) with private property of citizens, in that it made a levy on her funds contingent on a preliminary vote of *adeia* passed with a quorum of 6000 citizens present and voting. We learn from the accounts of the Tamiae-logistae that withdrawals took the form of loans with consequent obligation both to pay interest and make repayment to Athena. The reserve was, accordingly, Athena's money. Withdrawals of money with

---

[1] Kolbe (*Sitz. Ber. Akad.*, 1930, pp. 333 ff.) argues that after being raised appreciably in 427 B.C. the tribute was elevated to 1460 + talents by Cleon in 425/4 and maintained at that figure till the Twentieth was substituted for it in 414/3. West and Meritt dissent. Quite apart from the epigraphical question at issue (the correct dating of *IG*¹ I 543 and 37 frg. z), the problem whether the first figure of *IG*² I 63, l. 212, is to be restored with ⊓ or ✕ must be regarded as still unsettled. [See further on this point West, *Trans. Amer. Phil. Assoc.*, 1930, pp. 217 ff.] It seems to me probable that in 421 B.C. and later the Aristidean *phoros* was an alleviation to which Athens consented for political reasons in specific cases (*Thucy.* V 18 5; Xen. *Hell.* I 3 9?; above, p. 42, n. 3), not the general basis of the assessment.

[2] Andocides (III 8) states that 7000 talents were "carried up to the Acropolis" during this period, and that more than 1200 talents of tribute came in annually.

which to pay for the construction of "the Propylaea and the other buildings" (*Thucy.* II 13 3) between 447 and 431 B.C. and of the Erechtheum and the temple of Athena Nike between 434 and 415 B.C. did not constitute loans, since the edifices belonged to the Goddess. They were subtractions from the reserve, not additions to the debt, and hence, like the expenditures on the Erechtheum between 409/08 and 405/04 B.C., were doubtless unrecorded in the published accounts of the Tamiae.

A further provision of the decree of Kallias (the crucial lines 50–52, already referred to) required the Hellenotamiae "to deposit (κατατιθέναι) on the Acropolis [1] with the Tamiae the surpluses (restoring περιόντα), or the receipts (restoring γενόμενα), at hand at particular moments (ἑκάστοτε) in the course of the year (κατὰ τὸν ἐνιαυτόν)."[2] This requirement, if put into effect, involved the creation for the Empire of what we may call, using modern phraseology, "a checking account" of the Hellenotamiae with the Tamiae; for if sums reached the Tamiae in this way, they were not added to the reserve so as to replace the sums borrowed between 433/2 and 423/2 B.C. The interest on every loan recorded in *IG*[2] I 324 was computed from the date on which it was contracted to July 3d (Meritt), 422 B.C. (Wade-Gery, *Class. Rev.*, 1930, pp. 163 ff.). If γενόμενα is read, we certainly cannot interpret this provision as requiring the addition automatically of the *phoros* to the war-fund of Athena; for this

---

[1] New reading [πόλ]ι[ν (instead of [φόρ]ο[ν]) by Meritt.

[2] I agree with Beloch (*Griech. Gesch.*, II, 2, p. 349), De Sanctis (*Atthis*[2], p. 490), Levi (*Atti della Accad. di Torino*, 1920/21, p. 123), and Busolt (*Griech. Staatsk.*, II, pp. 1134, 1234), if I understand him aright, in maintaining that κατὰ τὸν ἐνιαυτόν cannot mean "yearly": that would require κατ' ἐνιαυτόν. But when Beloch declares the depositing of surpluses as they arose in the course of the year to be an absurdity, I cannot follow him. It is what is done by every modern man of business. It would be an absurdity only if the funds so deposited were "given" to Athena and were recoverable both in the course of the year and later only in the form of a loan. The procedure contemplated is intelligible if we recall that the Hellenotamiae did not possess an Opisthodomos of their own in which they could place for safe-keeping comparatively large sums of money. It may also be assumed that once imperial money had passed into the hands of the Tamiae the *demos* would have to be consulted before it could be expended. Such a check on the Hellenotamiae would have been timely in 434 B.C. Theretofore they had been governed by the decree, no longer operative because it was then fulfilled, which had laid down the conditions under which payments to the fund of 3000 talents should be made by them.

would force us to assume that Athens financed the war between 426/5 and 423/2 B.C. with only a fraction of its revenues from the Empire, since its borrowings from Athena and the Other Gods amounted to only 808 talents, 1241 drachmae [1] during the *penteteris* (Meritt's figures), whereas the yield of the tribute alone must have exceeded 3000 talents if anything like the assessment of over 960 (or 1460) talents annually (*IG*[2] I 63, l. 212) was received in 425/4–423/2 B.C. If περιόντα is read, our evidence for the period prior to 421 B.C. does not preclude us from interpreting this provision as contemplating additions of surpluses to the war-fund of Athena. With this reading discretion was left to the Hellenotamiae as to whether or not a surplus existed at any particular moment. The contingency was surely not contemplated that these officials would shorten themselves by the premature *traditio* of temporary surpluses; and during the Archidamian War it may be doubted whether they ever were in a position to make any deposits whatsoever with the Tamiae. It was to be foreseen that the campaigns would absorb all their receipts before the year ended, however untroubled the horizon might appear at any given moment. Moreover, the *phoros* came in with such great irregularity that temporary surpluses were probably at no time considerable.[2] But however

---

[1] This being so, *IG*[2] I 299, to which are now added (Wade-Gery, *JHS*, 1930, pp. 288 ff.) 294 and 308, with a total payment of more than 1267 talents, cannot belong to 426/5 B.C. It must be dated between 431/30 and 427/6 B.C. inclusive, probably in 431/0 B.C.

[2] Wade-Gery (*Class. Quart.*, 1930, p. 38) has called attention to the fact that on several occasions (*IG*[2] I 324, ll. 13, 20, 32) during the *penteteris* 426/5–423/2 B.C., and, indeed, in other years also (cf. *IG*[2] I 302, ll. 28 f.), loans were made by the Tamiae within a few weeks after the Dionysia, the time of the year when, according to the *scholion* on Arist. *Acharnians*, 503 (εἰς δὲ τὰ Διονύσια ἐτέτακτο Ἀθήναζε κομίζειν τὰς πόλεις τοὺς φόρους, ὡς Εὔπολίς φησιν ἐν Πόλεσιν), the tribute was due. Cf. Busolt, *Griech. Staatsk.*, II, p. 1353, n. 4. Why did the Hellenotamiae borrow money just when they should have been most flush with it, unless they deposited the tribute with the Tamiae so that it became the property of the Goddess immediately after its receipt in Athens? This, as we have pointed out, the restoration γενόμενα would permit; but the implications of such procedure are fatal (*above*, p. 158): we cannot imagine Athens waging war between 426/5 and 423/2 B.C. with less than a third of her war revenues. Wade-Gery's interrogation whether the tribute was used to wage war must be answered in the affirmative. For what other purpose was it levied? The explanation of these seemingly untimely borrowings lies, perhaps, in the situation revealed by *IG*[2] I 65 (c. 425/4 B.C.). The significant passage proceeds, after a mention of the Dionysia: [τὰς πό]λες haίτ[ινες

that may be, on the assumption of a checking account, even if
we read περιόντα, we can assume, what the reading γενόμενα
would necessitate, that deposits were made with the Tamiae
and withdrawn again by the Hellenotamiae without additions
being made at any time to the war-fund of Athena, that is to
say, to the fund from which money could be paid out only on
vote of the *demos* following a preliminary vote of *adeia* and with
the obligation to pay interest until replacement; for such transactions would, of course, not appear in the accounts published
by the Tamiae-logistae.

After the Peace of Nicias the situation was different. The
provision under consideration must then have created, through
the accumulation of "surpluses" or "receipts" from the *phoros*,
a fund of constantly increasing dimensions on deposit with the
Tamiae. By 415 B.C., as we have seen, it can easily have
amounted to 3000 talents. And there is now evidence which
forces us to conclude that, whereas the old war-fund belonged
to Athena, the new war-fund belonged to the state. Loans
from the Tamiae, that is to say, expenditures for military purposes of Athena's own money, were made with annual regularity
between 418/7 and 414/3 B.C. inclusive (*IG*² I 302, 297). But
the stones on which the records were cut are so badly damaged
that the figures for most of the items are lost and the totals
for two years alone (418/7 and 415/4 B.C.) are preserved. In
418/7 *c.* 56½ talents were disbursed, in 415/4 *c.* 353 talents.
The chief item in the latter year is one of 300 talents sent to
Sicily at Nicias' request (*Thucy.* VI 74 2, 93 4, 94 4). It is
dated on the third day of the eighth prytany (Anthesterion 22
= March 20, 414 B.C., according to Meritt; cf. *AJA*, 1930, p.
151), i.e., a fortnight or three weeks before the Dionysia.

ἂν ἀπο]δῶσι τ[ὸν φόρον καὶ αἴτιν]ες μὲ ἀπο[δῶσιν καὶ h]αἴτιν[ες ἂν κατὰ μέρε· ἐπ]ὶ δὲ τὰς ὀφ[ε-
λόσας πέ]μπεν πέν[τε ἄνδρας τὸς] ἐσπράχσον[τας τὸν φ]όρον. ἀναγ[ραφόντον δὲ οἱ hελλ]ενο-
τα[μ]ίαι ἐσσανίδι τὰς [πόλες τὰς ὑστερό]σας τὸ φό[ρ]ο. The inference is cogent that some
cities paid their tribute in part only, and others did not pay it at all, at the specified
time. It can be surmised that the Hellenotamiae received a fraction only of the tribute
at the Dionysia. On the other hand, the Dionysia marked the opening of navigation,
and hence the dispatch of transmarine military expeditions. We can assume that these
occasioned outlays for which the money in the hands of the Hellenotamiae at the
moment did not suffice.

Unfortunately the total expenditure for 416/5 B.C. is lost. Four items were involved in all, with Alcibiades, Lamachos, Nicias, and Antimachos of Hermos as the recipients (*above*, p. 23, n. 1). The amount of the first payment is lost. The second consisted of 30 talents (Meritt, *AJA*, 1930, pp. 150 f.). The third was of 14 talents and some drachmas. The fourth consisted of Cyzicene staters, we do not know how many, or their value in silver, which was added; but the sum cannot have been large, for the largest payment of electron of which we have knowledge — 4000 staters in 417/6 B.C. — amounted to only about 16 talents.[1] Certainly the figures are extraordinarily small for the year in which the great armada was outfitted; and it is, I imagine, with them in mind that Meyer and others conclude that the reserve was small at the time the decision was taken to send the fleet to Sicily.

It seems to me obvious that the Sicilian Expedition was financed only in small part by borrowings from Athena. But it *was* financed with very large sums. As Beloch has well pointed out (*Griech. Gesch.*, II, 2, p. 352), the magnitude of the outlays can be gauged by the fact that the expedition against Samos necessitated the borrowing from Athena of over 1200 talents; that the siege of Potidaea cost Athens 2000 talents (*Thucy.* II 70 2) or, according to Isocrates (XV 113), 2400 talents; and that the defense of Syracuse left the Syracusans with large debts after 2000 talents had been expended (*Thucy.* VII 48 5). The Sicilian expedition must have cost Athens far more than any of these sums. And what is more, during all the time Nicias was in Sicily, Athens was obliged to draw heavily on the tribute for military enterprises nearer home — in Thrace and the Peloponnese and elsewhere — and, after the occupation of Decelea by the Lacedaemonians, in Attica itself. As a matter of fact we have in *IG*[2] I 99 the mention of a sum of 3000 talents "set aside" for the Sicilian Expedition. The

---

[1] If the stater was worth 24 Attic drachmas, as commonly assumed (Woodward, *JHS*, 1914, p. 278; Wade-Gery, *Num. Chron.*, 1930, pp. 31 ff.). The huge expenditure of 61,697 + staters recorded in *IG*[2] I 307 is not a single payment, but a summation (κεφάλαια) of payments of electron made during a period — a year probably (*above*, p. 75, n. 3).

text is unfortunately badly mutilated. As restored by Hiller the essential lines run: λῦσαι δὲ [αὐτίκα κ]αὶ τὸ φσέφι[σμα τὸ πρὶν γενόμενον περὶ τ]ô ἔκπλο τôν ἐχσέ[κοντα νεô]ν ἑέος ἂν ἑ[ε στρατιὰ ἀπάρει, καὶ μὲ ἔναι ἐ]π' ἄλλο ἔργον με[δ' ἐπ' ἄλλεν] στρατιὰν [δαπα- νᾶν τι τôν ταλάντον τôν τ]ρισχιλίον. ἐ[ὰν δέ τις εἴπει ἒ ἐπιφσεφίσει χρêσθαι τοῖς χρέμασι τοῖ]ς ἐχσαιρ[έτοις ἐς τὸν στό]λον μ[ε - - -

Whatever uncertainty there may be regarding individual words, the sense of the text seems to have been won: the sum of 3000 talents was "set aside" for the Sicilian Expedition. The date is c. March, 415 B.C. The term used for this appropriation (ἐχσ- αιρέτοις) is the one employed by Thucydides (II 24 1; cf. *Andoc.* III 7) for the special reserve set apart for a naval crisis, which, too, was safeguarded by severe penalties against di- version to other uses "by motion or putting to vote" in sub- sequent Assemblies. And similarly the deposit of c. 28 talents made by the Treasurer of the Military Fund with the Tamiae in 344/3 B.C. was thus "set aside" (*IG²* II 1443, cf. *above*, p. 133). It is excluded that the reference is to a sum to be accumulated subsequently by the addition of the *phoros* of three or four consecutive years. Athens never contemplated such a dura- tion for the campaign against Syracuse. The decree, in fact, made some other arrangement regarding the *phoros* (frg. h). The question remains, from what fund was the 3000 talents segregated? If it was from the funds of Athena, the record of it must have appeared in *IG²* I 302. But that does not seem possible. The one item which comes in question, the first of the four (Cavaignac, *Études*, p. 142; Meritt, *AJA*, 1930, p. 130), was not a round sum. The figures are mostly lost, but the con- clusion of the set of numerals is preserved — 3 drachmas, 1 obol. It seems, therefore, excluded that the Tamiae of Athena dis- bursed the net sum of 3000 talents in 416/5 B.C. for the ex- pedition to Sicily.

The issue of this discussion is, then, that the surpluses of the imperial revenues were not used after the Peace of Nicias to pay off the debt of the state to the Goddess but to create an imperial fund in deposit with the Tamiae, expendable by the Hellenotamiae, at the order of the *demos*, without obligation for interest or repayment to Athena.[1] And with this determination we are able to explain why it was that in 418/7 B.C. the Tamiae began to make their loans in electron as well as in silver. When the peace arrived, the coined silver in their possession had become so depleted that, after possible further deductions for the Erechtheum and the temple of Athena Nike, they thought it wise to make payments in electron whenever money of this color could be used by the recipients (*above*, p. 23).

In these circumstances it seems odd that any moneys at all were borrowed from Athena in 418/7–415/4. And we have certain hints that it was not done without remonstrance. The Tamiae, quite exceptionally (*above*, p. 17, n. 2), note that *adeia* was voted by the *demos* in these years; and, equally exceptionally, they substituted "we loaned" (ἐδανείσαμεν) for "we disbursed" (παρέδομεν) in the account for 415/4 B.C. (*IG*² I 302, l. 56). Their insistence upon recording strict compliance with legal prescriptions and upon formal rectitude in naming their payment a loan and not a gift come near to being an expostulation against the people's decision to take the money from them. These deviations from set practice are also intelligible now that we have seen that there then existed in the custody of the Tamiae another fund from which withdrawals could be made without *adeia* and without borrowing. I surmise that the surpluses of the Hellenotamiae were protected by decree or law against drafts till 3000 talents — *the* 3000 talents of *IG*² I 99 — had been accumulated, and that this total was no sooner reached than it was segregated *en bloc* for use against Syracuse.

The case is not without parallel. In the absence of specific information we cannot hope to explain all the nuances of Athenian finance. We are in no position to say categorically why prior to 434 B.C. the state borrowed[2] *c.* 200 talents from the

---

[1] Andreades ('Ιστορία τῆς Ἑλληνικῆς Δημοσίας Οἰκονομίας, I, p. 275, n. 3) notes that these deposits were no longer gifts to Athena.

[2] Bannier (*Rh. Mus.*, 1926, pp. 184 f.) adduces parallels which show that ἀποδοῦναι τοῖς θεοῖς τὰ χρήματα τὰ ὀφελόμενα (*IG*² I 92, l. 2; cf. ll. 30 ff., 52 ff.) *can* mean "pay to the gods moneys due them" for some other reason than borrowing; but it is difficult to imagine what this other reason can be. There is no evidence or probability that the state had any standing obligation to contribute money to the temples. Its whole duty was fulfilled when it provided means for cultus, which could not be neg-

Other Gods. The borrowing was obviously a series of petty transactions, and it must have been effected at a time when there were thousands of talents in the quasi-public war-fund of Athena; for we cannot assume with De Sanctis (*Atthis*[2], pp. 488 ff.) that there was ever a moment during the *pentekontaetia* when this fund was entirely exhausted: the totals achieved in 434–431 B.C. are conclusive on this point. It seems probable that during some period prior to 434 B.C. the war-fund of Athena, like the war-fund of the state after 421 B.C., was protected by decree or law against withdrawals for other than designated purposes pending the accumulation of a total of the desired maximum. That the Athenians were conversant with such a policy is shown by lines 43 ff. of the decree of Kallias.

Thus the division between χρέματα ἱερά and χρέματα ὅσια predated the financial reorganization of 411 B.C.;[1] and, as we have seen (*above*, p. 3), it was carried farther when the *kolakretae* were abolished, in that the contingent expenses of the state were divided thereafter on this line between the Tamiae and the Hellenotamiae. We have, then, to recognize that between 411 and 404 B.C. the Tamiae dispensed primarily the revenues (ἐπέτεια) of Athena Polias, Athena Nike, and Hermes, but we have further to recognize that as a result of some public action taken after systematic preparation in 410 B.C. (*IG*[2] I 109, cf. *above*, p. 34) some means were found to replenish temporarily the practically exhausted treasury of Athena — with the result

---

lected, and saw to it that the temples got their revenues. As Bannier himself concedes, the ordinary translation of the phrase, "pay back to the gods moneys borrowed," accords with common Greek usage. The specific vote of 200 talents to cover the state's obligation to these deities — it was presumed to be less than that figure — can have formed part of Kallias' first motion (*IG*[2] I 91), or of a rider thereto, and the record of it can have been entered on the portion of the stone lost at the bottom.

[1] It first appears in 434/3 B.C. in the title ταμίαι τὸν ἱερὸν χρεμάτον τὲς Ἀθεναίας, which began to be used in that year, the restoration in *IG*[2] I 293 being in my judgment and in that of Meritt (letter) suspect. Meritt proposes to restore ταμίαι ἐκ πόλεος. The earlier title was ταμίαι hοι τὰ τὲς θεὸ ἐταμίευον (for variants see *above*, p. 104). After the legislation of 435/4 B.C. the Tamiae of Athena were to have the custody of other χρέματα that were ὅσια; but these were not dealt with in the inventories and accounts. Outside the inventories and accounts after 434 B.C. the Tamiae are commonly named Tamiae of the Goddess (*IG*[2] I 368; *SEG*, III, 40, 426/5 B.C.; *IG*[2] I 379, 420/19 B.C.; 106, 411–08 B.C.; 373, l. 91, 409/08 B.C.; 374, ll. 117, 187, 408/07 B.C.; II 1655, 407/06 B.C.). Cf., however, *IG*[2] I 313, l. 173, *above*, p. 27, n. 1.

that Athena was able to make considerable advances from income in 410/09 B.C. and to dispense in 409/08 B.C. from balance and income, by an effort which reached well to the bottom of her money-chests, a sum approximating 440 talents, of gold in coin and bullion, silver of native and foreign minting, and even of silver dedicated in the Parthenon (*above*, p. 24). Thereafter payments from funds in the Opisthodomos occupied a distinctly secondary and minor place in the financial operations recorded in the accounts of the Tamiae. 408/07 and 407/06 B.C. were doubtless lean years so far as the outlays of these magistrates were concerned. The dribs and drabs of income posted in *IG*² I 304B prove it for the latter of these two years. The accounts for 408/07 B.C. are lost. We notice, however, as indicative of financial straits, the steps taken to liquidate the cash of the Eleusinian Goddesses. But the imperial revenues can have maintained approximately their 409/08 B.C. level. And the return of Alcibiades in May, 407 B.C., added 100 talents which would not have reached Athens otherwise (Xen. *Hell*. I 4 8 ff.). But in 406 B.C. Athens lost control of the sea. Callicratidas could refer to Conon as an adulterer skulking in another's house. The crisis of Arginusae precipitated the policy of melting down the sacred vessels and the votives of the temples. From this point developments have been followed in some detail in the earlier sections of this work.

After 412/1 B.C. Athens lived financially from hand to mouth. The special effort made in 410 B.C. to recreate a temple reserve could not be repeated, and once its yield was used up, the Tamiae had little more than the *epeteia* to "lend" to the state: the Hellenotamiae had no longer their own war-reserve on which to draw. The revolution of 411 B.C. synchronized with the exhaustion of both war-funds (*Thucy*. VIII 76 6).

Less need be said about other provisions of the decree of Kallias. As has been pointed out already, it was not in order in 434 B.C. to require the Tamiae of Athena to publish annual statements of the loans made to the state. That was obligatory already (*IG*² I 293), and the earlier regulation appertaining thereto must have been addressed to the *logistae* and not to the Tamiae (*above*, p. 16, n. 1). In 407/06, or possibly in 411

B.C., this obligation was transferred to the Tamiae, who naturally used their own period of accounting, which ran from Panathenaia to Panathenaia. Two public statements were ordered by the decree of Kallias. The Tamiae of Athena were commanded to issue inventories of the three chambers of our Parthenon — the Pronaos, Hekatompedon, and Parthenon; and upon the Tamiae of the Other Gods was imposed the obligation to publish inventories-accounts of the money, sacred vessels, and *ex-votos* of value of all the shrines of Attica, which, simultaneously were to be assembled in the Opisthodomos. The first of these categories of public records aimed mainly at recording for safe-keeping the dedications which had already begun to accumulate in the new temple and which were bound to multiply in the future. A new situation required an extension of the responsibilities of this board of Treasurers. The centralizing of the sacred properties of the other shrines forestalled the imminent dispersion of the *c.* 200 talents about to be paid back to the Other Gods; but it went further. It mobilized on the Acropolis about 500 talents of money theretofore scattered about Attica; and it involved forwarding annually to the Opisthodomos the revenues of these shrines. With their money were included their sacred properties of gold and silver and the annual increase of such articles, so far as they were not needed for worship and the personal *kosmos* of the deities. Such a provision is intelligible as part of a general policy of making accessible for use in a great military crisis the entire minted and mintable property of the national gods and goddesses. It may be taken as certain that already in 434 B.C. Pericles regarded the outbreak of a decisive war with the Peloponnesian League as imminent.[1] "Victories in war," he affirmed, "were won by wise policy and abundance of money" (*Thucy.* II 13 2); and the issue showed that he was right.

[1] The decree of Kallias belongs about a year after the defeat of the Corinthians by the Corcyraeans at Leukimne — in the middle of the two-year period (*Thucy.* I 31 1) during which Corinth was making preparations for attacking Corcyra again (Adcock, *CAH,* V, p. 475). It was at this moment that Pericles warned the Athenians that "he already saw war bearing down upon them from the Peloponnese" (Plut. *Per.* 8 5; Meyer, *Gesch. d. Alt.,* IV, pp. 281 ff.).

Considered as a financial measure pure and simple the resolution of the Athenians of the great age to accumulate a reserve of 9700–6000 talents and to recreate it in large part after it was depleted by the Archidamian War deserves the highest praise. It was a feat which we should find it hard to parallel; and it discloses a providence on the part of the people and its leaders for which modern governments have neither the courage nor the necessity. Nine thousand seven hundred talents was a colossal sum of money. Its magnitude may be realized if we recall that in 378/7 B.C. the total property, movable and immovable, of all the citizens and resident aliens of Athens amounted to only 5750 talents (*Polybius* II 62 6; cf. *Dem.* XIV 19).[1] If the Periclean reserve had been divided among the free population of Attica, the wealth of every man could have been doubled. The temptation of the *demos* to enrich itself through jeopardizing its future was very great. How great it was the precautions taken by the people against its own instincts disclose. The reserve was *given* to Athena; and only when it had reached a total that seemed adequate for any eventuality[2] was the decision taken, not to divide the surpluses, but to accumulate a second reserve more freely disposable. As this programme worked out, Athena's fund was well-nigh exhausted by borrowings before the new fund began to be realized.

There cannot be much doubt that the amplitude of their financial preparations encouraged the Athenians to envisage

[1] After much vacillation I have come to the conclusion that 5750 talents represent in fact the total property of the Athenians and not, as Böckh (*Staatshaushaltung*[3], I, pp. 572 ff.) maintained, the aggregate of the fractions of it which, diminishing progressively from the first class to the third, were used as a basis for levying the *eisphora*. For a *précis* of the literature see Busolt, *Griech. Staatsk.*, II, p. 1213, n. 2. Add Glotz, *La Cité grecque*, pp. 402 f. We have accordingly to adjust our ideas to a financial predominance of the Athenian state over private individuals unparalleled in modern times.

[2] According to Kolbe's figures (*Sitz. Ber. Akad.*, 1929, pp. 280 ff.) it amounted to ±7000 talents in 434 B.C. Perhaps Isocrates' figure (8000 talents; VIII 126), which conflicts with that given by him elsewhere (VIII 693; XV 234) for the Periclean reserve (10,000 talents), is to be taken as a statement of its amount at this moment. Zimmern (*Greek Commonwealth*[2], pp. 410 ff.) comments on its inadequacy for the war that ensued; and this became palpable to the Athenians as early as 428 B.C. But what modern statesman in the year 1931 can see a way to finance a general war for so long a period as even four years?

with greater equanimity the resort to war in 431 B.C.; and it is equally certain that the availability of a sum aggregating at least from four to five thousand talents in 415 B.C. predisposed them to embark on the Sicilian adventure with lighter hearts. In ancient Athens war was financed in large part by the savings of the past; in the modern world, by the savings of the future. The Athenians did not possess a credit system by which they could borrow from the nation the money with which to wage war and thus shift to coming generations the burden of paying off war debts. To have retained the reserve in the treasury and issued bonds for an equivalent amount was not feasible. Men had first to become habituated to the use of paper securities in private business before the state could think of resorting to such expedients.[1] "Statesmen," says H. A. L. Fisher, "can only do business with the intellectual currency of their own age."

Considered as an economic measure the accumulation in the Opisthodomos of such a large portion of the specie of the Aegean world gives furiously to think. To say that it impaired the purchasing power of private individuals is to affirm that its dissipation in the course of the Peloponnesian War increased this capacity. Its dissipation was accompanied by the diversion of tens of thousands of men from profitable enterprises to military activities; and had the silver not flowed into the treasury of Athena in the first instance, it would doubtless have gone to pay the wages of non-Athenian crews and soldiers and the costs of local battleships and fortifications. It can be argued that its accumulation in the hands of the Tamiae freed men in the Empire from an inducement to devote greater energies to the production of non-economic goods. The withdrawal of specie from circulation tended to stabilize prices.[2] It un-

---

[1] The nearest approach to such a transaction known to me was made by Timotheos in the middle of the fourth century. During a temporary shortage of funds he issued to traders in payment for supplies tokens stamped with his seal and redeemed them at their face value when his money arrived (*Polyainos* III 10 1; cf. Regling, *Zeit. f. Num.*, 1929, pp. 199 ff.).

[2] It is generally assumed that a rise of wages — and prices — occurred during the period of the Peloponnesian War (Beloch, *Griech. Gesch.*, III, 1, pp. 339 f.; Tod, *CAH*, V, pp. 22 ff.). Kolbe (*Sitz. Ber. Akad.*, 1929, pp. 280 f.) contends that the opposite was the case. The data are meager and conflicting. On the one side we have the increase of the jurors' allowances from 1 or 2 obols daily to 3; on the other, the payment

questionably stimulated the trades and industries that furnished materials of war; but it did not increase the general prosperity. It created businesses that required the continuance of war for their successful conduct. Notably it bred mercenaries, and pirates (Ziebarth, *Beiträge zur Gesch. des Seeraubs und Seehandels im alten Griechenland*, pp. 12 ff.).

Had the alternative to hoarding specie in the Athenian Opisthodomos been its use in imperial or Athenian commerce, industry, and agriculture, the result must have been a considerable acceleration of economic productivity; but before this was possible the Greek states must have assuaged the fears and ambitions from which wars sprang and seen some way of safe-

of 3 obols daily stipulated for the Archons and *prytaneis* in the new constitution of 411 B.C. (Arist. *Ath. Pol.* 29 5), the *diobelia*, and the reduction in the wages of crews from 1 drachma per day in the first years of the war (*Thucy.* III 17 3) and 415 B.C. (*id.* VI 31 3) to 3 obols and $3\frac{3}{11}$ obols (*id.* VIII 29; 45 2) after 412 B.C. But these fluctuations are susceptible of various explanations. The wages of soldiers did not vary much. During the siege of Potidaea hoplites were allowed 2 drachmas daily — one for themselves and one for servants (*id.* III 17 3). In 420 B.C., 4 Attic obols (3 Aeginetan) were provided for *sitos* for hoplites, light-armed troops, and archers, and 8 for horsemen (*id.* V 47 6), for service in the Peloponnese. One drachma daily was the pay arranged for the Thracian mercenaries recruited for the Sicilian expedition of Demosthenes (*id.* VII 27 2). Rents, at least on Delos, were stable (Tarn, in *The Hellenistic Age*, by Bury and others, p. 116). The fifteen farms of the Temple yielded 7500–7600 drachmas yearly in 434 B.C. (*IG*² I 377), 7800 in 377–374 B.C. (*IG*² II 1635). For the wages paid workmen on the Erechtheum in 409/08–405/04 B.C. we have no comparable data for the pre-war epoch.

The most significant of these items, the reduction of the wages of crews, favors Kolbe. If he is right, we shall have to assume that the dissipation of the reserves, and the influx of Persian gold after 412 B.C., were more than compensated by increase of private hoarding due to the uncertainties of the war and the diversion of large sums to foreign and barbarian lands, there to be put to non-productive uses, and thus taken out of circulation. The war doubtless occasioned a multiplication of paid services and a corresponding increase in the use of the medium of exchange. The Acharnians, for example, when driven into Athens, had to buy food products instead of living off their own farms (Aristoph. *Achar.* 34 ff.). The tens of thousands of oarsmen, while serving on the fleets, received and paid out coin as never before. There cannot be much doubt that not only Athens, but its citizens, had much less money at the end of the war than at its beginning; and the pressure of the enemy, the forceful measures taken by its fleets, and its coercion of maritime trade may have enabled the state to keep wages and prices down to its ability to pay them. Its prohibition of local minting of silver followed by the paralysis of its own mining operations must have curtailed the output of new silver money; but this factor was offset by the activity after 412 B.C. of Chian and other mints (Gardner, *History of Ancient Coinage*, p. 287) and the new use of gold coins.

guarding their future other than by fighting. The alternative use of much of this reserve of silver in the unbusinesslike practice of private hoarding and in temple hoarding elsewhere than in Athens must also be reckoned with. There were forces at play in ancient Greece too strong for economics.

Granted the Empire, I think that we may say that the Athenians were wise in their day and generation in their financial policy of war insurance; and so important did it seem to them to have an ample margin for special efforts or emergencies that in 428 B.C., when it became clear that the war expenditures would speedily exhaust the reserve, they imposed a levy of 200 talents (2 per cent?) on capital and in 425/4 B.C. they doubled or tripled the tribute.

As the war entered upon its third decade and the revenues from the Empire dwindled with the loss by Athens of undisputed control of the sea and the outbreak of revolt among her allies, the imperial city experienced the disadvantages incident to the political regime she had created at home. Her marvellous democracy had been made possible by her ability to use freely her domestic revenues for the realization of her own social and political ideals. She now faced the dilemma which the fourth century presented with ever-increasing poignancy of abandoning her system of popular benefits or of starving her military operations. The reformers of 411–410 B.C. reserved all revenues for the prosecution of the war, and excluded from active participation in government all citizens who could not take part in the varied activities of public life without being indemnified for their time. Their position was untenable. Athens could not keep the element of its population disfranchised which manned the fleet by which alone the war could be waged successfully; and the recovery of her naval supremacy in 410 B.C. seemed to make it unnecessary. Though the expedients she used became increasingly more and more desperate, it must, nevertheless, be recognized that between Cyzicus and Aegospotami Athens *did* manage to finance both her domestic institutions and her military operations. In 410 B.C. she was unready to declare herself bankrupt. At that time she recognized in a practical way her obligation to repay to Athena the moneys due her (*IG*² I 109), and in 407/06 she treated temporary drafts on domestic revenues for military purposes as loans (*IG*² I 105). The citizens were buoyed up by hopes of reëstablishing in its entirety their Empire. But in 403 B.C. the state acknowledged its bankruptcy. Indeed the financial situation was then so desperate that even without the excuse of having war to finance moderate leaders like Phormisios tried to abandon the system of popular benefits (*Lysias* XXXIV; *CAH*, V, p. 373). Naturally the proposal was rejected, and Athens faced the future a democracy in the old sense.

During the fourth century no possibility existed for rehabilitating the war-fund either of Athena or of the state. The Athenians proved as tenacious as any other popularly organized people in holding on to and improving their inherited standard of living, cost it what it might. It had taken centuries of pious and persistent effort to accumulate through the revenues of, and gifts to, the Goddess Athena's quota of the fund available in the Opisthodomos at the outbreak of the Peloponnesian War. The attempt was not renewed. The sacred moneys (ἱερὰ χρήματα) handed over after 403 B.C. by one board of Tamiae to its successor cannot have amounted at any one time to more than a few talents (*above*, p. 140). On the occasions when the state made special deposits of public moneys with Athena they were expendable on order of the People, not gifts to Athena subject to use only by borrowing. They represent a continuance of the policy inaugurated in 434 B.C. and put into effect after the Peace of Nicias (*above*, pp. 159 ff.); but they failed to produce like results for the simple reason that Athens no longer levied tribute on an Empire. So far as we can see, Athens was unable at any time to accumulate a reserve through savings from domestic revenues. Until the collapse of the Empire no need was felt to realize such surpluses for this purpose. Between 403 B.C. and the time of Eubulos there was no agency concerned primarily with seeing to it that a margin existed between the revenues received annually and the sums allocated to, and spent by, the magistrates, Council, and People; and when Eubulos created such an agency it was recognized, as theretofore, that surpluses should be spent immediately for domestic purposes (*theorika*), thus leaving for military purposes (*stratiotika*), when war arrived, only current surpluses. No plan was formed for the systematic building up from domestic revenues of a war-fund of any kind, unless it was through the accumulation of public and private offerings of objects of gold and silver in the temples, for which the primary motive was piety and ostentation, not concern for military emergencies. Notoriously, Athens had to provide from her own resources her share of the expense involved in the undertakings of the Second Delian League. It created for this purpose a system — that of the symmories — for levying regularly a tax on income (378/7 B.C.); but the yield was insufficient, partly through evasions; nor could the other members of the League be got to contribute their share — the undertakings were often rather Athenian than confederate in aim — except under compulsion. Hence Athens, harassed by wars against its own associates, was unable to collect a reserve either from its own income tax or the contributions of its allies. Yet nothing had happened in the meanwhile to invalidate the contention of Pericles that "it is accumulated wealth, and not taxes levied under stress, that sustains wars" (*Thucy.* I 141 5).

APPENDICES

APPENDIX I

IONIC SCRIPT

PRIOR to 412 B.C. the Ionic script was used in the published copies of Athenian decrees in several instances: IG^2 I 16 (*c.* 465 B.C.); 17 (*c.* 450 B.C.); 38 (*a.* 446/5 B.C.); 55 (*c.* 431 B.C.); 25 (420/19 B.C.). The first of these regulates judicial procedure in cases in which citizens of Phaselis might be involved in consequence of business contracts entered into by them at Athens or because of commerical relations with Athenians. It was inscribed on stone at the expense of the Phaselitans, and it is to their account that we should probably ascribe the use of the foreign script. The fourth has as its object a certain Aristonus, whom Wilhelm (*Oester. Jahresh.*, 1898, Beibl., p. 44) has identified with the Aristonus who together with Polymedes, the head of a rival faction, led the cavalry which Larisa sent to the aid of Athens at the outbreak of the Peloponnesian War (*Thucy.* II 22 3). The end of the decree is lost. We may suspect that it, too, owes its presence on stone to private publication. The second is a treaty struck by Athens with a foreign state (unknown). We are not informed as to the circumstances of its publication; but the treaty struck with Chalcis in 446/5 B.C. is identical with it in phraseology, and in the Athenian decree in which this is embodied (IG^2 I 39) the charge of publication is placed upon the Chalcidians. Hence IG^2 I 17 also was incised in all probability at foreign expense. IG^2 I 38 gives us a decree written in Attic letters with which is incorporated a *lex* written in Ionic. A general rule governing the practice of Athens in the publication of such documents has been drawn up by Busolt (*Griech. Staatsk.*, II, pp. 819 f., n. 3) as follows: "Die Steine mit Beschlüssen, welche einzelne Bundesstädte betrafen, wurden von diesen als Interessenten bezahlt, Steine mit Verträgen mit auswärtigen Staaten seit der Ueberführung der Reichskasse nach Athen von den Hellenotamien." With the substitution of *kolakretae* for Hellenotamiae [1] I accept the principle, and deduce from it the occasional use of the Ionic script in Athenian decrees of this period.

The fifth example (*IG*² I 25) approaches the period when Ionic becomes a rival with Attic in decrees. This decree was incised by two different stonecutters, the first of whom used Attic, the second Ionic. Foreigners had nothing to do with it. Two other public documents incised prior to 412 B.C. are written with Ionic letters: *IG*² I 377 and 947. The first is an account of the Delian Amphictyons of the years 434/3 and 433/2 B.C.; the second is a list of soldiers who fell in battle written in Attic with the Ionic superscription Λημνίων ἐγ Μυρίνης (cf. *IG*² I 948). These two reflect foreign usage. The Ionic script was, so to speak, the *koine*; and its early use in Athens for private records is abundantly attested (*IG*² I 395, 400 II, 524, 618, 661, 732, 734, 760, 770, 770a, 772; *Riv. di Filol.*, 1930, p. 202; *IG*² I 787, 788, 826, 828, 864, 866, 904, 905, 906, 911, 916, 924, 1029–1085).[2] It is not surprising, therefore, that we find a number of decrees (*IG*² I 14/5, *a.* 446/5 B.C.; 34/5, *a.* 445 B.C.; 57, 424/3 B.C.; 80, 431–421 B.C.) into which an occasional Ionic letter (ordinarily $\eta = \bar{e}$) has slipped inadvertently, and a number of inscriptions (*IG*² I 369, 426/5 B.C.; 71, 423/2 B.C.; 280, 422/1 B.C.; 266, 420/19 B.C.; 328, 414/3 B.C.; 373, 409/08 B.C.; 316, *a.* 408/07 B.C.) which use both Ⴑ and Λ for lambda. See Larfeld, *Handbuch der attischen Inschriften*, II, pp. 430 ff.; Litchfield, *Harvard Studies Class. Phil.*, 1912, pp. 138 ff., 152.

After 412 B.C. the Ionic script is used in Attic decrees with some frequency: *IG*² I 93 (414/2 B.C.); II 174 (*c.* 412 B.C., cf. *SEG*, III, 80); I 103 (412/1 B.C.); II 12 (411/0 B.C.); I 106a, 108, 110a (410/09 B.C.); I 118 (408/07 B.C.), 116[3] and 117 (407 B.C.), 124 (406/05 B.C.), 125 (405/04 B.C.), 126 (405/04 B.C.). After 407/06 B.C. all the decrees we possess are Ionic (cf.

---

[1] The Hellenotamiae did not begin to pay the cost of inscribing decrees on stone till 411 B.C.

[2] For the use of Ionic in the writing on red-figured vases see Kretschmer, *Griech. Vaseninschriften*, pp. 103 ff.

[3] Preponderantly Attic but with an admixture of Ionic. Both *eta* and *omega* occur. Cf. also the superscription of *IG*² I 120 (408/07 B.C.), in which an *omega* occurs.

Palaios, *Polemon*, I, p. 174). Apart from one tribute-list (*IG²* I 231) which has an occasional *eta*, in the *Tabulae Magistratuum* the Ionic script was not used before 407/06 B.C., excepting for the Treasurers' accounts of Mnasilochos' archonship, that is to say, during the government of the Four Hundred (*IG²* I 298).[1] It is the only authentic utterance of that body which we possess. For the odd case of the inventory of the Hekatompedon, for 409/08 B.C. (*IG²* I 274), see *above*, pp. 46 f. After 407/06 B.C. the Ionic script is used in all the datable public documents except *IG²* I 255a, 290, 289. The accounts of the building Commissioners for the Erechtheum become Ionic in 407/06 B.C. (Paton, *The Erechtheum*, No. XXIX, p. 648: Dinsmoor's date),[2] and remain Ionic in 406/05 and 405/04 B.C. (*The Erechtheum*, Nos. XXVII, XXVIII: *IG²* II 1654, 1655 dated by Kirchner in and about 395/4 B.C.; but see *The Erechtheum*, pp. 460, n. 5, 649 f.; and *above*, pp. 48 f.). The accounts of the Tamiae are Ionic in 406/05 and 405/04 B.C. (*IG²* I 305 and 303?; II 1502, 1686, 1687?). The only Athenian documents which preserve the Attic letters after 407/06 B.C. are the inventories of the Tamiae, and all of these thus far identified are Attic. [Cf., however, *above*, p. 66, n. 1.]

The public documents of the year 407/06 B.C. are hesitating, showing now Attic (*IG²* I 105, 123, 122?, 314), now Ionic (*IG²* I 117, *The Erechtheum*, No. XXIX = *IG²* II 1655), now a mixture of both (*IG²* I 116, 304B, 274?).

The chief advocate for the introduction into Athenian official use of the Ionic script was Archinos, the most influential leader of the "moderates" after the democratic restoration in 403 B.C. (*CAH*, V, pp. 372 ff.). He issued a pamphlet in which he distinguished phonologically the sounds for which Ionic had letters and Attic none (Theophrastos, quoted by Syrianus,

[1] For the date of *IG²* I 303, see *above*, p. 26, n. 1. The *prytaneis* of Erechtheis for the year 408/07 B.C. used Ionic in the imperfect catalogue of their members which they had inscribed on the base of a dedication made to Athena (*IG²* I 398). The Athenian Amphictyons at Delos for 410/09 B.C. naturally drew up the record of their *acta* in Ionic (*BCH*, 1884, p. 283). Two *deme* records (*IG²* I 186/7, 189) are partly Ionic.

[2] The dating of No. XXVI (*The Erechtheum*, p. 416 = *IG²* I 374, ll. 406 ff.) in 407/6 B.C. is problematical.

p. 940b, 10 = *Commentaria in Arist. graeca*, VI, 1, Kroll, p. 191;
cf. Usener, *Rh. Mus.*, 1870, p. 591). This was obviously before
403 B.C., possibly in *c.* 412 B.C., and he may have achieved an
ephemeral success with his campaign in 411 B.C.[1] He practically
won his point in 407/06 B.C. All that remained was to have
Ionic made obligatory for all public documents; and to effect
this he introduced and had a measure passed in the archonship
of Eukleides.[2] The codification and republication of the laws
begun in 403/02 B.C. made the occasion unusually suitable for
giving the *coup de grâce* to the old native script.

[1] 410 B.C. is the critical date for the transition from ξυν to συν (Meisterhans, *Grammatik*[3], pp. 220 f.).

[2] Suidas, *s.v.* Σαμίων ὁ δῆμος: τοὺς δὲ Ἀθηναίους ἔπεισε χρῆσθαι τῶν Ἰώνων γράμμασιν Ἀρχῖνος - - - ἐπὶ ἄρχοντος Εὐκλείδου - - - περὶ δὲ τοῦ πείσαντος ἱστορεῖ Θεόπομπος (*FHG*, I, p. 306; *FGH*, IIB, p. 570). Cf. schol. *Eurip. Phoen.* 682.

APPENDIX II

EPIGRAPHICAL NOTES

THE publication in 1930 of a practically complete inventory of the Tamiae of Athena ('Αρχ. Δελτίον, 1927/8, p. 128) — the one for the year 369/8 B.C.[1] — enables us to fill out a good many passages in the fragmentary records of the general period. I append a few of the more obvious restorations. Lines 1–14 of *IG*² II 1425 (368/7 B.C.) may be completed tentatively as follows (omitting the figures of the weights):

[πρῶ]τ[ος ρυ]μ[ός· κεφαλή, στέφανη, ὅρμος],
[ἐνώιδια, ὑπ]οδ[ερίς, ἥλω δύο χρυσώ],
[χεὶρ ἀριστερά, ἀμφιδέα, χρυσία μικρά],
[στ]αθμόν·[
[δε]ύτερο[ς ρυμός· θώραξ, στρόφιον],
[πε]ρ[ιτραχηλίδιον, στολίδε δύο, χρυσία]
[μικ]ρά, [στ]αθ[μόν·
[τρίτ]ο[ς ρυμ]ός· [ἀπόπτυγμα, περόναι δύο, πόδε]
[δύ]ο, [χρυσία μικρά, σταθ ΧΓΗΗΗΗΔΔΔΓΗΗΗΙΙΙ]
[τέτα]ρ[τος ρυμός· χεὶρ δεξιά, ἀμφιδέα],
[κατωρίδε δύο, στέφανος, χρυσία]
[μικρ]ά, σ[ταθμόν·
[δ]ρα[χ]μ[ὴ] παρα[γί]γ[νεται]
[π]έ[μπ]το[ς ρυμός, ?]ἀ[κρωτήριον, χρυσίον]

The letters indicated as uncertain need verification from the stone or a squeeze, and I am troubled at the length of lines 8 and 9; but the reading of line 13 seems to me assured. In lines 133 ff. of this same inventory we should restore:

ὀ[μφαλοὶ φια]λ[ίω]ν [δύο, σταθμὸν ΓΗ]·
θυμιατήρι[α] ἀρ[γ]υρᾶ [τρία παρὰ τὴν τράπεζαν]
ἄστατα ἐπι[σκευῆς δεόμενα].

[1] It will appear shortly in *IG*² II, Add. under the number 1424a.

The ἀργυρᾶ of line 134 is vouched for by line 14 f. of *IG*² II 1413;
cf. *below*. In line 14 of Ἀρχ. Δελτίον, 1927/8, p. 126, I suggest
ἄ[σ] τατ[ο]ς : ἄγ[ραφ]ος; in line 216 f. [σ]ώρ[ακοι ΓΙΙΙ καὶ] ἡμι[σω-
ράκιον τοξευμάτων σαπρῶν ἀχρήστων]. In line 6 of *IG*² II 1415, I
restore [ἱερὰ Ἄμμ]ωνος; and in line 63 of *IG*² II 1421, Ἄμ[μωνος
φιάλη] (*above*, p. 131, n. 1). Despite the redundancy, in line 5
of Ἀρχ. Δελτίον, 1927/8, p. 128, col. I, the text may have run:
[τάδε χρυσᾶ· Νίκης χρυσῆς], τοῦ [χ]ρυ[σ]ο[ῦ σταθμόν]. Twenty letters are missing before τοῦ (Meritt). There is not room enough
after χρυσοῦ for ἀγάλματος; seven letters are probably the limit.
*IG*² II 1412 and 1413 can be restored more completely than
heretofore. (See below, pp. 181–183.)

   To meet the requirements I have had to assume that in *IG*² II
1413 the sixth and the seventh *hydriae* of Artemis Brauronia
were separated from the rest and placed first, the assumption
being that they were dedicated later; and that there is something amiss with the figure in line 16. Elsewhere (Ἀρχ. Δελτίον,
1927/8, p. 128, col. II, l. 92 ¹; cf. *IG*² II, 1412, l. 21, 1425, l. 180,
1429, l. 8) the weight of this pitcher is ΓΗΗΗΗΔΔΙΙ. The difference may be due to error, ancient (cf. Ἀρχ. Δελτίον, 1927/8,
p. 128, col. II, l. 91) or modern (*id*. l. 76 — where a Γ has been
omitted, cf. Εἰκ. 3 and *IG*² II 1425, l. 166 and 1413, l. 17), or to
reweighing. Another irregularity is the omission of πέμπτη in
line 23/4 of *IG*² II 1413. The first *hydria* in each series was left
unnumbered in this inventory, and no numbers at all were
assigned to the καιναί of Athena. In *IG*² II 1412 all are without
numbers, but the order shows that this is a matter of the inventory, not of the articles themselves. The sole irregularity
is that the fourth in the Nike series preceded the third, thus
preserving throughout the order of their weights. The omission
of σταθ in 1413, l. 26, is irregular, and l. 18 has 72 letters. *IG*²
II 1413 may be the earlier of the two: note the fuller specification of donors in the case of the θυμιατήρια, the separation of
the *hydriae* of Artemis into two lots, and the curious item in
line 29, which suggests that we are not far from 385/4 B.C.; but
the appearance of καὶ συνάρχοσι in line 17 of 1412, the singular

---

¹ Εἰκ. 3 (p. 129) shows that a Γ has been added erroneously in the transcription
of this line.

IG. II 1412 (384/3–378/7 B.C.)

στοιχ. 86

12 [. . . . .]θίπᾳπη ἀνέθηκε α[ὑδρίαι καιναί Ἀθηναίας· ὑδρία ἀργυρᾶ, στα]-
[θ ⊢ΗΗΗΗ⊦ΔΔΔΔ⊦]⊦· Ἀθηνάας ὑδρί[α ἀργυρᾶ, σταθ ⊢ΗΗΗΗΓ⊦⊦· ὑδρία ἀργυρᾶ, σταθ ⊢ΗΗΗΗΙΙΙ· θυματήριον χαλκᾶ ὑπερεί]-
[σματα ἔχον, ὃ Ἀ]ρι[σ]τόκριτος ἀν[έθηκε, σταθ ΧΧΗΗΗΔΔΔ· θυμιατήριον χαλκᾶ διερείσματ' ἔχον, ὃ Κλεοστράτη ἀνέθ]-
15 [ηκε, σταθ ΧΗΗ]Η[ΔΔ]· θυμι[α]τήριο[ν χαλκᾶ διερείσματα ἔχον, σταθ ΧΧΗΗΗΗΔΔΓ⊦⊦·
[. . . . .]ος χρυσός, ὃν Δημέ[ας
[. . . . . .] καὶ συνάρχοσι· Νίκης ὑ[δρία ἀργυρᾶ, σταθ : ⊢ΗΗΗΗ⊓Δ· ὑδρία ἀργυρᾶ, σταθ : ⊢ΗΗΗΗΗ⊓ΔΔΔ⊦⊦· ὑδρία ἀργυρᾶ, στ]-
[αθμὸν : ⊢ΗΗΗΗ⊓]ΔΔΔΔ⊦⊦· ὑδρία ἀ[ργυρᾶ, σταθ : ΧΓ· Ἀφροδίτης ὑδρία ἀργυρᾶ, ἣν οἱ ταμίαι παρέδωκαν, σταθ : ⊢ΗΗΗΗ⊓]·
[Ἀρτέμιδος] Βραυρωνίας ὑδρία [ἀργυρᾶ, σταθ : ⊢ΗΗΗΗ⊓ΔΔΓ⊦⊦⊦· ὑδρία ἀργυρᾶ, σταθ : ⊢ΗΗΗΗ⊓ΔΔΔ⊦⊦· ὑδρία ἀργυρᾶ, σ]-
20 [ταθμὸν : ⊢ΗΗΗΗ⊓]ΔΔΔΓ⊦⊦· ὑδρία ἀ[ργυρᾶ, σταθμὸν : ⊢ΗΗΗΗ⊓ΔΔΔΔ⊦· ὑδρία ἀργυρᾶ, σταθμὸν : ⊢ΗΗΗΗ⊓ΔΔΔ⊦⊦· ὑδρία ἀρ]-
[γ]υρ[ᾶ, στα]θ : [⊢ΗΗΗ]ΗΔΔ⊦⊦· ὑδρία ἀρ[γυρᾶ, σταθ : ⊢ΗΗΗΗ⊓Γ⊦⊦⊦⊦· Ἀνάκοιν ὑδρία ἀργυρᾶ, σταθ : ⊢ΗΗΗΗ⊓ΔΔΔ⊦⊦· ὑδρία ἀ]-
[ρ]γυρᾶ, σταθ[: ⊢Η]ΗΗ⊓ΔΔΔΔΓΙΙΙ· ὑδ[ρία ἀργυρᾶ, σταθ : ⊢ΗΗΗΗΔΔΔ⊦⊦· Δήμητρος καὶ Κόρης φιάλη ἀργυρᾶ, σταθ : . . . . .]
ταὐτη[ν] τὴμ [φι]άλην παρέδωκα[ν οἱ ταμίαι
⊓Γ⊦⊦⊦· ὑδρί[α] ἀργυρ[ᾶ], σταθμ[ὸν : ⊢ΗΗΗΗΗΔΔ⊦⊦⊦ΙΙΙ· ὑδρία ἀργυρᾶ, σταθ : ⊢ΗΗΗΗΔΔΔΓ⊦⊦⊦· ὑδρία ἀργυρᾶ, σταθ : ⊢ΗΗ]-
25 ΗΗΔΔΓ⊦⊦⊦[ΙΙΙ]· ὑδρία ἀργυρᾶ, [σταθ : ⊢ΗΗΗΗΗΔΔΔΓ⊦⊦⊦· ὑδρία ἀργυρᾶ, σταθ : ⊢ΗΗΗΗ⊓Γ⊦⊦⊦· . . . . .ἐγ κιβωτίω]-
[ι] χρυσίον ἀ[π]ὸ τὸ κανῶ, ἵνα τὰ [ἐλεφάντινα ξώιδια, σταθμὸν : ΔΔΔΔ⊦⊦·

[181]

IG. II 1413 (384/3–378/7 B.C.)

I [. . . . . . χερ]νιβεῖον ἀ[ργυροῦν

[. . · θυμιατή]ριον ἀργυ[ρὸν χαλκᾶ διερείσματα ἔχον, ὃ . . . . ἀνέθηκεν, σταθ XXHHHHΔΔΓ⊢]-   στοιχ. 71

[⊢ :]θυμιατήριον ἀργ[υρὸν χαλκᾶ διερείσματα ἔχον, ὃ 'Αριστόκριτος 'Ανακαιεὺς ἀνέθηκεν],

[σταθ : XXHH]HΔΔΔ ∴: θυμ[ιατήριον ἀργυρὸν χαλκᾶ διερείσματ' ἔχον, ὃ Κλεοστράτη Δεξιμένο ? ἀ]-

5 [νέθηκε, σταθ]μὸν XHHH[ΔΔ·

[οἰνοχόη χρυ]σῆ ῥαβδω[τὴ

[θιοπίδες τέτ]ταρες, σ[ταθμὸν ⊓HHHHΓ|||·

[. . . . .]ηκε στα[θμὸν   φιάλαι 'Αι]-

[. . . . . . .]ρος ἦν η]   ὑπόστατον χρ]-

10 [νσὸν τῶι κρατ]ῆρι, ἄστ[ατον· κρατῆρ] ἐ[πίτηκτος ἐπίχρυσος ἄστατος·

[. . . . .]ΔΓΗ||| στ[έφανος χρυσ]ὸς ὃν ἡ Νικη ἔχει ἐπὶ τῆς κεφαλῆς ἡ ἐπὶ τῆς χειρὸς τὸ ἀγαλ]-

[ματος τὸ χρυ]σõ, ἄστα[τος· στέφανο]ς χρυ[σõς

[. . . . .], σταθμ[ὸν . . . .]⊢|| || C[

[. . . . .]τὸ κρα[τῆρος τὸ μεγάλο ἀπὸ τῆς χειρὸς τῆς Νικης   θυ]-

15 [μιατηρα ἀργ]υρᾶ τρ[ία παρὰ τὴν τ]ράπεζα[ν, ἄστατα, ἐπισκευῆς δεόμενα· ἀργυραῖ : 'Αρτέμιδο]-

[ς Βραυρωνίας ὑ]δρία, [σταθμὸν ⊓HHH]HΔΔΔΓ[⊢· 'Αρτέμιδος Βραυρωνίας ὑδρία ἑβδόμη, σταθ ⊓HHH]-

[H⊓Γ⊢⊢⊢· ὑδρία]ι και[ναὶ 'Αθηναίας]· ὑδρία, σ[ταθ ⊓HHH⊓ΔΔΔΔ⊢⊢· ὑδρία, σταθ ⊓HHH⊓Γ⊢· ὑδρία, στ]-

[αθμὸν ⊓HHHHH||· 'Αθη]να[ίας Νικης ὑδρ]ία, σταθ [⊓HHHH⊓Δ· ὑδρία δευτέρα, σταθ ⊓HHHH⊓ΔΔΔ⊢· ὑδρία]

[τρίτη, σταθ XⲒ· ὑδρία τετάρτη, σταθ]μὸν ⊓HHHΗ[⊓ΔΔΔΔ⊢· 'Αφροδίτης ὑδρία μία, σταθμὸν ⊓HHH]-

20 [ΗΓ· ᾽Ανάκου ὑδρία, σταθμὸν ΓΗΗΗΓΔ]ΔΔΗΗ· ᾽Α[νάκου ὑδρία δευτέρα, σταθ ΓΗΗΗΓΔΔΔΔΓ]ΙΙΙ· ᾽Ανάκο]-
[ιν ὑδρία τρίτη, σταθμὸν ΓΗΗΗΗΔΔΔ]ΙΗ· ᾽Αρτέμ[ιδος Βραυρωνίας ὑδρία, σταθμὸν ΓΗΗΗΗΓΔΔΓΗ]-
[ΗΗ·· ᾽Αρτέμιδος ὑδρία δευτέρα, σταθ]μὸν ΓΗΗ[ΗΓΔΔΔΗ· ᾽Αρτέμιδος ὑδρία τρίτη, σταθμὸν ΓΗΗ]-
[ΗΗΓΔΔΔΓΗ· ᾽Αρτέμιδος Βραυρωνία]ς ὑδρία [τετάρτη, σταθ ΓΗΗΗΗΓΔΔΔΔΗ· ᾽Αρτέμιδος ὑδρία],
[σταθ ΓΗΗΗΗΓΔΔΗ· Δήμητρος καὶ Κόρ]ης ὑδρία, [σταθμὸν ΓΗΗΗΗΔΔΔΙΙΙ· Δήμητρος καὶ Κόρης ὑ]-
25 [δρία δευτέρα, σταθ ΓΗΗΗΗΔΔΓΗΗ]· Δήμητρος [καὶ Κόρης ὑδρία τρίτη, σταθ ΓΗΗΗΗΔΔΓΙΙΙ· Δή]-
[μητρος καὶ Κόρης ὑδρία τετάρτη, Γ]Η ΗΗΗΗΔΔΔ[ΓΙΗ· Δήμητρος καὶ Κόρης ὑδρία πέμπτη, σταθ Γ]-
[ΗΗΗΗΓΙΗΙΗΙ· ....ἐλε]φαντίνην[
[.........ἀκινάκη]ς σιδερδ[ς τὴν λαβὴν χρυσῆν ἔχων, τὸ δὲ κολεὸν ἐλεφάντ]-
[ινον ἐπίχρυσον, τὸ πυγλίον χρυσόν], καὶ ὁποτ[έρας τῆς ἀρχῆς ἐστιν ἄδηλον
30 [· θρόνοι μεγάλοι ΙΙΙ, οὐχ ὑγιές, ἀνακλί]σες ἔχο[ντες ἠλεφαντωμένας· ἕτερος θρόνος, ἀνάκλισ]-
[ιν οὐχ ἔχων...........]θήραιον[
[...................]έ]χει φα[
[...................]ς λυχν[εῖον
[...............κλῖνα]ι Μιλη[σιουργὲς
35 [................]ἀσπ[ίδες
[..............]ΔΓ[

sequence of the *hydriae* of Nike, and the failure to isolate all the *hydriae* in one section, give us pause. Because of the δοκιμεῖα (ll. 9 ff.) and the arrangement of the items I am inclined to date *IG*² II 1415 after 378/7 B.C. and near the series of inventories *IG*² II 1421/4 (374/3 B.C.) and following. In that event it must belong in 375/4 B.C., since the thicknesses of the stones (0.15 *vs.* 0.115) and the number of letters to the line (54 *vs.* 55) prevent us from joining it with *IG*² II 1411. Then *IG*² II 1412, 1413 and 1414 belong in 384/3–378/7 B.C. For the father of Kleostrate (1413, l. 3), see Kirchner, *PA*, 8617. For the ἀκινάκης (1413, ll. 28 f.), see Johnson, *AJA*, 1914, pp. 15 f. In *IG*² II 1460 τὸ δέ has fallen out before πυγλίον (l. 14). The δέ may have been omitted in 1413, l. 29, because of the following καί.

ADDENDUM

THE study of the Financial Decrees of Kallias promised by Wade-Gery (*above*, pp. 17, n. 1, 153, n. 1) has now appeared (*JHS*, 1931, pp. 57 ff.). It contains the new readings of the first line of IG² I 92, which show that IG² I 91 and 92 were passed on the same day of one and the same year. His reasons for concluding that this year is either 434 or 422 B.C. seem to me sound. Those for preferring the latter year I cannot accept. They strengthen rather than weaken my conviction that 434 B.C. is alone possible. Most of them have been met already in this work. If, despite IG² I 231 (*SEG* V 25, cf. p. 22) and IG² I 218 (*SEG* V 28, cf. p. 24), which leave the question open, the use in IG² I 91/2 of three dative plurals in -αις and one in -ασι favors 422 B.C., as Wade-Gery concludes from a very careful collection and analysis of the evidence, we can assume simply that our copy of the decrees of Kallias was inscribed after the Peace of Nicias. It was then and then only that the provision for creating a public war-fund was put into effect. But I am still unconvinced that it cannot have been cut on stone in 434 B.C. We must not demand at any time of the Athenian stone-cutters too much uniformity in spelling.

GENERAL INDEX

GENERAL INDEX

Index of Inscriptions

(An asterisk signifies a restoration.)